Heaven Help Us

Quarto is the authority on a wide range of topics.

Quarto educates, entertains and enriches the lives of our readers—enthusiasts and lovers of hands-on living.

www.quartoknows.com

This edition published in 2016 by
CHARTWELL BOOKS
an imprint of Book Sales
a division of Quarto Publishing Group USA Inc.
142 West 36th Street, 4th Floor
New York, New York 10018
USA

Conceived, Designed, and Produced by:
Quirk Books
215 Church Street
Philadelphia, PA 19106

ISBN-13: 978-0-7858-3465-6

Typeset in Mrs. Eaves
Designed by Doogie Horner
Production management by John J. McGurk

Image credits: Cover images from left to right: Saint Anthony the Great, Saint Francis of Assisi, Blessed Virgin Mary, Copyright: Zvonimir Atletic/Shutterstock. Page 44 (no. 3): The martyrdom of St.Erasmus, 1474, oil on panel, Netherlandish School. Society of Antiquaries, London, UK/Bridgeman Art Library. Page 304 (no.1): Icon of St. Spiridon with scenes of his life, egg tempera on panel, Theodoros Pulakis (fl. 1650). Benaki Museum, Athens, Greece/The Bridgeman Art Library.

Previously published as *This Saint Will Change Your Life.*

10 9 8 7 6 5 4 3 2 1

Printed in China

Heaven Help Us

300 Patron Saints to Call Upon for Every Occasion

Thomas J. Craughwell

CHARTWELL
BOOKS

Contents

Introduction

This life is a valley of tears. Success eludes us in our chosen careers. Our families, love life, and friendships are disappointing. We suffer from headaches, stomach trouble, and the occasional hangover. We fall prey to con men and make easy marks for panhandlers. We are afraid of snakes. We are dumb in science. We are bad dancers.

We can sit quietly in our homes and offices, seething with dissatisfaction, or we can seek help. And help is not only at hand, it's free. I'm talking about patron saints. A few years back, the blockbuster best seller *The Prayer of Jabez* assured us that it's perfectly fine to pray for money. Yet why limit yourself to praying for relief from financial worries when heaven is just teeming with men, women, and children (not to mention angels) who are ready—eager, even— to weigh in and solve just about every problem that afflicts the human race. All we have to do is ask.

For example, did you know there are patron saints for gamblers and alcoholics; for thieves, card sharps, and fallen women; for wives saddled

with unfaithful husbands and parents stuck with disappointing children?

There are patron saints for bartenders, diplomats, and conscientious objectors; for vegetarians and eco-warriors; for coin collectors and rock climbers. There are saints to protect you from the devil, from witches, and from being hanged; saints to shield you from an attack of appendicitis and to nurse you through bowel disorders; saints to ward off poverty, encourage discretion, and put a stop to riots.

The Internet has a patron saint. Television does, too. And let's not forget the animal kingdom. Cats, dogs, and birds all have patron saints, as do cattle, pigs, horses, whales, wolves, and even salmon.

This religious phenomenon is extraordinary, but its origins are entirely secular. In ancient Rome, there were patrons and there were clients. Patrons were wealthy, powerful, influential individuals from the upper class who, in a spirit of noblesse oblige, gathered around them a small circle of clients. These clients were Romans who tended to be short on cash and light on luck. Every morning, as a sign of respect, the clients made a brief call at their patron's house. If the client had any petition to present—perhaps he was looking for a government job or he needed protection from creditors or he hadn't the money for his son's tuition—he would turn to his patron for help, and the patron would solve the problem.

The Roman patron-client relationship became the model for the relationship of affection and confidence that exists between Christians and their patron saints. For about the first one thousand years of the Catholic Church's history, a Christian's patron saint mirrored the old Roman system: whichever saint answered a Christian's prayers became his or her patron saint. In the early Middle Ages, the notion surrounding patron saints shifted, and certain saints came to be regarded as specializing in particular causes. By the sixteenth century, the era of the Protestant Reformation and the Catholic Counter-Reformation, patron saints had proliferated to such an extent that scarcely an ailment, animal, profession, or condition of life didn't have its very own patron saint.

The enthusiasm for patron saints survives today. Open the classified section of any newspaper and you'll encounter column upon column of thank-you notices to St. Jude, the patron saint of impossible situations. Religious-goods stores thrive selling small plastic statues of St. Joseph, who, among his many other attributes, has become the patron saint of successful real-estate transactions. And with patron saints for astronauts, ecology, and AIDS, it's obvious that this ancient devotion is keeping up with the times.

Accountants

ST. MATTHEW

FIRST CENTURY • FEAST DAY: SEPTEMBER 21

During the Roman Empire, tax collecting was one of the most lucrative jobs a person could have. With the emperor's tacit approval, collectors were free to wring all they could from their district's taxpayers and then keep a portion of the proceeds for themselves. Caesar didn't mind the profiteering as long as the total assessed tax was delivered to his treasury. But Jewish taxpayers forced to pay the exorbitant sums weren't quite so forgiving, especially when the tax collector was a fellow Jew, like Matthew. Jewish tax collectors were regarded as loathsome collaborators and extortionists who exploited their own people. It's little wonder, then, that in the gospels tax collectors are placed on par with harlots, thieves, and other shameless public sinners.

Matthew collected taxes in Capernaum, a town in the northern province of Galilee and the site of a Roman garrison. Christ was a frequent visitor there, performing such miracles as healing the centurion's servant, curing Peter's ailing mother-in-law, and raising Jairus's daughter from the dead. One day, while passing the customs house where Matthew was busy squeezing extra shekels from his neighbors, Christ paused to say, "Follow me." That was all it took to touch Matthew's heart. He walked out of the customs house forever, giving up his life as a cheat to become an apostle, the author of a gospel, and eventually a martyr.

As a tax collector, St. Matthew had to be good with figures. Consequently, accountants, bankers, stockbrokers, finance professionals, and, of course, tax collectors have adopted him as the saint they call on to help them advance in their profession.

See holy card, page 41

ST. JOHN BOSCO

1815–1888 • FEAST DAY: JANUARY 31

John Bosco, the youngest son of a peasant family near Turin, in northern Italy, was a bright, athletic boy with an engaging personality. One day when John was about ten years old, a small traveling circus pitched its tent near the family's farm. After just one performance John was mesmerized. He spent all his spare time with the jugglers and acrobats, who taught him a few tricks and then, when he proved he had talent, revealed their more sophisticated techniques.

After the circus moved on, John Bosco put on his own show for his family, juggling, using simple sleight of hand, and walking a tightrope strung between trees. Once he'd polished his act, he invited some of the tough neighborhood kids to watch. They liked John's one-man circus act and his down-to-earth personality. As they became friends, John found opportunities to suggest that the boys should watch their language, stay away from liquor, go to confession, and attend Mass. That was the start of John Bosco's vocation to rebuild the lives of troubled kids.

As a priest, Don Bosco dedicated his life to reclaiming orphaned and abandoned boys. (In Italy, priests are addressed as "Don" rather than "Father.") He built complexes in which the boys could grow up in a safe environment, receive an education, learn a trade, and even train for the priesthood.

Rome has never formally declared John Bosco to be the patron saint of circus performers. In 2002 Father Silvio Mantelli, an amateur magician, took a request to make the patronship official to Pope John Paul II, to whom he presented a magic wand. It didn't do the trick. Rarely does the pope formally appoint a patron saint. For Don Bosco to become a patron, Father Mantelli and his friends need only venerate him and spread that devotion to others in their profession.

See holy card, page 41

ST. GENESIUS

DIED ABOUT 300 • FEAST DAY: AUGUST 25

On West Forty-ninth Street, in the heart of Manhattan's Broadway theater district, lies the little church of St. Malachy, the unofficial chapel of New York's theatrical community. St. Malachy's has played host to Hollywood's faithful since the 1920s—at Sunday Mass, it wasn't unusual to share a pew with stars such as George M. Cohan, Spencer Tracy, Perry Como, Irene Dunne, Elaine Stritch, Danny Thomas, Bob and Dolores Hope, and Ricardo Montalban. One of the side chapels is dedicated to St. Genesius, a martyr with a special relationship to thespians and their craft.

Genesius was an actor and a pagan in Rome during the reign of Diocletian, the emperor who tried to exterminate Christianity once and for all. Anti-Christian persecution was in full swing when Genesius and his troupe were commanded to perform before the imperial court. Naturally, the actors wanted to impress the emperor, so they wrote a new piece inspired by the events of the day—a comedy lampooning Christianity. Genesius was cast as a convert.

The play began, and it was immediately a hit. Romans of every class enjoyed a farce, and the troupe's scurrilous mockery of all things Christian delighted Diocletian and his guests. Genesius was center stage for the baptism scene, the play's climactic moment. But as the actor playing the priest poured water over Genesius's head and recited the words of the Christian rite of baptism, something extraordinary happened. Divine grace flowed through Genesius, and in an instant he recognized that everything the Church taught was true. Filled with zeal that he could scarcely understand, Genesius began to berate Diocletian for his cruelty to the Christians. At first the emperor laughed, thinking the daring speech was part of the play. But as Genesius continued his tirade, Diocletian realized that this audacious actor spoke in earnest. Enraged, the emperor had

Genesius arrested and immediately sentenced him to death by torture.

As the executioners tore Genesius with iron hooks and burned him with torches, they urged him to renounce his new-found faith, but he replied, "Were I to be killed a thousand times for my allegiance to Christ, I would still go on as I have begun."

The Christians of Rome buried their unexpected martyr in one of the catacombs outside the city walls. Today the relics of St. Genesius are enshrined in the Church of Santa Susanna, the parish for American residents and visitors to Rome.

See holy card, page 41

ST. PELAGIA

FIFTH CENTURY • FEAST DAY: OCTOBER 8

St. John Chrysostom, a fifth-century patriarch of Constantinople, was preaching about the mystery of grace (which brings even the worst sinners to repentance) when he enlivened his sermon with an example that everyone in the congregation would recognize. He reminded listeners about the era's best-known actress, a woman whose talents on stage were celebrated throughout the eastern Roman Empire. Although famous for her acting, she was infamous as a seductress who "went beyond all in lasciviousness," as John put it. For her sake, rich men squandered fortunes and fathers abandoned children. She'd even ensnared the empress's brother.

How did she do it? John speculated that she drugged or bewitched her victims. Yet, as wicked as she was, she repented, asked to be baptized, and entered a convent. There her repentance was so sincere and her devotion to prayer and good works so complete that she developed a new reputation as a saint. "Let no man who lives in vice," John concluded, "despair."

It's an uplifting story, but one part is missing: the actress's name. Apparently she was so well known in Constantinople that St. John felt no need to mention it. The notorious actress became known as Pelagia, thanks to an expanded fictionalized account of her life told by James the Deacon.

In James's version of the story, Pelagia is an actress of such extraordinary beauty and powerful sexual allure that even bishops found it hard not to look at her when she passed by. He recounts that, by chance, she overheard a bishop's sermon that moved her to renounce her sinful pleasures and begin a new life—not in a convent but in a monastery, where her acting skills enabled her to pass as a eunuch monk for the rest of her life.

See holy card, page 41

ST. BERNARDINE OF SIENA

1380–1444 • FEAST DAY: MAY 20

In today's Christian churches, the monogram IHS is almost as ubiquitous as the cross. But that wasn't always so. The letters are the abbreviation of the Greek name for Jesus, and they appeared occasionally on Byzantine icons beginning in the fourth or fifth centuries. The monogram was virtually unknown in western Europe until the fifteenth century, when it became an important part of the impassioned sermons of the wandering Franciscan friar St. Bernardine of Siena, a fierce advocate for Christianity and spokesman for peace.

At that time, Italy was not a single nation but a patchwork of squabbling principalities, dukedoms, and city-states often at war with one another. Bernardine made it his mission to visit the warring factions, bringing his message of peace. To overflowing crowds in town churches and piazzas, Bernardine taught that Christ detested bloodshed and that all Christians must live in peace. His sermons portrayed Jesus as a loving brother and generous friend who is betrayed by an ungrateful humanity with each war people wage. He tailored his message to appeal to a congregation's faith, reason, and emotions; between his arguments he told stories that made listeners laugh or weep. At each sermon's climax, when Bernardine held his audience's rapt attention, he would suddenly raise a wooden tablet on which the letters IHS were painted in gold. This dramatic gesture never failed to draw an outpouring of religious fervor.

The IHS device became Bernardine's personal "logo." Certainly, it would be demeaning to characterize St. Bernardine only as a genius of saturation marketing. However, he did manage to elicit a response from his target audience that modern advertising professionals dream of, leading them to venerate him as their patron saint.

See holy card, page 42

ST. COLMAN OF STOCKERAU

DIED 1012 • FEAST DAY: OCTOBER 13

During the Middle Ages, prisoners in danger of being hanged, justly or otherwise, prayed to St. Colman to win them a reprieve. Colman was a pilgrim from either Ireland or Scotland. We can't say for sure because, in the Middle Ages, German speakers used the same term, *Schottisch*, for both the Scots and the Irish.

Whatever his nationality, Colman was making his way to Jerusalem when he passed through the Austrian town of Stockerau, about six miles from Vienna. He could not have passed through the country at a worse moment. The Austrians were at war with the Moravians and Bohemians (the people who today make up the Czech Republic), and Coleman's arrival aroused the suspicion of war-paranoid local authorities. They convinced themselves they had a spy in their midst, rationalizing that his pilgrim garb was a clever disguise and that his inability to understand German was simply a ruse. So they ordered Colman's arrest and had him dragged off to a dungeon.

Colman was stretched on the rack and interrogated, but he couldn't understand the questions of his German-speaking torturers, and they couldn't understand his Gaelic requests for an explanation. Frustrated by the prisoner's refusal to give up playing the role of foreigner and admit that he was being paid by the Moravians and the Bohemians, a local magistrate ordered Colman to be hanged from a dead elder tree. As a warning to other spies, the citizens of Stockerau left his body swinging in the breeze.

As the days passed, however, Colman's body was amazingly unaffected by any of the grotesque things that usually befall a corpse left hanging outdoors. No crows pecked out his eyes; no wild dogs gnawed off his feet. In fact, his body showed no signs of decay at all. And then the dead elder tree came back to life! For eighteen months Colman's body hung from the revived tree, looking as fresh as the day the hangman slipped the noose around his neck. Conceding that they had killed an innocent man, the people of Stockerau cut down Colman's body, buried it at nearby Melk Abbey, and venerated him as a saint.

Once St. Colman was enshrined in Melk Abbey, his story spread throughout the German-speaking lands of Bavaria, Swabia, Austria, and Bohemia. Prisoners and criminals prayed to him to save them from the gallows, while pilgrims to the tomb invoked the saint for a host of other needs: to cure their ailments, to help unmarried women find suitable husbands, even to protect their horses and cattle. In 1713, when an epidemic was raging through the area around Melk, the monks made a seventy-pound beeswax candle and kept it burning continuously before his shrine until the plague abated. St. Colman's reputation as a worker of miracles spread as far as Rome, where four popes encouraged the faithful to go on pilgrimage to his shrine.

See holy card, page 42

ST. ALOYSIUS GONZAGA

1568–1591 • FEAST DAY: JUNE 21

Because St. Aloysius Gonzaga died when he was barely twenty-three years old, artists—whether Old Masters or creators of laminated holy cards—have traditionally depicted him as a frail, almost effeminate, youth. In this case, however, art does not imitate life. Aloysius Gonzaga was aggressive and unyielding, with a pronounced antagonistic streak. As a member of Italy's infamous Gonzaga family, he came by these qualities naturally; where the Medici were the connoisseurs of Renaissance Italy, the Gonzagas were its warlords. Aloysius brought the same ferocious energy to religious life that his ancestors had carried onto the battlefield.

As the eldest son and heir, Aloysius was expected to marry well, raise a family, expand the Gonzagas' wealth and influence, and, if the opportunity arose, slaughter their enemies. He had been trained for this role and appeared to be dutifully following that path. Yet secretly he was planning to renounce his title and become a Jesuit priest. At age fifteen, he revealed his intentions to his parents. The news sent Aloysius's father into a rage. He blamed his wife as well as his son's chaplain for filling the boy's head with pious nonsense, and he threatened to flog Aloysius unless he renounced his ambition. Aloysius refused, and the standoff continued more than two years. In the end Aloysius got his way. He gave up his inheritance and set off to become a Jesuit novice in Rome.

The Jesuits were a practical order, cultivating spiritual life through not just prayer and meditation but also good works. Suspecting that the young nobleman needed to learn the virtues of obedience and humility, the Jesuit superior sent Aloysius to work in one of the city's hospitals. Aloysius did as he was told, but he loathed every minute of it. The filthy wards and bedding infested with lice and fleas were bad enough—but the patients, with their hideous wounds or awful diseases, truly frightened him. It took all his Gonzaga willpower to get through each day.

Aloysius had a change of heart, however. Many of the patients he tended had been abandoned by their families and friends, and quite a few were dying. Where once he had felt only fear and revulsion, eventually he began to experience genuine compassion and tenderness.

In January 1591 a terrible epidemic of plague struck Rome. Soon the city's hospitals were overwhelmed with patients, so convents and monasteries threw open their doors. Even the Jesuit superior left his office to take up nursing duties. Had the outbreak come a year earlier, Aloysius might have run away; but, emboldened by his new strength, he went out every day to collect the sick and dying. He found beds for them, washed them, fed them, comforted them, and prayed with them. Sadly, his heroic service lasted only a few weeks; Aloysius himself soon fell victim to the epidemic and died.

In recent years, AIDS patients and their caregivers have adopted as their patron St. Aloysius Gonzaga, the man who overcame his fear of the sick and the dying and became their most kindhearted nurse.

See holy card, page 42

OUR LADY OF LORETO

SHRINE ESTABLISHED BEFORE 1472 • FEAST DAY: DECEMBER 10

Italy's Basilica of Our Lady of Loreto is not as well known as Lourdes and Fatima, but at least fifty popes have visited the shrine during the last six hundred years (John Paul II visited three times during his twenty-six-year pontificate). Inside the magnificent basilica is a small stone building that is said to be the house in which Jesus, Mary, and Joseph lived while in Nazareth.

Plenty of historic buildings have been dissembled and rebuilt elsewhere, but the story of Loreto is far more extraordinary. In 1291, after a Muslim army drove the last Crusaders from the Holy Land, angels appeared in Nazareth, lifted the Holy House off its foundations, and carried it to safety in Italy.

Of course the story has its share of doubters. Skeptics point out that the first mention of the presence of the Holy House at Loreto dates from 1472, almost two hundred years after the angels would have deposited it there. Why are there no eyewitness accounts of the miracle? Believers counter that lots of historical documents have been lost or destroyed over the centuries; besides, the style of construction is not typical of Italy, and the stones used are virtually unknown in that region but are common in Galilee. And so the debate continues.

The pope has never pronounced the authenticity of the Holy House. But in 1920, just seventeen years after the Wright brothers achieved the first successfully manned flight, Pope Benedict XV named Our Lady of Loreto the patron of airline pilots and their passengers, a patronage that has been extended to flight attendants.

See holy card, page 42

ST. MATTHIAS

FIRST CENTURY • FEAST DAY: MAY 14

Sometimes the link between a saint and the area of patronage is tenuous. Such is the case with Matthias, the patron saint of alcoholism. We know little about the apostle; he's mentioned only once in the New Testament, in the Acts of the Apostles (1:15–26), when the eleven surviving apostles named him as a replacement for the traitor Judas. This sole episode is all that is certain about St. Matthias. Legend has it that he preached to cannibals in Ethiopia and was martyred there; conflicting lore claims he was battered with stones and beheaded in Jerusalem. With so little known about his life, and no mention of any alcohol troubles, how did he come to be the patron saint of recovering alcoholics?

The answer lies in a letter written by St. Clement of Alexandria (died 217), an Egyptian theologian. Clement quotes St. Matthias as saying, "We must combat our flesh, set no value upon it, and concede to it nothing that can flatter it." It appears that Matthias is invoked against alcoholism because of this single quotation urging Christians to practice self-control.

A more plausible patron for recovering alcoholics is on the horizon, though. Rome is reviewing the case of Venerable Matt Talbot of Dublin, Ireland. Talbot, who came from a family of heavy drinkers, was drunk every day from the time he was twelve years old until he swore off alcohol at age twenty-eight. He overcame his alcoholism by following a daily schedule of hard physical labor, intense prayer, and good works. Since Talbot's death in 1925, the cause for his canonization has moved slowly. Stay tuned.

See holy card, page 43

ST. JOHN BERCHMANS

1599–1621 • FEAST DAY: AUGUST 13

$\mathfrak{J}$f sanctity is ever ordinary, then John Berchmans was an ordinary saint. The son of a Flemish shoemaker, from an early age John loved God and his neighbor and longed to serve them as a priest. As the first step, he volunteered as an altar boy, as do many young boys who hope (or whose parents hope for them) to have a religious vocation.

From the first time he served Mass, John knew he was meant for the priesthood. He never felt so close to God as when he was in the sanctuary of his parish church, praying the responses and bringing the priest everything necessary to say Mass. He loved it so much that he volunteered to serve as many as five Masses each day.

At age seventeen, John joined the Jesuits and began his formal studies for the priesthood. From their beginnings, the Jesuits were renowned as intellectuals, teachers, preachers, and missionaries, and by the turn of the seventeenth century they had already given the Church a fresh crop of mar-

tyrs, the result of western Europe's Reformation. The Jesuits appealed to John because they emphasized an orderly, down-to-earth approach to spiritual life. John, whose favorite religious devotions were the simple acts of praying before a crucifix, saying the rosary, and, of course, attending Mass, felt entirely at home among them. Laypeople who met John liked him and appreciated his matter-of-fact devoutness, and he impressed his fellow Jesuits as someone genuinely holy, a low-key kind of saint.

Given John's down-to-earth nature, it's ironic that he became the star pupil at his seminary. The Jesuit superiors sent him to prepare for the priesthood at their college in Rome. There, he astonished his philosophy teachers by absorbing all they taught him and finishing the course in just three years instead of the usual four or five. Public disputations between seminarians from rival colleges were a popular form of recreation in seventeenth-century Rome. When the students of the Greek college challenged those from the Jesuit college to a debate, the Jesuits agreed that John should represent them. Thanks to John, the Jesuit college team was able to triumph.

Tragically, the celebration ended abruptly. The day after the debate John fell seriously ill with dysentery, a high fever, inflammation of the lungs. As it became clear he was dying, a steady stream of visitors passed through John's room to say goodbye. On August 13, 1621, twenty-two-year-old John Berchmans died.

Upon his death, his cult began in his homeland, in what is now Belgium, where people felt a strong attachment to him. Engravers produced holy pictures of him, but they could not keep up with the demand. Within a couple months they had sold some twenty-four thousand copies of John's portrait in the Low Countries alone. So, although he didn't die a martyr, or live in abject poverty, or preach to multitudes, for his steadfast faith and devotion to the Mass, John Berchmans is honored as a saint and the patron of altar servers.

See holy card, page 43

BLESSED KATERI TEKAKWITHA

1656–1680 • FEAST DAY: JULY 14

Cruising along the interstate through New York's Mohawk valley, most drivers don't even notice they've passed the holiest piece of real estate in the United States. On a hill above the highway is Ossernenon, a Mohawk village where three Jesuits saints were martyred—Saints Isaac Jogues, Rene Goupil, and John de LaLande—and where Blessed Kateri Tekakwitha, the first Native American saint, was born.

Kateri's mother was an Algonquin Christian who had been captured in a Mohawk raid, and her father was a Mohawk who followed his tribe's traditional religion. Kateri was four years old when a smallpox epidemic took the lives of her parents and infant brother, leaving her in the care of an uncle and two aunts, relatives of her father. Smallpox afflicted the village throughout her childhood until tribal elders finally decided to move to a new site called Caughnawaga, north of the Mohawk River and near modern-day Fonda, New York. Not

long after the move, in 1675, Father Jacques de Lamberville, a Jesuit missionary, arrived in the village. Although the Jesuits had enjoyed tremendous success converting the Hurons, the Mohawks did not welcome the priests. Father de Lamberville succeeded in converting just one soul at Caughnawaga—twenty-year-old Kateri, whom he baptized on Easter Day 1676.

Kateri's conversion infuriated her family and her tribe. Her aunts seized any excuse to beat her. If she stepped outside her lodge, children chased her, throwing stones. One day a warrior ran at her with his hatchet drawn. Kateri was certain she was about to die, but at the last moment her attacker stopped and walked away. Anxious and exhausted by the constant harassment, Kateri didn't know what to do. For her safety, Father de Lamberville urged her to leave Caughnawaga for the Algonquin Christian village at the mission of St. Francis Xavier, across the St. Lawrence River from Quebec. Kateri set out alone on July 14, 1677. It was a two-hundred-mile journey and she walked the entire way, arriving at the mission in October, three months later.

By a wonderful coincidence, at the mission she met an Algonquin Christian named Anastasia Tegonhatsihonga, who had known Kateri's mother. Anastasia invited Kateri to live with her. Safe at last and in an environment where other Indians understood her, Kateri practiced her new faith without fear. She attended two Masses every morning, returning to the mission chapel for vespers at day's end. Kneeling at the altar to receive Communion, she looked so saintly that congregants elbowed each other aside to kneel next to her. Kateri had an unquenchable desire to know all she could about Christianity; what she learned from the Jesuit priests she then taught to friends.

Just days before Easter 1680, Kateri fell ill. As two French settlers and a mission priest, Father Pierre Cholenec, prayed beside Kateri's deathbed, a remarkable change came over her body: All her smallpox scars vanished. Father Cholenec testified, "Within a moment [her face became] so fair and beautiful that I cried out in surprise."

Convinced that they had known a saint, the Jesuits collected the documentation necessary for canonization. The documents are preserved in Rome and include a decorated deer hide signed with the names and marks of Algonquin men and women petitioning the pope to declare Kateri Tekakwitha to be a saint.

See holy card, page 43

Amputations

ST. ANTHONY OF PADUA

1195–1231 • FEAST DAY: JUNE 13

Whoever wonders wants to see,
Let him invoke St. Anthony.

For nearly eight hundred years, St. Anthony has enjoyed an unassailable reputation as one of the chief wonder-working saints. He wrought so many miracles during his lifetime, and so many more through his intercession immediately after his death, that Pope Gregory IX declared Anthony a saint less than a year after he died, the fastest canonization on record.

Anthony was mild and compassionate—none of his miracles are of the fire-and-brimstone variety. For instance, he once tried to persuade a community of heretics to return to the Catholic Church. When they refused to listen Anthony walked to the banks of the Brenta River and began to preach there. As he spoke, fish swam to the surface to hear him.

Another example of Anthony's miracles occurred while he was traveling with a fellow Franciscan.

A poor woman invited the two friars to spend the night in her house. Her one luxury was a small barrel of wine, and her prize possessions were two glass wine goblets. In honor of the occasion, the woman brought out her glasses and filled them with wine. Anthony's clumsy companion dropped and shattered his glass. In the ensuing commotion, the poor woman failed to notice that she hadn't shut off the wine barrel's tap. Distraught by the trouble and loss he had brought to his hostess, Anthony began to pray. A moment later the wineglass was restored, the tap shut off, and the wine barrel was full to the brim.

It was in an unguarded moment that St. Anthony became the patron of amputations. A young man named Leonardo got into a nasty argument with his mother, and in his anger and frustration he kicked her. As soon as he had committed such a disrespectful act, Leonardo was filled with remorse. He hurried to church, where St. Anthony was hearing confessions, and admitted what he had done. "That foot deserves to be cut off," Anthony said flippantly. He didn't mean it literally, of course, but that's how Leonardo understood it. Overwrought, the young man ran out of the church, grabbed the first axe he found, and chopped off his own foot. When word of the outrage reached Anthony, he performed one of his more spectacular miracles—he went to Leonardo's house, took the severed foot, and miraculously reattached it.

See holy card, page 43

ST. RENÉ GOUPIL

1608–1642 • FEAST DAY: OCTOBER 19

St. René Goupil gave up a successful surgical practice in France to serve with Jesuit missionaries in Canada. For two years he worked in the hospital in Quebec, treating French settlers and members of various tribes of the Algonquin nation. Then, in July 1642, Goupil met St. Isaac Jogues, a Jesuit priest recruiting volunteers to assist him in the wilderness, working among the Hurons. Goupil offered his services, and, on August 1, Jogues, Goupil, and about twenty Christian Hurons climbed into their canoes and set out for the mission. Less than twenty-four hours later they were ambushed and captured by a war party of seventy Mohawks. It marked the beginning of a gruesome ordeal for the two Frenchmen and their companions.

The Mohawks tore out all Goupil's fingernails, crushed his fingers with their teeth, and made him repeatedly run the gauntlet, during which his face was so battered that he became unrecognizable. The Mohawks burned at the stake almost all the captured Huron warriors, but they dragged Goupil and Jogues from village to village, torturing them as they went. One night Goupil was staked out on the ground so that Mohawk children could drop hot coals onto his naked body. Because of these horrific tortures St. René Goupil has become the patron of anesthesiologists.

The weeks of torture came to an end, at last, when Goupil and Jogues were given as slaves to the chief of the Mohawk village of Ossernenon, in modern-day New York. But the two Frenchmen had been there only a few days when Goupil made the mistake of teaching a four-year-old boy to make the sign of the cross. Thinking the gesture invoked evil spirits, the child's uncle split Goupil's skull with a tomahawk, ending his suffering forever.

See holy card, page 44

ST. FRANCIS OF ASSISI

1181–1226 • FEAST DAY: OCTOBER 4

𝕴t is the rare Christian who does not get all syrupy about St. Francis of Assisi's love for animals. Blame it on all those garden statues of Francis with a bunny curled up at his feet and little birds chirping on his shoulder. In real life, Francis's view of animals was theological rather than sentimental. Animals form part of God's creation, and, as the book of Genesis tells us, everything in creation is good. No doubt Francis loved bunnies and birds, but he also loved spiders and snakes—and that is the challenge. Francis saw the world as an immense God-ordered system in which everything plays the role assigned to it by the Creator, and therefore every creature, whether it's cute 'n cuddly or not, has value.

There are many stories about Francis and animals. One tells how, while Francis and his friends were walking through the Spoleto Valley, they encountered a large flock of birds. Francis stopped and began to preach to the flock. "My brothers and sisters, praise your Creator and always love him," he said, "for he clothed you with feathers and taught you to fly so you could make your home in the pure air." At this the birds all began to chirp and sing and flap their wings.

Another story tells how a Franciscan brother found a rabbit caught in a trap and brought the poor animal to Francis. The saint released the animal and healed its wounded leg, then set him on the ground with a warning that, in the future, he should watch his step. Instead of scampering away, the rabbit hopped back into Francis's lap. He wouldn't leave until Francis carried the rabbit into the woods and sent him on his way.

One story in particular spotlights Francis's belief in restoring the balance between man and beast. The town of Gubbio was plagued by a ferocious wolf that had carried off lambs and calves and other livestock—it had even killed small children. Afraid that the wolf would attack them, too, the citizens refused to go outside the city walls to tend their fields.

Then Francis came along. Declaring he was not afraid, Francis went outside the town in search of the wolf. He hadn't gotten very far from the gate when the animal, snarling and snapping its jaws, rushed out of the woods and straight for him. The people of Gubbio screamed in horror as they watched from behind the city walls, but Francis stood his ground. As the wolf came close, Francis commanded, "Stop!" The animal skidded to a halt and sat on its haunches, just as if it were a well-trained dog.

"Brother Wolf," said Francis, "you have been stealing livestock that does not belong to you and frightening your neighbors. In the name of the Lord of Heaven, I command you to stop." The wolf drooped its head and lay on the ground at Francis's feet. Then the saint turned to the townspeople. "Brother Wolf will not trouble you or your animals, but in return you must feed him every day." The people of Gubbio agreed, and every day the wolf came to town for a meal. He became the city's unofficial pet, and when he died the heartbroken towns-people had a sculpture of him carved and placed over the door of one of the town's churches. It is still there.

See holy card, page 44

ST. ERASMUS

DIED ABOUT 303 • FEAST DAY: JUNE 2

We know that a martyr named Erasmus was bishop of Formiae, in southern Italy. That's about it; any other facts about the saint have been lost. So, as often occurs when facts are few, legend has stepped in to fill the void.

According to the old stories, Erasmus was arrested during Emperor Diocletian's persecution of the Church. A magistrate commanded the bishop to sacrifice to a statue of Hercules. Erasmus refused. The magistrate then condemned him to an especially grisly death. Executioners bound Erasmus to a board, slit open his stomach, and tacked one end of his intestines to a reel. With each excruciating turn, the intestines were wound slowly around a spool. (If you're having trouble visualizing the ghastly ordeal, it is depicted in a large mosaic located over a side altar in St. Peter's Basilica in Rome.)

St. Erasmus's martyrdom made him the natural choice as the patron of stomach ailments. The suffering call on him to relieve such abdominal complaints as appendicitis, cramps, nausea, and seasickness, among others. During the Middle Ages, St. Erasmus was invoked as one of the Fourteen Holy Helpers, a group of patron saints considered especially effective for help with common problems.

Sailors also regard St. Erasmus (or St. Elmo, as they call him) as one of their patron saints because the reel used to wind his intestines reminded them of a ship's windlass. The electric discharge known as St. Elmo's Fire may be named after the Catholic saint as well. Sailors are particularly familiar with the phenomenon, which resembles a bright pink-purple glow and is often emitted from pointed structures, especially ships' masts during lightning storms at sea.

See holy card, page 44

ST. DAMASUS & ST. HELEN

ABOUT 304–384 • FEAST DAY: DECEMBER 11
249–329 • FEAST DAY: AUGUST 18

Of archaeology's two patron saints, only St. Helen was a digger. Today we would call St. Damasus a preservationist.

The son of a Christian family, Damasus was born in Rome at the end of the last major Christian persecution. The persecutions had resulted in martyrs by the thousands, perhaps even tens of thousands, and Rome itself had witnessed the infamous deaths of St. Agnes (forced to stand naked in a brothel, then beheaded), St. Anastasia (burned alive), and St. Sebastian (shot full of arrows). Damasus memorized the martyrs' stories during his youth. As a young priest he was assigned to the basilica built over the tomb of St. Lawrence (who died tied to a grill and roasted over a fire), which served to strengthen his devotion to the saints who had given their lives for their faith.

In October 366 Damasus was elected pope, and the project dearest to his heart was the restoration and beautification of the tombs of Rome's martyrs. To enable more pilgrims to visit the underground burial chambers, he ordered new stairways to be constructed and shafts to be dug to bring natural light and fresh air into the tunnels. He had artists adorn the catacombs with marble, mosaics, and frescoes, and Damasus himself wrote epitaphs for more than sixty of Rome's most beloved saints.

St. Damasus, then, is patron of the type of archaeologists who restore ancient sites and make them accessible to visitors.

St. Helen is patron of archaeologists who search for forgotten ancient sites and long-lost treasures. She was the mother of Constantine, Rome's first Christian emperor. Helen didn't convert to Christianity until age sixty, an unexpected event that helped influence both Constantine's own conversion and the relaxation of Christian persecution in the Roman empire.

Once the Christian faith was free

and flourishing, Helen traveled to the Holy Land to pray at sites associated with Christ's life, death, and resurrection. In Jerusalem she visited Calvary and the Holy Sepulcher, both of which lay beneath a temple of Venus erected by the emperor Hadrian two hundred years earlier. Helen had the temple demolished and then ordered the workmen to start digging. They uncovered three wooden crosses at the site and the cave in which Christ had been buried. But which was the cross on which Christ had died? A test was performed: Some say that all three crosses were touched to a sick or blind boy, whereas others claim that a dying woman was laid upon each. Both stories concur that, when touched by the True Cross, the ailing person was healed instantly.

Upon learning of his mother's discovery, Constantine sent funds to build a basilica on the site. Meanwhile, Helen moved on to other holy places, locating the cave in Bethlehem where Christ had been born and the spot on the Mount of Olives where he ascended into heaven. On these sites, too, Constantine built churches.

Like Howard Carter, the archaeologist who unearthed the tomb of the Egyptian pharaoh Tutankhamun, St.

Helen knew what she wanted to find and would permit nothing to get in her way until she found it.

See holy cards, page 61

ST. SEBASTIAN

DIED ABOUT 300 • FEAST DAY: JANUARY 20

How a saint becomes patron of a particular cause is usually predictable. Cosmas and Damian are the patron saints of doctors because that was their profession. St. Apollonia is the patron saint of toothaches because all her teeth were knocked out during her martyrdom. Native Americans invoke Blessed Kateri Tekakwitha because she was a member of the Mohawk tribe.

Sometimes, however, this principle operates in reverse. Such is the case for St. Sebastian, the Roman martyr who is always depicted as a handsome, nearly naked young man tied to a stake and pierced with arrows. St. Sebastian is the patron saint of archers, not because he was an archer himself but because he was their unfortunate target.

Sebastian was a member of the Roman Praetorian guard, an elite troop who served as the emperor Diocletian's bodyguard. When Diocletian began his persecution of the Church, Sebastian, a Christian, took advantage of his status and visited imprisoned Christians. That was dangerous business, and it was not long before he was denounced to the emperor. Enraged that one of his own bodyguards was a Christian, Diocletian ordered the Praetorians to take Sebastian to their camp and shoot him to death with arrows.

In the Middle Ages, archers prayed to St. Sebastian to make them better marksmen. Apparently they didn't see the irony in invoking an arrow-riddled saint to ensure that their own projectiles hit the mark.

See holy card, page 61

ST. BERNWARD

ABOUT 960–1022 • FEAST DAY: NOVEMBER 20

In the late 1800s and early 1900s, the United States was full of bricks-and-mortar bishops, busy men who scrambled to erect new churches, schools, convents, rectories, hospitals, and orphanages to meet the needs of the country's booming population of Catholic immigrants. A thousand years earlier, St. Bernward, a bricks-and-mortar bishop himself, not only spearheaded massive construction projects, he also drew the buildings' architectural plans.

Bernward was very young when his parents died. His uncle, Bishop Volkmar of Utrecht, took him in and supervised his education. Although Bernward excelled at mathematics and engineering, he entered the priesthood rather than pursue a career as an architect. He soon became a chaplain at the palace of the Holy Roman emperor and, in 993, was appointed bishop of Hildesheim, in northern Germany. This was wild country, the target of frequent raids by Slavic tribes from the east and Vikings from the north. To protect his diocese, Bernward drew upon his architectural skills, designing and supervising the construction of castles at strategic locations and erecting fortifications around the main cities and towns. He also built many churches and monasteries, the most famous being the Abbey of St. Michael in Hildesheim, a masterpiece of Romansesque architecture. Somehow this incredibly prolific bishop also found time to design and forge sacred gold and silver vessels for his cathedral as well as a magnificent pair of bronze doors that survive to this day.

In tribute to his wide-ranging talents, architects, goldsmiths, and metalworkers of all kinds have taken St. Bernward as their patron.

See holy card, page 61

ST. MAURICE &
THE THEBAN LEGION

DIED ABOUT 287 • FEAST DAY: SEPTEMBER 22

As their name implies, the Theban Legion came from in and around the Egyptian city of Thebes. Maurice, their *primicerius*, or chief officer, was a Christian, as were all the legionnaires. Emperor Maximian sent the legion from Egypt to Switzerland to crush a Gallic tribe that had rebelled against Rome; before the army marched into battle, the emperor commanded that every soldier sacrifice to the gods of Rome. With Maurice as their spokesman, the Christian legion refused.

To break their spirit, Maximian ordered a decimation in which loyal Roman troops killed every tenth Christian legionnaire. When they still refused to obey caesar's command, Maximian ordered a second decimation, again without success. The emperor then ordered his troops to massacre the Theban Legion, martyring ten thousand Christian soldiers at once.

It's a dramatic story—so many Christians slaughtered in one day.

Combine the tragedy with the courage, fidelity, and discipline of Maurice and his men, and it's only natural for them to be acclaimed as the patron saints of armies.

As the legion's commander, St. Maurice has enjoyed the most attention. Churches throughout central Europe are dedicated to him, and in France more than fifty towns and villages are named "St. Maurice." He also serves as one of the patron saints of Austria as well as of the pope's Swiss Guard.

See holy card, page 62

ST. JAMES THE GREATER

FIRST CENTURY • FEAST DAY: JULY 25

One of the first apostles to join Jesus, St. James was also the first to be martyred. Of the twelve apostles, St. James, his brother St. John the Evangelist, and St. Peter formed a privileged inner circle. Christ allowed them to witness miracles the other apostles only heard about later: the raising from the dead of Jairus's young daughter, the healing of St. Peter's mother-in-law, and Christ's display of his heavenly glory at the Transfiguration.

From time to time James and John's privileged status among the apostles went to their heads. When Samaritan villagers refused to welcome Jesus, the brothers urged him to call down fire from heaven and destroy the town. On another occasion their mother, with James and John's approval, asked Jesus to reserve in heaven the places on his right and on his left for her sons.

While the other disciples carried the gospel to far-off lands, James stuck close to home, preaching in Judea and Samaria. Consequently, when King Herod Agrippa began to round up Christians, James was easy to find. He was arrested, given a quick trial, and beheaded.

Legend tells us that as the king's men led James outside Jerusalem for execution, he passed a man crippled by arthritis or rheumatism who was sitting by the side of the road. The man begged James to cure him. Pausing for a moment on his way to martyrdom, James said, "In the name of Jesus Christ, for whom I am being led to execution, stand up and bless your Creator." As the soldiers dragged James away, the crippled man stood and then ran to the temple in the city to give thanks to God. That's the type of cure even people who suffer only minor twinges of arthritis pain pray for.

See holy card, page 62

ST. LUKE THE EVANGELIST

FIRST CENTURY • FEAST DAY: OCTOBER 18

rtists never satisfied with their work—those who think just a few brushstrokes more will make it perfect—should invoke St. Luke. Legend has it that St. Luke was given the especially daunting commission of painting a portrait of the Blessed Virgin Mary and the Christ Child. A sweet detail of the story asserts that the sitting took place in the Holy Family's house in Nazareth and that St. Luke painted the picture on Mary's kitchen table.

He must have created the same image quite a few times because churches claiming to possess Lucan portraits of the Virgin and Child are found all across Europe: there's one in Santa Maria Maggiore in Rome as well as the famous Black Madonna at the Polish monastery of Czestochowa.

St. Luke's gospel provides so many detailed stories about the Virgin Mary—more than the three other gospels combined—that New Testament readers have wondered whether Mary was one of Luke's

sources. This presumed relationship later segued neatly into the legend of the sacred portrait.

No one today would seriously claim that St. Luke painted the likeness of Jesus and Mary. Nonetheless, during the late Middle Ages and the Renaissance, artists created the Guild of St. Luke, which counted among its members Leonardo da Vinci, Raphael, and Jan Vermeer. In the fifteenth century, artists in Rome founded the Academy of St. Luke as a school for painters. It still operates there today.

See holy card, page 62

1.

2.

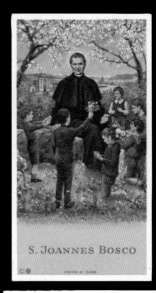

S. JOANNES BOSCO

3.

S. Genesio Martire

4.

Die hl. Pelagia, Bischerin.

1. Accountants • St. Matthew 2. Acrobats and Jugglers • St. John Bosco
3. Actors • St. Genesius 4. Actresses • St. Pelagia

1. **Advertising Professionals • St. Bernardine of Siena** 2. **Against Being Hanged • St. Colman of Stocherau**
3. **AIDS Patients and Caregivers • St. Aloysius Gonzaga** 4. **Airline Pilots and Passengers • Our Lady of Loreto**

S. Mattia. - S. Matías.

Sanctus Mathias, Apostolus

S. Mathias. - H. Mathias.

S. Giovanni Berchmans

S'Antoine guérit un jeune homme, pénitent, qui avait frappé sa mère et s'était coupé le pied en punition de son péché.

1. Alcoholism • St. Matthias 2. Altar Servers • St. John Berchmans
3. American Indians • Blessed Kateri Tekakwitha 4. Amputations • St. Anthony of Padua

S. RENATUS GOUPIL (*)
(1608-1642)

S. IOANNES DE LA LANDE (**)
(† 1646)

COADIUTORES TEMPORALES S.I.
MARTYRES

FEST. 26 SEPT.

EXTRAIT DE VIANDE DE LA Cⁱᵉ LIEBIG

SAINT FRANÇOIS D'ASSISE · 4.

Reproduction interdite. Voir l'explication au verso

3.

OPVS THEODORICI BOVTS ANNO MCCCCLXVIII

1. Anesthesiologists • St. René Goupil 2. Animals • St. Francis of Assisi
3. Appendicitis • St. Erasmus

ST. JOSEPH CUPERTINO

1603–1663 • FEAST DAY: SEPTEMBER 18

People are often surprised when the Catholic Church refuses to embrace phenomena that appear to be supernatural, whether a weeping statue, an apparition of the Virgin Mary, or the manifestation of Jesus's face on a freshly fried tortilla. But such skepticism is wise. Too often "miracles" prove to be wish fulfillment, a figment of the imagination, or even fraud. But the case of St. Joseph Cupertino is unusual: Although the Vatican has never explained his extraordinary behavior, neither has anyone ever declared it to be supernatural.

St. Joseph Cupertino levitated. Well, perhaps a better word is *flew*, because he didn't just hover a few inches off the ground, he truly moved through the air. And not just once—seventy episodes were recorded during a seventeen-year period.

His religious superiors at the Franciscan monastery tried to keep him out of the public eye, but some visitors just couldn't be turned away.

Spain's ambassador to the papal court brought his wife and a large entourage to see Joseph. Reluctantly the superior conceded and the guests were escorted to a chapel. Upon entering, Joseph rose off the floor, flew over the visitors' heads to a statue of the Virgin Mary, and remained momentarily suspended in midair before flying back to the chapel entrance and landing gently.

In 1638 the Inquisition investigated to determine if Joseph was faking the levitations or using some form of black magic. Joseph levitated while the inquisitors questioned him. Pope Urban VIII commanded that the Franciscan superior bring Joseph to see him. During his papal audience, Joseph levitated again.

Because St. Joseph Cupertino's slow, fluid movements through the air resemble those of an astronaut walking in space, he has become the patron of astronauts.

See holy card, page 62

ST. DOMINIC

1170–1221 • FEAST DAY: AUGUST 8

At Dominic's baptism, family, guests, and the officiating priest saw a star-shaped light shining from the infant's tiny forehead. In later artistic representations, the star became one of St. Dominic's emblems; this association led to his veneration as the patron of astronomers.

Famous for founding the Dominican religious order, Dominic sought to revive religious devotion among Catholics and bring the Cathar heretics back to the fold. The Cathars taught that the physical world was evil and, consequently, that the creator of the universe (the Catholics' God) was a demon.

Dominic emphasized preaching effectively and knowledgeably to ensure success in converting the nonbelievers. He traveled extensively in southern France, where the Cathars were especially numerous. He converted some but was not as successful as he'd hoped. In his discouragement, Dominic turned to Mary, who, according to tradition, appeared holding a rosary. She promised Dominic that if he prayed the rosary daily and taught others to do so as well, the Cathar heresy would be overcome. (Contrary to popular belief, St. Dominic did not introduce the rosary to Catholics—they had been using prayer beads for centuries—but he and his Dominicans spread the devotion.) Although the Dominicans succeeded in bringing many Cathars back to the Catholic faith, some lords and bishops felt the missionary effort was taking too long. They launched a war that, by the end of the thirteenth century, had nearly wiped out the Cathars.

Thirteen years after Dominic's death, he was canonized by his friend Pope Gregory IX, who said he doubted Dominic's sanctity no more than he doubted the holiness of Saints Peter and Paul. For the canonization process to take only thirteen years is unusual; most drag on for a century or more.

See holy card, page 63

ST. SEBASTIAN

DIED ABOUT 300 • FEAST DAY: JANUARY 20

In the story about the patron saint of archers (see page 36), we left St. Sebastian tied to a stake and perforated with arrows. The Praetorian Guard who made him their target assumed Sebastian was dead. So did everyone else who heard of his martyrdom. After sunset, a Christian woman named Irene crept into the Praetorians' camp to retrieve the body and give it a Christian burial. As Irene and her serving woman cut down Sebastian, they heard him groan. Incredibly, he was still alive.

Instead of carrying him to the catacombs for burial, the two women brought Sebastian to Irene's house, where they nursed him back to health. When he was able, Sebastian went off to confront Diocletian. He found the emperor on the steps of the imperial palace. Enraged that his former bodyguard was still alive, Diocletian demanded of his entourage, "Did I not sentence this man to be shot to death with arrows?" But Sebastian answered for the emperor's courtiers. He had been made a target for archers, yes, "But the Lord kept me alive so I could return and rebuke you for treating the servants of Christ so cruelly."

This time Diocletian took no chances: He ordered his guard to beat Sebastian to death there on the palace steps while the emperor watched. Once certain that Sebastian was dead, Diocletian ordered that the martyr's body be dumped into the Cloaca Maxima, Rome's main sewer. Yet Christians recovered it and buried Sebastian in a catacomb known ever since as San Sebastiano.

St. Sebastian is invoked for the conversion, or at least the confounding, of atheists and all enemies of Christianity because, at the risk of his own life, he faced his persecutor and tried to persuade him to turn to God.

See holy card, page 63

BLESSED PIER GIORGIO FRASSATI

1901–1925 • FEAST DAY: JULY 4

Pier Giorgio Frassati shattered the traditional notion that saints are meek, mild, frail creatures. The many photographs of him show a young man with almost movie-star good looks—dark hair, strong jaw, broad shoulders. As a boy, he was an exceptional athlete, and he never lost his love for strenuous physical activity. With a group of friends who called themselves "The Shady Characters," Pier Giorgio went on long hikes and mountain-climbing expeditions and competed in wild, even reckless, skiing races on the slopes of the Italian Alps.

Alfredo Frassati, Pier Giorgio's father, was one of the wealthiest and most influential men in Italy. He was a senator, Italy's ambassador to Germany, and publisher of the newspaper *La Stampa*. Both father and son were committed antifascists; as Benito Mussolini's power increased, Alfredo Frassati used his newspaper to amplify his criticisms of the dictator. One evening in 1924, a gang of Mussolini's black-shirt thugs broke into the Frassati home, thinking they could intimidate the family into silence. Instead, Pier Giorgio attacked the intruders, and the attackers fled. On another occasion Pier Giorgio was participating in an antifascist demonstration in Rome when policemen who supported Mussolini attacked the demonstrators. Using a banner pole as a weapon, Pier Giorgio clobbered some of the cops. He was arrested and spent the night in jail.

Pier Giorgio's approach to religious life was equally uncompromising. He prayed the rosary while hiking, often to the exclusion of talking to his friends. He began each day with Mass and Holy Communion. And he spent part of each day helping the poor and the desperate of Turin, his hometown.

Although the Frassatis were wealthy, Alfredo doled out meager allowances to his children, afraid that easy access to money would spoil them. Since he had no funds to give to the poor, Pier Giorgio adopted a more hands-on approach to charity. In his pocket, he kept a notebook with the names, addresses, and particular needs of impoverished people who came to rely on him for help. When he learned that an elderly woman had been evicted from her apartment, he found her a new home. He went from factory to factory with an ex-convict until he managed to persuade a foreman to give the man a job.

In 1925, a few weeks after his twenty-fourth birthday, Pier Giorgio felt unwell. He tried to ignore it, but by early summer he was very ill. After examining the young man, the doctor told the Frassatis that Pier Giorgio had contracted an especially virulent form of polio for which there was no treatment and that in a few days he would be dead. Stunned and grief stricken, the family refused to believe the diagnosis. But Pier Giorgio's condition deteriorated with each passing day.

On his deathbed Pier Giorgio gave his name-filled notebook to his sister Luciana, begging her not to forget the people he had tried to help. On July 4, 1925, Pier Giorgio Frassati died.

On the day of the funeral, the Frassatis were stunned when more than one thousand strangers, almost all from the slums of Turin, came to the church for the Requiem Mass. The family knew that Pier Giorgio had been blessed with a kind heart, but they were unaware that his acts of charity and compassion had touched so many.

See holy card, page 63

ST. UBALDO BALDASSINI

(ABOUT 1100–1160) • FEAST DAY: MAY 16

A utism was not diagnosed in the twelfth century, but early biographies of St. Ubaldo Baldassini describe his mother as suffering from some type of developmental disorder, which in recent years has led to Ubaldo being venerated as the patron of anyone on the autism spectrum.

Ubaldo was born in Gubbio, in the Italian province of Umbria. There were many noble families in the town: a few years before Ubaldo was born, Gubbio sent a thousand knights to fight in the First Crusade.

Ubaldo's parents sent him to study at the Monastery of Ss. Marian and James; there he began to consider joining the priesthood. After Ubaldo's ordination the bishop appointed him prior of the canons, the clergy that staffed Gubbio's cathedral. The canons had been lax in performing their religious duties, so Ubaldo (with a few canons who had not been corrupted) set the example, which over time other canons imitated.

Ubaldo's successful reform of the canons of Gubbio spread to the surrounding cities. When the bishop of Perugia died, the clergy of that city elected Ubaldo to be their bishop. Ubaldo hid in the countryside and then traveled to Rome to beg Pope Honorius II to spare him the burden of being a bishop. The pope granted his request, but two years later, when the bishop of Gubbio died, Honorius insisted that Ubaldo submit to the will of the clergy and the townspeople and become their bishop.

Ubaldo was saintly as well as courageous. During a bloody street brawl he elbowed his way into the middle of the fight, which so surprised the combatants that they stopped to trying kill one another and allowed Ubaldo to talk sense to them.

See holy card, page 63

THE HOLY INNOCENTS

FIRST CENTURY • FEAST DAY: DECEMBER 28

Even in the Christmas story, there is a touch of tragedy, and that is the massacre of the infant boys of Bethlehem. St. Matthew's gospel records that when the Magi stopped in Jerusalem to ask the whereabouts of the King of the Jews, Herod, the king of Judea, sent them to Bethlehem with instructions to return once they had found the Christ Child so that he, too, could pay homage. Warned by an angel that Herod was up to no good, the Magi returned home via a route that bypassed the city and its conniving king.

Once Herod realized the Magi were on to him, he sent troops to Bethlehem with orders to kill every boy aged two and younger. But the same angel warned Joseph to take Mary and Jesus south to Egypt for safety. By the time Herod's troops charged into the village, the Holy Family was long gone.

No one knows how many babies were massacred that day. Bethlehem was a small village, so the victims probably numbered about a dozen. Tradition, however, has always imagined much more catastrophic totals. Greek Christians claimed the tally was 14,000; the Syrians said 64,000; and western European Christians asserted 144,000.

Heart-wrenching as it is to contemplate the slaying of children, the Holy Innocents have always been regarded as the protectors of babies. In art they are shown in heaven, playing with the infant Jesus and the palm fronds that symbolize their having died for Christ. By 400, the Church celebrated December 28 as their feast day, and about that time the poet Prudentius composed a hymn in their honor. It begins:

All hail! ye infant martyr flowers
Cut off in life's first dawning hours:
As rosebuds snapped in tempest
    strife,
When Herod sought your Savior's
    life.

See holy card, page 64

ST. CASIMIR

1460–1483 • FEAST DAY: MARCH 4

𝕵n the Middle Ages every member of a royal family was expected to secure an advantageous marriage. The exceptions were those princes and princesses who opted to become priests or nuns. So, confirmed bachelors like St. Casimir were extraordinary. The third of thirteen children born to King Casimir IV and Queen Elizabeth of Poland, as a younger son Casimir would have been allowed to enter religious life. But, although intensely devout, he had no such calling. He was perfectly content to live as an unmarried layman. (His parents never gave up hope, however; they arranged to have a German princess waiting for him in case he changed his mind.)

Remaining a prince rather than becoming a priest had its advantages: Casimir enjoyed a large income, which he used to help the poor, ransom captives, and assist destitute pilgrims who had no means of returning home. He was not reticent about bringing injustice and oppression to the king's attention, demanding that such inequities be rectified.

Casimir also cultivated a profound prayer life. In addition to attending Mass every morning, he returned to the palace chapel seven more times during the day to follow the monastic cycle of prayer. Sometimes he even got up in the middle of the night to go to church. If the doors were locked, he prayed on the steps.

When in 1481 King Casimir was called to Lithuania to settle that country's political problems, he placed his son in charge of Poland in his absence. During the two years young Casimir reigned in his father's name, he brought a new level of justice and mercy to the country. He was on his way to Lithuania to visit his father when he died of tuberculosis at age twenty-four.

See holy card, page 64

ST. AMAND

ABOUT 584–ABOUT 676 • FEAST DAY: FEBRUARY 6

St. Amand never tended bar or bought a round of drinks, and he certainly had no idea how to pour the perfect pint. Yet he is still the patron saint of bartenders for reasons that have nothing to do with his profession but everything to do with his location.

For most of the seventh century, Amand preached the gospel in Belgium, northwest Germany, and the area around Bordeaux, France. Amand didn't have an easy time persuading the region's pagan tribes to renounce their heathen customs, and he ran into real trouble convincing the morally degenerate king of the Franks, Dagobert I. When Amand tried to bring the ruler to repentance, Dagobert exiled the missionary from the kingdom. But the king quickly changed his mind when his wife gave birth to a son. He gave up his wicked ways and insisted that only the holiest priest in the land should baptize his child. That person, of course, was Amand, so back he went to the region with which he's be-

come most identified.

Known in his time as a great missionary, St. Amand ostensibly founded several monasteries in present-day Belgium.

As the man who almost single-handedly planted the Christian faith in these remote corners of Europe, St. Amand became a regional favorite, a sort of Franco-Belgian-German version of St. Patrick. Since the area is renowned for its production of superior beers and wines, virtually everyone involved in making and distributing the beverages, including bartenders, took St. Amand as their patron.

Today St. Amand's fame has spread worldwide to encompass beer and wine connoisseurs who appreciate the fine sauternes produced by the Château St.-Amand, in the Bordeaux region, and the excellent St. Amand French country ale brewed along the Franco-Belgian border.

See holy card, page 64

ST. AMBROSE

ABOUT 340–397 • FEAST DAY: DECEMBER 7

S t. Ambrose began as a lawyer, not a priest, and while studying law he learned the art of presenting an argument in a convincing and appealing way. He put those skills to good use years later when he shifted careers from the courts to the Church. Where he had once used his eloquence to win court cases, he now relied on these talents to urge sinners to repent, to bring converts to the Church, and to inspire Christians to a more fervent practice of their faith. Ambrose was so eloquent and persuasive that he's been called "the honey-tongued doctor," a quality that, through the centuries, artists have conveyed by depicting Ambrose with a beehive. This association has led beekeepers to take St. Ambrose as their patron.

When Ambrose was a teenager, his sister Marcellina (also later a saint) became a nun. She took her vows in St. Peter's Basilica in Rome, receiving the veil from the pope himself. For the rest of his life, Ambrose was outspoken in his admiration for women who chose convent life. His preaching on the subject was so persuasive that, after hearing his sermons, large numbers of young women decided to become nuns. Mothers who wanted their daughters to marry learned to steer clear of any Mass celebrated by Bishop Ambrose.

The smooth eloquence and compelling logic of St. Ambrose changed the world. Presenting the Christian faith in a way that was convincing, attractive, and rational, he succeeded in converting a reluctant North African philosopher named Augustine—as in St. Augustine, the second most influential theologian the Church has ever known (after the apostle St. Paul).

See holy card, page 81

54

ST. JEROME

ABOUT 345–420 • FEAST DAY: SEPTEMBER 30

St. Jerome was a Latin scholar in love with the art of fashioning words into beautiful phrases. About the year 366 he became secretary to the newly elected pope, St. Damasus. It was Damasus's dream to produce a new Latin translation of the Bible—one based on the original Greek and Hebrew manuscripts yet still pleasurable to read—and he recognized Jerome's flair for language. The pope believed his secretary was the man for the job, and, when asked to take on the daunting task, Jerome responded enthusiastically. During the next three years Jerome produced beautiful, accurate translations of the psalms, the four gospels, all the epistles, and the Book of Revelation. Pope Damasus was delighted.

To improve the then-current translation of the Old Testament, Jerome studied Hebrew. At first he complained that Hebrew contained "hissing and broken-winded words" but kept at it and eventually mastered the language in which God had spoken to the prophets. It took Jerome twenty-six years to complete his translation. In that time Pope Damasus, his friend and patron, died. Jerome moved from Rome to Bethlehem. Then in 410, the city of Rome fell to barbarians. One of his letters survives from this time, when Roman refugees were pouring into the Holy Land. "I have set aside my commentary on Ezekiel, and almost all study," he wrote to a friend. "For today we must translate the words of the Scriptures into deeds."

See holy card, page 81

Bicyclists

OUR LADY OF GHISALLO

SHRINE DATING FROM ABOUT 1135 • FEAST DAY: OCTOBER 13

On the summit of a steep hill near Lake Como in Italy, on the route of the Tour de Lombardy bicycle race, sits a small chapel dedicated to Our Lady of Ghisallo. The first race was organized in 1905, by which time devotion to Our Lady of Ghisallo was nearly eight hundred years old. Originally the site was a simple wayside shrine. But during the Middle Ages, the Count of Ghisallo erected a small chapel in gratitude to Mary for saving him from robbers who had attacked him nearby.

In the 1940s Father Ermelindo Vigano, the parish priest as well as a cycling enthusiast, asked Pope Pius XII to make the Madonna of Ghisallo the patron saint of cyclists. The pope agreed and issued a formal declaration in 1949. Since then the chapel has become a destination for cyclists, and the shrine's administrators have opened a small museum of religious and cycling artifacts. Among the bicycling relics on display is the wrecked bicycle Fabio Casartelli was riding when he died as a result of a crash during the 1995 Tour de France.

Every year on November 2, All Souls Day, Mass is offered for the repose of the souls of cyclists who have died. On Christmas Eve, the shrine's church is crowded with cyclists as well as local people who make the perilous trek up the mountain for Midnight Mass.

See holy card, page 81

56

ST. MILBURGA

DIED 727 • FEAST DAY: FEBRUARY 23

During the eighth century, the royal families of England produced a bumper crop of holy men and women. Milburga's mother, Ermenburga, her two sisters Mildred and Milgitha, and, of course, Milburga herself are all venerated as saints.

Though born a princess, Milburga chose the life of a nun and entered Much Wenlock Abbey, a convent her father had founded in Shropshire, near the Welsh border. Those living in the abbey's neighborhood regarded Milburga as a saint, attributing all manner of miracles to her, including the raising of a little boy from the dead.

Once, just before harvest, an enormous flock of birds alighted on the farmers' fields and began gobbling up all the grain. Nothing the farmers did frightened off the birds, so Milburga began to pray. With the sound of a tremendous flapping of wings, the flock rose above the fields and flew away. This story led to Milburga's status as the saint who wards off the ravages of wild birds, but she has since become the patron of pet birds, too.

For more than eight hundred years, St. Milburga's tomb in Much Wenlock Abbey was a holy place cherished by local people and served as the destination of pilgrims from every corner of England and Wales. All that came to an end, however, when Henry VIII broke with Rome, closed all the abbeys, and sent his men to dismantle the saints' shrines. The king's commissioners arrived at Much Wenlock in 1540. They stripped St. Milburga's shrine of its valuables, pried open her coffin, carried her bones outside the church, and burned them.

See holy card, page 81

ST. CHARLES BORROMEO

1538–1584 • FEAST DAY: NOVEMBER 4

It's hard to read a biography about St. Charles Borromeo and not wonder if the author is exaggerating. How could one man have accomplished so much before his death at age forty-six?

One answer is that the Counter-Reformation, the Catholic Church's sixteenth-century effort to reform itself in the wake of the disastrous Protestant revolt, focused Charles's attention; it even gave him a practical "to do" list for reorganizing his diocese. Pope Pius IV, Charles's uncle, had made him the cardinal archbishop of Milan, giving him authority over a vast territory that extended from northern Italy into southern Switzerland. Although not the most corrupt diocese in Europe, Milan had its share of problems. Many of the difficulties could be attributed to Charles's predecessors, who had been content to live in Rome (or other congenial, cosmopolitan cities), collect revenue from Milan, and let an auxiliary bishop or monsignor deal with the daily headaches of running the archdiocese.

Charles was the first archbishop to reside in Milan in fifty years. He began his work there by reforming the priests, targeting those who kept mistresses or viewed their life in the Church as a way to amass a personal fortune. He also insisted that priests say Mass properly and reverently and use their sermons to explain to their congregations the essentials of the faith. Next, Charles focused on the nuns. Some cloistered convents had been receiving too many male visitors. Charles commanded that every convent install in its parlor a grill or partition to keep the nuns on one side and visitors on the other.

He then took on the religious orders as well. Too many members had strayed, refusing to obey their superiors and leading scandalous lives, so Charles insisted that all live by the rules of the order. Opposition to his reform was fierce: One group, inaptly named the Humiliati, hired an assassin who shot Charles in the back while he was praying in his chapel. (The shot didn't kill him.)

His reforms and good deeds didn't end there. Charles also sold most of the property the archbishops of Milan had acquired and gave the money to charity. After a bad harvest, he fed three thousand people every day until the famine ended. When the plague struck Milan, Charles led penitential processions through the streets, walking barefoot and with a noose around his neck to demonstrate that even cardinals need God's mercy. For the formation of holy priests, Charles founded a seminary. For the instruction of children in the faith, he established the Confraternity of Christian Doctrine, known in Catholic parishes today as the CCD program.

By 1584, after twenty-one years on the job, Charles showed symptoms of exhaustion (and no wonder!). By autumn he was running a persistent fever, and on October 30 he was found unconscious on a chapel floor. His doctors insisted that he remain in bed, but, true to form, Charles kept up his hectic schedule until two days before his death, on November 3, 1584.

Perhaps it's unfair to bishops that St. Charles Borromeo is their patron. Who could repeat all that he accomplished in such a short time? Yet Charles remains a model of what is most important in a bishop's work—producing holy priests and nuns, teaching the faith to the laity and helping them live holy lives, caring for those who cannot help themselves, and setting the example of trust in God.

See holy card, page 82

ST. KEVIN OF GLENDALOUGH

ABOUT 498–618 • FEAST DAY: JUNE 3

The son of a noble Irish family, young Kevin began living among monks at age twelve. Ordained a priest as an adult, he traveled into the Wicklow Mountains, south of Dublin, where he settled in a beautiful valley called Glendalough. He intended to live as a hermit, but his solitude didn't last long; soon he had so many disciples he had to build a monastery to accommodate them all.

As is often the case with Irish saints, Kevin's life has been embellished with a host of legends. One story tells of a young man, suffering from severe epilepsy, who received a vision telling him he would be cured by eating apples. Since no apple trees grew in Glendalough, Kevin commanded a willow tree to bear fruit, and twenty apples immediately appeared on the branches. The young man ate some and was healed. In another tale, as Kevin was praying, a cow licked his robe. Later, at milking time, the cow produced fifty times more milk than any other in the dairy.

Kevin's patronage of blackbirds comes from yet another miracle story. One day during Lent, Kevin was praying with his arms outstretched, his body forming a cross. A blackbird alighted on his hand, laid an egg, and flew off. Out of pity for the unborn bird, Kevin remained for weeks in the cruciform position until the egg hatched and the new blackbird was strong enough to fly.

See holy card, page 82

Der hl. Damasus.

„So leuchte euer Licht vor den Menschen, auf
daß sie eure guten Werke sehen, und euren Vater
preisen, der im Himmel ist." Matth. V. 16.

Bemühe dich, deiner Umgebung gutes Beispiel
zu geben durch dein Handlungen und Worte.

Bete um Abwendung der Aergernisse.

Kath. Anstalt von Joh. Kravogl in Innsbruck.

K. BEURON   1061

3-208   PRINTED IN ITALY

R. Margreiter   GL. 1065

ST. BERNWARD

1. Archaeologists · St. Damasus   2. Archaeologists · St. Helen
3. Archers · St. Sebastian   4. Architects · St Bernward

Sanctus Mauritius Martyr.

S. Giacomo. - Santiago.

Sanctus Jacobus, Apostolus.

S. James. - H. Jacobus.

S. Luca. - S. Lucas.

Sanctus Lucas, Evangelista.

S. Luke. - H. Lucas.

SAINT JOSEPH CUPERTINO
CONVENTUAL MINOR FRIAR
HELPER IN EXAMINATIONS
OSIMO (ANCONA) ITALY

Armies • St. Maurice and the Theban Legion 2. Arthritis and Rheumatism • St. James the Greater
3. Artists • St. Luke the Evangelist 4. Astronauts • St. Joseph Cupertino

ST. DOMINIQUE.

S. Sebastian.

For I am sure that neither death, nor life, nor principalities, nor powers, nor any other creature shall be able to separate us from the love of God. Rom. VIII. 38. 39.

1. **Astronomers • St. Dominic** 2. **Atheists • St. Sebastian**
3. **Athletes • Blessed Pier Giorgio Frassati** 4. **Autism • St. Ubaldo Baldassini**

ŚWIĘTY KAZIMIERZ.

1 Babies • The Holy Innocents 2. Bachelors • St. Casimir
3. Bartenders • St. Amand

FOURTEEN HOLY HELPERS

FEAST DAY: AUGUST 8

In October 1347, several Genoese merchant ships returning from the Middle East limped into the port of Messina, in Sicily. All the sailors on board were either dead or dying of an unknown disease characterized by a never-before-seen symptom—large blackish swellings on the neck and in the groin and armpits. The strange malady notwithstanding, the people of Messina did what seemed natural: They carried the dying to hospitals, took the dead to church for a funeral, and looted the ships of their valuable cargo. In this way the Black Death arrived in Europe. Between one- and two-thirds of Europe's population would be wiped out before this first outbreak had run its course three years later. It was not uncommon for the entire population of a village, monastery, or convent to die. In Florence the population fell from about 120,000 to about 50,000. Such statistics were typical in urban areas across Europe.

Confronted with such a terrible disease, many Christians turned to Heaven for help. In France, the Low Countries, and German-speaking lands there existed a devotion to a group of well-loved saints known collectively as the Fourteen Holy Helpers. Now the people in these regions turned to the Fourteen Helpers to spare them from the epidemic. Given the extent of the calamity, having fourteen heavenly intercessors all at once would have been a comfort. The fourteen are Saints Acacius, Barbara, Blaise, Catherine of Alexandria, Christopher, Cyriacus, Denis, Erasmus, Eustace, George, Giles, Margaret of Antioch, Pantaleon, and Vitus, and all (except Pantaleon) appear in this book.

Devotion to the Fourteen Holy Helpers has diminished over the centuries, except in the tiny village of Bad Staffelstein in southern Germany, where pilgrims still pray at the spectacular rococo church dedicated to them.

See holy card, page 82

ST. AUGUSTINE

(354–430) • FEAST DAY: AUGUST 28

Before Augutine's conversion, when he was still a Manichean and living with his mistress, he taught philosophy and rhetoric in schools in North Africa and Italy. If he published during that period, those writings have not survived. But after his conversion, and especially after he was consecrated bishop of Hippo (in what is now Algeria), Augustine became an extremely productive writer.

In addition to his *Confessions*—which is, by the way, the world's first autobiography—he wrote many books on Christian doctrine and philosophy; the virtues of faith, hope, charity, chastity, and patience; and on music as well.

Augustine waded into the religious controversies of his age, correcting the unorthodox opinions of the Arians, the Pelagians, the Donatists, and, of course, the Manicheans—a heresy he knew especially well. In his books on how to interpret sacred Scripture, he suggested that readers be prudent: in his discussion of how to read the Book of Genesis, hesuggested, "We must be on our guard against giving interpretations that are hazardous or opposed to science, and so exposing the Word of God to the ridicule of unbelievers."

His magnum opus is The City of God, in which he answers the criticism of pagans who claimed that Rome had fallen to the Goths in 410 because the Roman people had abandoned the old gods for Christianity. This work took Augustine thirteen years to complete.

We have 270 of his letters (there were probably many more that have been lost over time) and 363 of his sermons. In the first few years of the twenty-first century, bloggers, who tend to be prolific and address a host of topics, chose St. Augustine as their patron.

See holy card, page 82

ST. JANUARIUS

DIED ABOUT 305 • FEAST DAY: SEPTEMBER 19

When St. Januarius was beheaded around the year 305, some Christian women who were on the scene collected a little of the bishop's blood in a glass vial and placed the relic in his tomb. Although it's easy to connect this act with today's practice of blood banks collecting and storing blood, a much more dramatic story explains why Januarius is honored as the patron of blood donors. Called "the miracle of the liquefaction," the phenomenon began occurring after the bishop's bones were moved from their original burial place to a shrine inside the cathedral of Naples. At some point, the cathedral clergy noticed that the blood in the little bottle acted strangely—and it still does.

Here's what happens: Every September 19 a solemn ceremony is held in front of St. Januarius's shrine. The small glass vial is the center of attention. Four inches tall and a bit more than two inches in diameter, the vial holds a solid dark red mass that is believed to be the same dried blood collected by the women at the scene of Januarius's martyrdom. In front of a throng of laity and clergy, the archbishop of Naples carries the vial to a reliquary that contains the skull of the saint, and then the miraculous phenomenon occurs: The solid mass inside the vial becomes liquid. Once the red mass has liquefied, the archbishop holds the relic aloft, turning it this way and that, so that the crowd can see the liquid sloshing around inside the vial. The archbishop cries, "The miracle has happened!" and everyone in the church surges forward to kiss the relic.

Various attempts have been made to find a scientific reason that explains how a solid should suddenly become a liquid, but none have proved satisfactory. In-depth study of the phenomenon has been stymied by Neapolitan church officials who refuse to allow scientists to break the vial's seal and take a sample. Furthermore, the Vatican has made no official declaration that the liquefaction is a supernatural event. *Something* happens—even skeptics concede as much—but exactly what or why remains a mystery.

On some occasions, the blood has not liquefied, which Neapolitans take as a warning from the saint or as a sign of his displeasure. (For example, the relic remained solid the year Naples elected a Communist mayor.) But incidents have also occurred when the blood has liquefied spontaneously, as when the late Cardinal Terence Cooke of New York visited the shrine in 1978. Cardinal Cooke, by the way, is currently a candidate for sainthood himself.

See holy card, page 83

ST. COLUMBA

ABOUT 521–597 • FEAST DAY: JUNE 9

By recognizing St. Columba as the patron of bookbinders, the Church is in fact rehabilitating him. He'd really be more suitable as the patron saint of copyright infringement, plagiarists, and people who borrow books but never return them.

Columba was born a prince of the O'Donnell clan of County Donegal in northwest Ireland. Like so many Irish Christians of this period, Columba was an avid collector of beautiful books. Not long after being ordained a priest, Columba called on Finnian, abbot of Clonnard Abbey. Finnian had just returned from Rome, where he had bought a copy of St. Jerome's translation of the Psalms. Filled with superb hand-lettering and border decorations, the book was a work of art. As Columba turned the pages of this treasure, he knew he had to have it. So, every night after Finnian and his monks had gone to sleep, Columba sat up making an exact copy. He had just finished when Fin-

nian got wind of what his guest had been up to. Since the copy was unauthorized, Finnian demanded that Columba hand it over. Columba refused. Their argument grew heated, forcing the monks to step in and suggest that the case be arbitrated by Diarmaid, Ireland's high king.

Off Finnian and Columba went to the king's court, where each presented his side of the story. Diarmaid considered the case and then pronounced his verdict: "To every cow its calf, and to every book its copy." Barely able to conceal his rage, Columba surrendered his hard-earned replica. Now he nursed a double grudge—against both Finnian and Diarmaid.

Upon returning home, Columba summoned the O'Donnell clan's chiefs and warriors. He made a rousing speech, claiming that the king and the abbot had insulted him and that the clan's honor was at stake. Stirred by their kinsman's fiery oratory, the O'Donnells went to war against Diarmaid and Finnian. The two armies met on a plain beneath a mountain called Ben Bulben, where the O'Donnells inflicted a crushing defeat on Columba's enemies, leaving three thousand dead in their wake. The fight was regarded as a great victory in O'Donnell country, but Columba's private war didn't meet with much approval in the rest of Ireland.

At a special synod assembled to discuss the unfortunate event, bishops and abbots agreed that if every thin-skinned priest went to war each time his pride was wounded, Ireland would become a slaughterhouse. Most wanted to make an example of Columba by excommunicating him. St. Brendan, however, argued for a less severe penalty and urged merely exiling him from Ireland for life. The synod was persuaded and voted Columba out of Ireland. They also commanded him to convert three thousand pagans—one for each man who had died in his war.

The penalty of leaving his home forever brought Columba to his senses. Repentant and obedient, he sailed for the isle of Iona off Scotland's western coast. From there, he launched a mission to the land of the Picts that, by the end of his life, brought many more into the church's fold than the three thousand converts the synod had demanded.

See holy card, page 83

ST. JOHN OF GOD

1495–1550 • FEAST DAY: MARCH 8

Peddling books was just one of many careers attempted by the man who came to be known as St. John of God. He worked as a shepherd and at odd jobs on the estate of a Spanish count; he enlisted in the army but was nearly hanged after leaving his post guarding a cache of valuable loot. He traveled to Morocco with the high-minded intention of ransoming Christian slaves from Moorish captivity, but since he had no money he never managed to redeem a single one.

Finally John opened a small shop in Granada from which he sold books and holy cards. Between customers he reflected on the sinful life he'd led while in the army. All that drinking, gambling, and whoring preyed on his mind—so much so that he became mentally unhinged. He took to running through the streets howling with penitential grief, so city authorities had him locked up.

By luck St. John of Avila, a renowned preacher and spiritual counselor, happened to be in town. He visited John, soothed him, and listened to what must have been a long, frenzied confession. Then he commanded John to give up his hysterical displays and please God by doing something useful for humanity.

Assured by John of Avila that the volatile bookseller was once again in full possession of his senses, the asylum guardians released him. John put his confessor's advice into action by opening a small hospital for the poor in which he did all the nursing, cooking, and cleaning. Eventually the people of Granada came to realize that John was not a madman but their own homegrown saint. They began calling him John of God. Due to his late-in-life dedication to the sick, in addition to being the patron of booksellers, St. John of God is also the patron of hospitals and hospital workers.

See holy card, page 83

ST. BONAVENTURE

1221–1274 • FEAST DAY: JULY 15

St. Bonaventure was attending a church council in Lyon, France, when he was seized by excruciating stomach pains and died. Some biographers say he died of a ruptured bladder; others claim he was poisoned by extremist members of his own religious order, the Franciscans. Whatever the cause, St. Bonaventure has become the patron of those suffering from gastrointestinal problems.

Bonaventure was a prodigy of the Middle Ages. Mystic, prolific author, inspiring preacher, and zealous advocate of the Franciscan order, he helped "mainstream" the friars into universities and the highest levels of the church (Bonaventure himself was appointed a cardinal).

St. Francis's original principle of absolute poverty had worked well when the Franciscan movement was limited to a dozen men. But after his death, the Franciscans numbered in the thousands and their missions spread across Europe. Bonaventure realized that if the friars were required to keep living in rags, without shelter or knowing where their next meal would come from, they'd become a public nuisance and the movement would eventually be crippled. He argued for a modification that would permit each Franciscan community to have a permanent home. The friars would still own nothing personally and their lives would remain austere, but they would no longer be begging on the streets.

Bonaventure further argued that the Franciscans mustn't be aloof. At his urging, many friars entered universities and became professors. They accepted appointments from the pope to serve as bishops and cardinals and used their new positions to set the example of St. Francis's spirit of humility, patience, and charity. The Franciscan model envisioned by St. Bonaventure is the one that endures to this day.

See holy card, page 83

ST. GEORGE

DIED ABOUT 303 • FEAST DAY: APRIL 23

During the Middle Ages, everyone knew the story of St. George and the dragon. Our hero was a valiant knight who happened to be riding through Libya on the very day the king's daughter was to be sacrificed to a dragon. George offered to fight the beast, and the king offered him gold and silver for saving the maiden's life. But rather than riches, George requested that Libya become a Christian kingdom. After slaying the dragon, he then proceeded to baptize the Libyans.

St. George has been the model of selfless chivalry for at least one thousand years. He was martyred in what is now the city of Lod, Israel; he may have been a soldier. By 500, the emperors of Byzantium had made him a patron of their armies. When the Islamic armies conquered the Holy Land, the Palestinian Christians took George as their heavenly protector. During the first Crusade, western European knights adopted him as their guardian and carried his legend back home. Germany, Malta, Portugal, and England are just a few of the European kingdoms that later chose George as their patron saint.

Although clearly just a myth, the dragon-slaying episode can still be salvaged, with the dragon representing sin, temptation, and all the baser aspects of human nature that St. George overcame by his faith and practice of Christian virtues. Because of his constancy and heroic martyrdom, St. George serves as an appropriate model for boys and young men. It's only natural that the Boy Scouts—who pledge to do their duty to God and country; help others at all times; and keep themselves physically strong, mentally alert, and morally upright—would take him as their patron. To honor Catholic adults who promote the ideals of scouting, the U.S. National Catholic Committee on Scouting awards the St. George Emblem.

See holy card, page 84

ST. AGATHA

DIED ABOUT 250 • FEAST DAY: FEBRUARY 5

Many history textbooks describe the ancient Romans as noble, enlightened, and civilized—even though their judicial system perpetrated some of the most gruesome crimes imaginable. The Romans believed that criminals (a category that included Christians) were less than human, so brutalizing them was perfectly acceptable. This rationale allowed them to crucify thousands of slaves who rebelled with Spartacus; it also justified smearing pitch on dozens of Christian men, women, and children before setting them ablaze to illuminate Nero's garden.

By these standards, the agonies experienced by St. Agatha were just business as usual. Her troubles began with a consul named Quintianus. As the man who governed Sicily, Quintianus could have whatever he wanted—and he wanted Agatha. But she was a wealthy Christian who had consecrated her virginity to God, and she turned him down flat. Enraged by the rejection, Quintianus ordered Agatha to be arrested and stretched on the rack. Despite excruciating pain, she refused to renounce her faith or accept him as a lover. He then instructed the executioners to slice off her breasts.

Agatha was unconscious as the jailers carried her to a prison cell and left her to die. Then St. Peter arrived, descending from heaven, and restored her breasts. When the jailers reported that Agatha was alive and healthy, Quintianus had her rolled over hot coals until she died.

Devotion to St. Agatha began in Sicily and spread throughout the Christian world. Because of the mutilation endured during her martyrdom, she has always been the patron of women suffering from any type of breast ailment. In recent years, she has been invoked especially against breast cancer.

See holy card, page 84

Brewers

ST. WENCESLAUS

907–929 • FEAST DAY: SEPTEMBER 28

This saint's beer-making connection becomes clear upon learning that he grew up in the Bohemian town of Budweis. The region has a centuries-old tradition of fine beer making, and Bohemian Budweiser is among the world's best lagers. (As for American Budweiser, let's concede that it's the world's best-selling beer and leave it at that.)

Wenceslaus's father, the duke of Bohemia, was a Christian; his mother was a pagan. As a young boy, the little duke went to live with his grandmother Ludmilla (later also a saint), who raised him as a devout Catholic. After Wenceslaus's father's death, his mother ordered the teenager to return home. She then allied herself with the nobility's anti-Christian faction, made it clear she preferred her younger son Boleslav, and even had her mother-in-law, Ludmilla, strangled.

Wenceslaus and his mother never reconciled. Upon coming of age, he gave his grandmother a royal funeral, encouraged the spread of the Catholic Church, and made peace with Germany (one of Bohemia's traditional enemies).

In September 929 Boleslav lured his brother to his castle by inviting him to participate in a church dedication. Early the next day, while on his way to a prayer service, Wenceslaus was intercepted by Boleslav, who struck him across the face. As the brothers fought at the church door, Boleslav's henchmen attacked Wenceslaus from the rear, killing him.

Immediately the Christians of Bohemia venerated their murdered duke as a martyr. His body was enshrined in the Prague cathedral, and Wenceslaus was declared Bohemia's patron saint. Brewers took St. Wenceslaus as their patron because he'd spent so many years in the country's prime beer-producing region. Professional and home brewers who want to make Bohemian-quality beer would do well to pray to St. Wenceslaus.

See holy card, page 84

75

ST. LOUIS IX OF FRANCE

1214–1270 • FEAST DAY: AUGUST 25

St. Louis was fourteen years old and already king of France when he married thirteen-year-old Margaret of Provence. In many ways, Louis was unlike other royal husbands: He loved his wife, treated her with respect, and never cheated on her. Although he was undoubtedly pious, within his marriage Louis definitely didn't try to live like a monk. His contemporaries tell us that all his life he had a strong sex drive; indeed, in forty-two years of marriage, Louis and Margaret had eleven children. Add to all this Louis' wealth, rank, and power, and no wonder he's venerated as a model bridegroom.

Louis believed that God had made him king so that he could do good for his kingdom, the Church, and the Christian world. He insisted that his judges treat all French citizens fairly and that they temper justice with mercy. He volunteered to arbitrate in everything from private disputes to civil wars. In his kingdom he encouraged the growth of universities and was a lavish patron of the arts—his most famous commission is that jewel of Gothic architecture, Paris's Sainte Chapelle, as an exquisite shrine to hold a relic he believed to be the true Crown of Thorns. Louis was also exceedingly generous to the poor and helpless, passing out baskets full of food to all who came to the palace gates.

But St. Louis is best known as a Crusader. In the early 1240s, Europe was under attack from hordes of Mongol invaders, and the Christians of the Holy Land were on the verge of complete annihilation at the hands of the Saracens. In 1248 Louis and his army of Crusaders captured the Egyptian city of Damietta in the Nile Delta. Since Egypt was the launching point for invasions of the Holy Land, the Crusaders believed that, by capturing or at least immobilizing the region, they could force the armies of Islam to make peace. But in 1250, in a great battle at Mansourah, the Crusaders were routed and Louis was taken prisoner. To free himself and his fellow Crusaders, the king had to pay an enormous sum in gold and return Damietta to the sultan of Egypt.

For the next twenty years, Louis focused his attention on France. But when the sultan attacked the Holy Land again, Louis prepared for yet another crusade. He got as far as Tunis in North Africa when he succumbed to typhus and dysentery. Even on his deathbed, he tried to do good: He summoned the ambassadors from Constantinople to urge them to work for the reconciliation of the Orthodox and Catholic churches.

St. Louis' dynasty lasted another five hundred years, coming to end with the French Revolution when his descendant, Louis XVI, was guillotined. As the blade fell, the king's chaplain exclaimed, "Son of St. Louis, ascend into heaven!"

See holy card, page 84

ST. DOROTHY

DIED 311 • FEAST DAY: FEBRUARY 6

A list of martyrs compiled by St. Jerome in the fourth century says that a young woman named Dorothy was executed in Cappadocia on February 6, 311. A charming legend has grown up around this succinct entry.

St. Dorothy was arrested during the Roman emperor Diocletian's persecution of the Church. His magistrate promised to spare her life if she sacrificed to the Roman gods, but Dorothy refused. The magistrate made her a second offer: If she married a pagan, he would spare her life. Dorothy replied that she had taken a vow of virginity, and her only spouse would be Jesus Christ.

The guards then took Dorothy to prison, where two wicked old women tried to corrupt her. Instead, Dorothy converted them to Christianity and baptized them. The next day, as Dorothy was led out to execution, a pagan lawyer named Theophilus mocked her. "Bride of Christ!" he called out, "send me some fruit and flowers from your bridegroom's garden."

As Dorothy knelt down at the chopping block, a little boy appeared beside her. Over his arm he carried a basket full of magnificent roses and beautiful apples. Dorothy lifted three of each from the basket, wrapped them in her veil, and gave it to the child. "Take these to Theophilus," she said. "Tell him I will meet him in the garden." A moment later the executioner struck off her head.

When the mysterious little boy presented Theophilus with the fruit and flowers and repeated Dorothy's message, the scoffer suddenly declared that Dorothy's God was the only God and that he, too, was a Christian. The magistrate handed over the lawyer to the executioner, and Theophilus went to join Dorothy in her bridegroom's garden.

See holy card, page 101

ST. BENEZET

ABOUT 1163–1184 • FEAST DAY: APRIL 14

St. Benezet was a shepherd who tended his flock outside the French city of Avignon. When he was about fifteen years old, God appeared to him in a vision and instructed him to perform a heroic work for the people of the region by building a bridge across the Rhône River. Of course, Benezet had no training as an engineer or architect, nor any money to start the job. He asked the bishop of Avignon for help, but the bishop dismissed him as a dreamer.

Benezet, however, did not give up. He collected a team of determined volunteers and began assembling materials for the bridge. It's said that angels guarded Benezet's sheep while he worked at the construction site and that he proved the supernatural character of his mission by lifting a massive block of stone, carrying it to the river, and setting it in place for the foundation of one of the piers.

Eventually the bishop and city authorities came around, supplying the funds and engineers Benezet needed to finish the bridge. Sadly, he didn't live to see the structure completed: He died six years after his work began, at age twenty-one. The bishop buried him in a little chapel on the bridge; the people of Avignon proclaimed him a patron saint of their city; and five years later, at the founding of the bridge, the Guild of Bridge Builders adopted St. Benezet as their patron, too.

In 1669, after a flood washed away part of the bridge, St. Benezet's body was moved to the cathedral of Avignon, then to the city's Church of St. Didier. His ruined bridge still stands, and devotion to St. Benezet remains strong in Avignon.

See holy card, page 101

ST. GABRIEL THE ARCHANGEL

FEAST DAY: SEPTEMBER 29

The Bible mentions only three archangels by name: St. Michael, the warrior who drove Lucifer and the rebel angels out of heaven and into hell; St. Raphael, the guide and guardian of Tobias; and St. Gabriel, God's favorite messenger.

St. Gabriel's news is always momentous and often startling. He is most famous as the angel who told the Blessed Virgin Mary that God had chosen her to be the mother of Christ. His greeting to Mary has become the opening line of the most popular and best-known prayer in the Catholic world: "Hail Mary, full of grace, the Lord is with thee." In addition to telling Mary that she would be the mother of the Messiah, Gabriel revealed that her cousin Elizabeth, who had never been able to conceive and was long past childbearing age, was pregnant as well. Elizabeth's son would be St. John the Baptist.

St. Matthew's gospel doesn't give the angel's name, but tradition has always assumed that it was Gabriel who told St. Joseph to marry Mary, announced the birth of Jesus to the shepherds of Bethlehem, warned the Magi not to return to King Herod but to go home by a different route, commanded Joseph to take Mary and the Christ Child to safety in Egypt, and returned to the Holy Family a couple years later with the news that Herod was dead and it was safe for them to return home to Nazareth.

Since St. Gabriel played such a large role in the gospels as the bearer of important news, who better to be the patron of broadcasters, postal workers, messengers, and couriers of all kinds.

See holy card, page 101

S. Ambrosius.

ST. JÉRÔME

1. Beekeepers · St. Ambrose 2. Bible Study · St. Jerome
3. Bicyclists · Our Lady of Ghisallo 4. Birds · St. Milburga

St. KEVIN

Die heiligen 14 Nothhelfer.

1. Bishops • St. Charles Borromeo 2. Blackbirds • St. Kevin of Glendalough
3. Black Death • Fourteen Holy Helpers 4. Bloggers • St. Augustine

SAN GENNARO

SAN GIOVANNI DI DIO
PADRE DEGLI INFERMI

S. Bonaventura.

Wer die Wissen
schaft der Heiligkeit
vorzieht, wird nicht
glücklich werden.
S. Bonaventura.

1. Blood Donors and Blood Banks · St. Januarius 2. Bookbinders · St. Columba
3. Booksellers · St. John of God 4. Bowel Disorders · St. Bonaventure

ST. GEORGIUS

R. Margreiter   GL 1055

ST. AGATHA

Hlg. Wenzel

S. Lodovico Re di Francia
protettore dei *** transalpini
Il Signore mi conduce,
nulla mi mancherà

1. Boy Scouts • St. George 2. Breast Ailments • St. Agatha
3. Brewers • St. Wenceslaus 4. Bridegrooms • St. Louis IX of France

84

ST. JOHN THE EVANGELIST

DIED ABOUT 100 • FEAST DAY: DECEMBER 27

The theologian Tertullian (about 160–220) is the first to tell the story of an unsuccessful attempt to martyr St. John the Evangelist. About ad 90, the elderly apostle was arrested in Ephesus and sent to Rome for trial and execution. The emperor Domitian had no pity for the old man and condemned him to a horrific death—boiling in oil.

A huge cauldron was erected beside the city's Latin Gate. As the oil began to bubble, the executioners stripped John naked and threw him in. But when the apostle regained his footing and stood up in the kettle, his body showed no signs of scalding. The frustrated executioners built up the fire until the oil reached a searing, rolling boil, yet still St. John stood unharmed. When at last the executioners admitted defeat and John climbed out of the sizzling liquid, his skin was unmarked and he looked as fresh as if he'd just stepped out of a relaxing bath. But Domitian was unaffected by the miracle and condemned John to exile on Patmos, a small, rocky island in the Aegean.

A small church in Rome now stands near the Latin Gate, built on the presumed site of the miracle. It's called San Giovanni in Oleo, or St. John in Oil. A shrine to the saint has stood on this spot since at least the fifth century. For many centuries, the Church observed on May 6 a special feast day, St. John before the Latin Gate, commemorating the miracle that preserved the brave apostle from being scalded to death. Under the current ecclesiastic calendar, that feast day has been suppressed.

See holy card, page 102

ST. HOMOBONUS

DIED 1197 • FEAST DAY: NOVEMBER 13

St. Homobonus was a citizen of Cremona, Italy. He was hardworking and honest, religiously devout and generous, and a successful entrepreneur. His entrepreneurship is the reason businessmen have venerated him as their patron for nine hundred years.

Homobonus inherited his father's tailoring business at a time when Italian cities were growing rich from the manufacture of fine fabrics. Recognizing the wave of the future, Homobonus shifted his business from making clothes to selling cloth.

Starting a new business venture is a time-consuming task, yet every week Homobonus found a moment to visit the poor, delivering whatever they needed. At the end of each working day, before returning home to his family, he went to Mass at the Church of St. Egidio.

At age fifty Homobonus was wealthy enough to retire and devote himself exclusively to charitable works. On November 13, 1197, he was attending evening Mass as usual when suddenly he flung out his arms and fell facedown on the church floor. At first the congregants around him thought it was just a flamboyant gesture of piety. But when Homobonus didn't stand up to hear the reading of the gospel, some members grew concerned. Bending over him, they found the good man was dead, most likely from a massive heart attack.

The bishop of Cremona traveled to Rome to tell Homobonus's story personally to Pope Innocent III, who was so impressed that he began the process of making Homobonus a saint. Two years later, it was official. The canonization caused a furor because, in the twelfth century, sainthood was rare for laymen who had not died as martyrs. But Innocent III was a practical, results-oriented man, and Homobonus's straightforward approach to sanctity appealed to him.

See holy card, page 102

ST. MARGARET CLITHEROW

ABOUT 1553–1586 • FEAST DAY: MARCH 25

Margaret Middleton Clitherow grew up among hardworking businesspeople. Her parents earned a nice living as candle makers in York, England, and from them she learned to run a shop and keep the books. When she was about eighteen years old, Margaret married John Clitherow, a butcher and one of the wealthiest businessmen in town. She took up the management of his shop, and the Clitherow meat business enjoyed even greater success.

Margaret had been raised Protestant, but John had grown up in the Catholic faith. Life under the rule of Elizabeth I was dangerous for Catholics, so John conformed to the Anglican Church to settle the religious question in his own household. Or so he thought.

John's brother William was a frequent visitor to the Clitherow home. William had remained a Catholic and was resolved to become a priest. Very likely it was he who first drew Margaret back into the "old religion."

In 1574 Margaret converted to Catholicism, and she was determined to hear Mass daily and give her children a Catholic education. To accomplish her agenda, she helped win the release of a young Catholic from prison and boarded him as a private tutor. She then directed carpenters to build a secret room to accommodate a priest as well as hidden cupboards in which to conceal the vestments, sacred vessels, and other altar furnishings necessary for Mass.

The Clitherow house became a dodgy place to live, what with a priest and a Catholic tutor in residence, local Catholics slipping in and out for Mass, and Margaret herself tending to imprisoned faithful or sneaking out at night to pray at the gallows where priests had been executed. Yet, thanks to the loyalty of family, servants, and even Protestant neighbors, Margaret's Catholic outpost survived for twelve years.

Then, in March 1586, authorities stormed unannounced into the house.

The tutor fled and the priest managed to escape to his secret room, but the raiders seized an eleven-year-old boy living with the Clitherows. They threatened to beat him with a cane if he didn't talk. The terrified child admitted that Mass was celebrated daily in the house, and he revealed the secret cupboards and the priest's room. Margaret was arrested for the crimes of attending Mass and harboring a priest. When the court asked for her plea of guilty or not guilty, her shrewdness and heroism came to the fore.

If she were given a trial, her children, husband, and servants would be compelled by threats or torture to testify against her. To spare them this ordeal, Margaret exercised a right few were willing to claim: She refused to say whether she was guilty or innocent. In so doing, her family and friends were off the hook, but Margaret herself was condemned to a terrible penalty. Under English law, prisoners who refused to plead one way or the other were crushed to death, slowly. Her judges reminded her of that fact, but Margaret remained resolute.

On March 25 the jailers came for her. Before a large crowd, the executioners staked her on the ground in the form of a cross, laid a heavy wooden door over her, and then piled some eight hundred pounds of stone atop the door. It took fifteen minutes for Margaret to die, but she never lost consciousness. Her only cry was, "Jesu, Jesu, Jesu! Have mercy on me!"

All three of Margaret's children remained faithful Catholics. In fact, her daughter became a nun and her two sons became priests. Her house still stands in York, in the street known as the Shambles.

See holy card, page 102

ST. BARTHOLOMEW

FIRST CENTURY • FEAST DAY: AUGUST 24

The gospels of Matthew, Mark, and Luke all include Bartholomew among the twelve apostles. But, aside from these brief mentions, he doesn't play a major role in these writings. Readers get some sense of the man in the gospel of St. John, who calls him Nathanael, which was undoubtedly his first name. (Bartholomew means "son of Tolmai.")

According to John's writings, Nathanael was resting in the shade of a fig tree when his friend Philip came along. Flush with excitement, Philip declared he had met the Messiah—the man's name was Jesus and he came from the village of Nazareth. The world-weary Nathanael replied, "Can anything good come from Nazareth?" But, to humor his friend, he went along to meet Jesus for himself.

As Philip and Nathanael approached, Christ called out, "Behold, an Israelite indeed, in whom there is no guile!" Confused, Nathanael asked Christ how he knew him. Jesus answered, "When you were under the fig tree, I saw you." The astonished Nathanael exclaimed, "Rabbi, you are the Son of God! You are the King of Israel!" "You will see greater things than these," Christ promised. "You will see the heavens open and the angels of God descending and ascending upon the Son of man."

Butchers took Bartholomew as their patron saint because of the apostle's grisly martyrdom—tradition says he was flayed alive. Not surprisingly, other groups who also venerate St. Bartholomew are tanners and leather workers who peel the hide off animals before the carcasses are sent to the butcher.

See holy card, page 103

Cab Drivers

ST. FIACRE

DIED 670 • FEAST DAY: AUGUST 30

In the seventeenth century, Paris's Hotel Saint-Fiacre owned a fleet of carriages for the convenience of their guests. These were the first hired cabs in the city; they became known as *fiacres*, and the drivers adopted St. Fiacre as the patron who would keep them safe as they drove around town, preserve the good health of their horses, and bring them passengers who gave generous tips.

St. Fiacre never drove a cab. He was an Irish monk who left home to live as a hermit in whatever far-off land he ended up in. His boat found its way to France, where, encouraged by the bishop St. Faro, he settled in the forest at Breuil. He built a hut for himself, an oratory dedicated to the Virgin Mary, and a guesthouse for travelers. According to legend, he was blessed with a healing touch that could cure fevers and restore sight to the blind. Fruit, vegetables, and medicinal herbs flourished in Fiacre's garden, and he shared the bounty with the hungry and the sick.

Gardeners have also taken St. Fiacre as their patron because supposedly when he decided to plant a garden, a touch of his spade was all it took to knock over a tree or uproot shrubs.

After his death St. Fiacre's hermitage-and-garden complex became a pilgrimage site that evolved into the village of Saint-Fiacre in the province of Seine-et-Marne. The shrine was especially popular during the seventeenth century. St. Vincent de Paul believed he had been cured of an illness through the intercession of St. Fiacre, and France's Queen Anne always attributed the birth of her son, the future Louis XIV, to the prayers of St. Fiacre.

See holy card, page 103

ST. PEREGRINE LAZIOSI

1260–1335 • FEAST DAY: MAY 1

eregrine Laziosi's conversion came about in the middle of a street brawl. He was one of the young hotheads of Forlì, an Italian town that had sided with the Holy Roman Emperor in his power struggle with the pope. The Forlians' rejection of papal authority was so extreme that the pope placed the town under interdict: All churches were locked up, no Masses could be said, and none of the sacraments were to be administered until the citizens repented. But, instead of making the Forlians think twice about their situation, the interdict only enraged them more. They refused to back down.

In an attempt to persuade Forlì to see reason, Pope Martin V sent St. Philip Benizi as his ambassador. Standing before a massive crowd in the town's largest piazza, St. Philip urged the Forlians to come back to the Church. But the townspeople were so embittered that even an appeal from a man widely regarded as a living saint didn't move them. The more St. Philip spoke, the more restless the crowd became, until finally a riot erupted.

Peregrine Laziosi was right in the middle of the uproar. He charged across the piazza, grabbed the front of St. Philip's religious habit, and struck him hard across the face. In response Philip turned the other cheek, waiting for another blow. Faced with such perfect Christlike meekness, Peregrine's rage turned to shame. Too mortified to apologize, he pushed his way through the crowd and ran home.

In that moment, Peregrine became a new man. He decided to join Philip Benizi's religious order and become a Servite priest. Peregrine strove to imitate Benizi: He became a gifted preacher and a patient, compassionate spiritual director to troubled souls.

For many years Peregrine suffered from an acute pain in his right leg. Initially doctors diagnosed it as an especially bad case of varicose veins;

when a nasty wound opened up on Peregrine's knee, however, his doctor realized it was cancer. In a last-ditch effort to save the priest's life, the physician planned to amputate.

The night before surgery, the suffering Peregrine dragged himself to the life-size crucifix that hung in the chapter room of the monastery. He sat at the foot of the cross and prayed until he fell asleep. He dreamt of Christ climbing down from the cross and touching his cancerous limb. When he awoke, the wound on his knee had healed and not a trace remained of the cancer that had infected his leg just hours before.

See holy card, page 103

ST. BERNARD OF CLAIRVAUX

1090–1153 • FEAST DAY: AUGUST 20

It takes four steps to get from St. Bernard, the "Mellifluous Doctor of the Church," to candle makers: 1) *mellifluous* means "honey-sweet"; 2) honey is produced by bees; 3) bees also make beeswax; 4) beeswax is used to make candles.

But the link is not quite the stretch it first appears to be. In his writings St. Bernard often developed the idea of the "sweetness" of the sacred, and he even used bees, honey, and wax as metaphors. Wisdom, he once wrote, is "like a bee bearing both wax and honey, [it] is able to kindle the light of knowledge and to pour in the savor of grace."

Bernard lived during the first flowering of Gothic art and architecture, a time when the ideals of chivalry and the poetry of the troubadours were spreading across Europe. This was the era of the Crusades, the revitalization of religious life in the Church, and the great outpouring of devotion to the Blessed Virgin Mary. And St. Bernard was involved in it all.

At age twenty-two he joined the Cistercians, a new monastic order, but he didn't remain an anonymous monk for long. Bernard's abbot recognized his leadership skills and sent him to build a sister abbey at Clairvaux. Austerity was the hallmark of Cistercian life, and Bernard found a way to translate that principle into stone. Unlike other churches and monasteries of the time, with their strange, grotesque, and sometimes even naughty images, Bernard insisted that the architectural style of his church and abbey be the simplest example of the new Gothic style, with minimal decoration and tall, clear-glass windows to flood the interior with light.

Bernard believed fervently that Christian shrines belonged in Christian hands and that the only way to defend Europe against a Muslim invasion was by controlling the Holy Land. But the atrocities committed by Crusaders broke Bernard's heart. Convinced that the Christian army would not triumph if they were not holy, he became one of the chief promoters of the Knights Templar, a unique religious community of warrior monks who pledged themselves to defend the Holy Land and all Christians therein.

By the twelfth century, many of the monastic orders in Europe had grown lax. Bernard upheld his Cistercians as the model of monastic life. Led by their abbot, the Cistercians followed a simple, orderly routine of prayer, work, and study, always emphasizing growth in virtue rather than the acquisition of real estate.

So many saints since Bernard have been devoted to Mary that his deep love for her is often forgotten. Yet his books and sermons began the movement to honor her as the essential object of veneration in Catholic life. "In dangers, in doubts, in difficulties," he wrote, "think of Mary, call upon Mary."

See holy card, page 103

ST. MACARIUS THE YOUNGER

DIED ABOUT 401 • FEAST DAY: JANUARY 2

Young Macarius was a successful businessman who made and sold candy and sweet pastries in Alexandria, Egypt. In 335, inspired by stories of St. Anthony of the Desert and other holy men who had fled civilization for a life of prayer and penance, Macarius gave up his candy concession and traveled south to a region of Egypt known as the Thebaid, near modern-day Aswan. He lived there for forty years in a bare, one-room dwelling known as a cell, even studying for a time under his hero, St. Anthony. He then moved to the deserts of northern Egypt, where he lived as a hermit.

The hermit monks of Egypt were renowned for their extreme sanctity and penitential practices. Macarius lived on raw vegetables, bread, and water. On holy days he celebrated by adding a little olive oil. Once he forced himself to remain awake for twenty days and twenty nights. He later admitted, "My mind dried up because of lack of sleep, and I had a kind of delirium. So I gave in to nature and returned to my cell."

Upon the death of one of his hermit neighbors, Macarius and some fellow recluses discovered one hundred gold coins in the dead man's cell, sparking a lively debate—should they distribute the gold among the poor or give it to the Church? Macarius argued that it should be buried with the hermit to teach them all a lesson on the evils of hoarding.

Macarius never modified his austere life. A century later, when Saints Benedict and Scholastica drafted a rule of life for monks and nuns, they rejected the extremes practiced by St. Macarius and his fellow hermits. Nonetheless, in the Eastern Church especially, St. Macarius is so greatly esteemed that he is invoked by name in the Coptic rite of the Mass.

See holy card, page 104

ST. CAMILLUS DE LELLIS

1550–1614 • FEAST DAY: JULY 14

By the time Camillus de Lellis was twelve years old, he was such a hulking, violent boy that even his own mother was afraid of him. He refused to go to school. He refused to go to Mass. Everyone in his family agreed that his temperament would allow him to pursue only one trade. So, at age seventeen, Camillus left his home in Abruzzi, in central Italy, to join his father as a mercenary, fighting for Venice against the Turks.

Camp life came easily to the boy. He liked the whoring and the drinking, and he was blessed with a gift for gambling and swearing. At six feet four inches tall, rippling with muscles, Camillus was fearsome on the battlefield. Father and son became professional mercenaries, traveling across Europe to render their services to whichever prince offered the best pay. Between wars, they supported themselves by running cons and cheating at cards.

But Camillus's luck ran out when he turned twenty-five. His father died, and he developed an open sore that wouldn't heal. In this darkest hour, as if by a miracle, he met St. Philip Neri, then the most famous priest in Rome. Philip helped the one-time mercenary and compulsive gambler banish his vices and learn to love God.

Camillus had barely given up his old habits when he conceived the idea of opening a hospital in one of Rome's slums. Philip told him he was making a serious mistake—the neighborhood was full of temptations, and he feared Camillus would fall back into his old habits. When Camillus insisted upon his plan, the once warm friendship turned chilly.

But Philip misjudged his friend. Camillus did not return to his old sinful life. His hospitals for the poor were a tremendous success, and by the end of his life he was one of the most beloved men in Rome.

See holy card, page 104

ST. JOSEPH

FIRST CENTURY • FEAST DAYS: MARCH 19 AND MAY 1

The gospels tell us that St. Joseph, husband of the Blessed Virgin Mary and foster father of Jesus Christ, was a carpenter. Consequently, laborers in general—and carpenters in particular—have taken him as their patron saint.

In 1955 Pope Pius XII emphasized St. Joseph's patronage when he instituted a new feast day, the Feast of St. Joseph the Worker. The pope chose May 1, giving Christians a counterbalance to the extravagant May Day celebrations organized by the Communist Party. Marxism scoffs at the idea that there's a spiritual dimension to life, let alone to labor. But, in St. Joseph, the Church upholds the model of a man who loved and obeyed God, was devoted to his family, and served as a productive, responsible member of society.

The May 1 feast day is the mid-twentieth-century Church's answer to the Marxists. But the idea of St. Joseph as the patron saint of laborers originates all the way back in the 1400s. For centuries the Church had downplayed Joseph, largely because of the seemingly endless string of heresies that mangled its teachings on the nature of Christ. To ensure that Christians understood that God was the father of Jesus, the Church minimized Joseph's role in the salvation story. But devotion to Joseph gained momentum during the late Middle Ages, when influential saints wrote and spoke about their affection for the humble carpenter. Local bishops began to authorize public Masses to be said in St. Joseph's honor and finally, in 1479, Pope Sixtus IV established March 19 as his feast day. Today a statue or picture of St. Joseph holds a place of honor in virtually every Catholic church.

See holy card, page 104

ST. ROBERT BELLARMINE

1542–1621 • FEAST DAY: SEPTEMBER 17

St. Robert Bellarmine put his tremendous intellect to practical purposes. He lived during the sixteenth-century Counter-Reformation, when the Catholic Church tried to reclaim the souls it had recently lost to Luther, Calvin, and other leaders of the Protestant revolt while clearing away the abuses and scandals that had gotten the Church into trouble in the first place. Bellarmine joined the Jesuits, the dynamic new religious order dedicated to preaching, writing, education, and the personal example of its priests and lay brothers. He hoped they would help him present the Catholic side of the argument in the most persuasive and attractive way possible.

Bellarmine found that Catholics with a meager understanding of their faith were often easy targets for Protestant preachers. To correct the prevailing ignorance, he wrote two handbooks: One was short volume for children explaining the basics of Catholicism in an easy-to-understand way; the second was a guide for catechism teachers to help them better understand their faith and show them how to present it to young people compellingly. He tested his methods by serving as a catechism teacher in Rome and instructing Jesuit novices. Bellarmine's fundamental principle sounds simple, but it required hard work: If one understands the basis of Catholic doctrine—drawn from the Bible and the writings of the early Church fathers—one will be able to defend it.

As a reward for a lifetime of service teaching and defending the faith, the pope made Bellarmine his personal theologian, a cardinal, and the head of the Vatican library. And, given his love for reading and research, St. Robert probably appreciated his duties at the library the most.

See holy card, page 104

ST. ELIZABETH ANN SETON

1774–1821 • FEAST DAY: JANUARY 4

For two hundred years American parochial schools have provided countless children with a solid education while teaching them how to be faithful Catholics and good citizens. Parish schools aren't as numerous as they were forty years ago, and the teaching nuns that once staffed them are almost all gone. But the situation is still not nearly as dire as it was in St. Elizabeth Ann Seton's day.

Mother Seton's life coincides with the birth of the United States and the rise of the Catholic Church in America. She was born a year before the battles of Lexington and Concord, during an era when Catholicism was outlawed in every colony except Pennsylvania. In British America, there were no bishops, nuns, Catholic schools, or seminaries. Only about twenty priests lived in the colonies, most slipping by incognito and using aliases to escape harsh anti-priest laws.

Mother Seton grew up the daughter of a prominent, well-to-do Anglican family on Staten Island. During the Revolution the Setons walked a fine line between loyalty to the king and support for the rebels. But, whatever her family's true sympathies may have been, they were firmly in the American camp by the time George Washington was elected president: Indeed, fifteen-year-old Elizabeth danced at the first inaugural ball.

At age nineteen she married William Seton, a wealthy New York merchant. The couple had five children—three girls and two boys—and enjoyed a life of comfort and privilege. After eight years of marriage, William's business went bankrupt; sadly his misfortunes continued, for he then contracted tuberculosis and died. (The Setons, along with their daughter Rebecca, were in Italy at the time.) On William's death, Elizabeth and Rebecca moved in with his business associates, the Filicchi family. The Filicchis owned a private chapel that provided Elizabeth with her first exposure to the Catholic faith. Two things especially impressed her: the family's reverence during Mass, and the comfort they received from confession. Upon returning to New York, she sought out the pastor of St. Peter's Church on Barclay Street and asked to convert to Catholicism.

With few exceptions, Elizabeth's Protestant family and friends turned their backs on her. She struggled to support herself and her children until Bishop John Carroll invited her to open a Catholic school in Baltimore. There Elizabeth began to consider entering the religious life. But she didn't want to be a nun in the European model, living a mostly cloistered life with only a few hours each day devoted to teaching girls who boarded at the convent. With so much work to be done for the Church in America, Elizabeth wanted to be active. With Bishop Carroll's encouragement, she founded a new order of teaching sisters, and together they opened America's first parish school in Emmitsburg, Maryland, on February 22, 1810.

The parochial school system founded by Mother Seton passed the faith from generation to generation; eased the passage of Catholic immigrant children into American society; and served as the seedbed for countless vocations to the priesthood and the religious life. Furthermore, her teaching order offered a new model for religious women—sisters who were "in the world, but not of it." In the history of the Catholic Church in America, Mother Seton is the indispensable woman.

See holy card, page 121

Nr. 321   VLA

HL. DOROTHEA
(6. FEBER)

St Bénézet.

Dieu tient l'homme intérieur comme une mère tient la tête de son enfant pour la couvrir de baisers et de caresses.

(Extr. de la Vie du Curé d'Ars)

Déposé.

St. Gabriel.

1. Brides • St. Dorothy   2. Bridges • St. Benezet
3. Broadcasters • St. Gabriel the Archangel

S. OMOBONO

"I have trodden the wine-press alone."

The Martyrdom of the Ven: MARGARET CLITHEROE,
"the Pearl of York" who suffered on March 25th 1586.

1. Burns • St. John the Evangelist 2. Businessmen • St. Homobonus

Sanctus Bartholomeus.

Carl Poellath, Schrobenhausen.

SCÈNES DE LA VIE MONASTIQUE

St FIACRE
DÉFRICHE SON CHAMP.

ÉDITION DE LA TRAPPE DE N.D. d'AIGUEBELLE. (2-6me)

S. PEREGRINE LAZIOSI
O. S. M.
Patron of malignant growths

S. Bernardus.

Von Der Ser.IV.v₂   B. Kühlen, M.Gladbach.

1. Butchers • St. Bartholomew 2. Cab Drivers • St. Fiacre
3. Cancer • St. Peregrine Laziosi 4. Candle Makers • St. Bernard of Clairvaux

S. Macaire l'Arménien, Patriarche d'Antioche.

S. CAMILLUS de LELLIS

Sanctus Joseph, patronus Ecclesiæ universalis.

1. Candy Makers • St. Macarius the Younger 2. Card Sharps and Con Men • St. Camillus de Lellis
3. Carpenters • St. Joseph 4. Catechism Teachers • St. Robert Bellarmine

ST. GERTRUDE OF NIVELLES

ABOUT 626–659 • FEAST DAY: MARCH 17

Upon learning that her convent's grain supply was infested with mice, St. Gertrude eliminated the pests through the power of prayer. At least, that's what legend says. Artists depict St. Gertrude with a cat at her feet, the rationale being that anyone who can get rid of mice must surely be a cat person.

Gertrude was the daughter of Blessed Pepin, the steward of the king of the Franks, and Blessed Itta, who served as a model of piety, charity, and love of learning. When Pepin died, Itta used the fortune she inherited to found both a monastery and a convent on her estate at Nivelles, in Belgium. Then, both mother and daughter took the veil (that is, they became nuns).

After Itta's death, Gertrude became the convent's superior. Famous for her generosity to the poor and the sick, Gertrude was especially kind to pilgrims and other travelers seeking safe lodging. All who met her felt they'd experienced an encounter with a living saint. According to one story, several monks from a neighboring monastery were sailing in the North Sea when a terrible storm arose. Certain they were about to drown, the monks prayed to Gertrude as if she were already a saint, and the storm abated.

St. Gertrude was only thirty-three when she succumbed to a fatal illness. Before her death the chaplain, an Irish priest, assured her that St. Patrick himself would lead her soul to heaven as a reward for her holy life. As it happened, Gertrude died on St. Patrick's Day.

See holy card, page 121

SS. PERPETUA AND FELICITY

DIED 203 • FEAST DAY: MARCH 7

One of the treasures of early Christian literature is the prison diary of St. Perpetua, a Roman noblewoman, wife, and mother who lived with her family in Carthage, in North Africa. At the time of her arrest, Perpetua was twenty-two years old and had recently given birth to a boy. Imprisoned with her was Felicity, one of Perpetua's slaves, who was eight months pregnant.

Because Perpetua was still nursing, her son remained with her in prison, and soon Felicity gave birth to a girl there. Once the two women were condemned, Perpetua's father came for her son and a Christian woman adopted Felicity's daughter. Perpetua's diary takes us to the night before her martyrdom; the rest of the story was completed by an unnamed Christian, an eyewitness to the women's tragedy.

On the birthday of Emperor Septimius Severus, Perpetua and Felicity, along with three Christian men—Saturninus, Saturus, and Revocatus—were led into the town's arena to be exposed to wild beasts. The men were mauled to death by a leopard and a bear, while the women were gored and thrown by a wild heifer before being finished off by a gladiator. Because Perpetua and Felicity are often depicted with the heifer that wounded them, they have become the patron saints of cattle.

Their story, so detailed and poignant, has been a favorite among Christians for eighteen hundred years. During the fourth century in North Africa, portions of Perpetua's diary were read at Mass. As bishop of Hippo, St. Augustine had to remind the priests and people of his diocese that as fine as Perpetua's book was, it must not be placed on par with sacred scripture.

See holy card, page 121

ST. CALLIXTUS

DIED ABOUT 222 • FEAST DAY: OCTOBER 14

Callixtus didn't have a prayer of becoming a saint—or so it seemed. The slave of Carpophorus, a Roman Christian, Callixtus had a head for numbers. When his master started a type of bank for fellow Christians, Callixtus was charged with managing the accounts. But he soon proved to be nothing but trouble, pilfering money and making bad investments. Angry and humiliated, Carpophorus set Callixtus to work turning the stone wheel at a gristmill.

Depositors anxious to recover even a portion of their savings convinced Carpophorus to release Callixtus if the wayward slave vowed to recover the funds he'd invested with Jewish merchants. So, one Saturday morning, Callixtus interrupted the Sabbath service at Rome's synagogue and demanded that the merchants repay the money. In the ensuing uproar, Callixtus was attacked and the brawl spilled onto the street.

Callixtus was arrested and then shipped off to work in the mines on Sardinia. But soon he was back in Rome, released in a general amnesty for Christian prisoners. (One can imagine the groans of dismay among the city's Christians and Jews alike.)

Pope Victor finally interceded. He offered Callixtus a stipend and set him up in a small house far outside the city's walls and away from trouble. It was there, perhaps under the pope's influence, that Callixtus's conversion began. The pope gave the new convert a job supervising catacombs that Roman Christians used as their burial ground, hence Callixtus's position as the patron saint of cemetery workers. Later ordained a priest, Callixtus served as adviser to Pope Zephyrinus.

But greater things were yet to come: Callixtus was eventually elected pope himself. After a brief five-year pontificate he died a martyr, beaten to death in the street by a pagan mob.

See holy card, page 121

Charitable Organizations

ST. VINCENT DE PAUL

1581–1660 • FEAST DAY: SEPTEMBER 27

A haphazard quality characterizes St. Vincent de Paul's lifetime of charity. His temperament was such that he could never turn away from a person in need, no matter what the need was. The list of troubles he sought to alleviate is astounding. He brought food and medicine to penniless sick people, comforted convicts condemned to row the galleys, and sheltered orphans, the elderly, and soldiers incapacitated by war wounds. He opened hospitals, took in abandoned babies, and taught catechism to children. He founded an order of nuns to serve the poor and another for priests to teach and encourage religious devotion among the urban poor and country peasants.

St. Vincent's first group of volunteers was made up of upper-middle-class ladies. Well intentioned but squeamish, the women lacked the physical stamina to work in the slums. A peasant himself, Vincent learned to recruit emotionally tough, physically robust young women from the country to serve the poor.

An unexpected benefit of his ambitious programs was the renewal of religious life in seventeenth-century France. The young priests Vincent trained were so well educated in the faith, so gifted at making Christian doctrine accessible and appealing to any audience, and so exemplary in their personal lives that bishops saw the "Vincentians" (as they came to be called) as a model, and they instituted St. Vincent's training program in their own seminaries.

One of St. Vincent's legacies is the St. Vincent de Paul Society, an organization of laypeople who quietly tend to needy populations in their own parishes.

See holy card, page 122

ST. NICHOLAS

DIED ABOUT 350 • FEAST DAY: DECEMBER 6

Clement Clarke Moore did St. Nicholas no favors. Since the publication in 1823 of his poem "A Visit from St. Nicholas" (better known as "'Twas the Night Before Christmas"), devotion to one of the most beloved saints on the Christian calendar has taken a nosedive. How could anyone be expected to pray to a saint described as "a right jolly old elf"? Thanks to Moore, people falsely believe that St. Nicholas's Santa Claus persona is what makes him the patron saint of children. But his link to children is centuries older than Moore's poem, and the connection exists for reasons that aren't nearly as whimsical.

St. Nicholas was bishop of Myra, in what is now Turkey. Once, while traveling, he stopped at an inn for the night. Proud of the opportunity to entertain a bishop, the innkeeper declared that he would serve Nicholas a splendid meal featuring meat delivered fresh that very day. Bishop Nicholas did not reply; he pushed the innkeeper aside and went straight to the kitchen. In the middle of the room stood a large wooden tub full of freshly butchered meat. Without saying a word, Nicholas made the sign of the cross over the tub. The meat vanished, and in its place appeared three little boys whom the innkeeper had murdered and planned to serve to his guests.

Look at almost any painting, statue, or stained-glass window from the Middle Ages or Renaissance that depicts St. Nicholas, and you're likely to see him with the three resurrected (and reassembled) boys. Our ancestors loved this story; for them, it manifested St. Nicholas's special care for children. Squeamish folk that we are, however, we have chosen to forget the whole thing.

See holy card, page 122

ST. GREGORY THE GREAT

ABOUT 540–604 • FEAST DAY: SEPTEMBER 3

Everyone has heard of Gregorian chant; it's named for St. Gregory the Great, the pope who made it the cornerstone of church music. Though it's unlikely Gregory composed any chant, he did arrange some existing music for the ecclesiastical choirs of Rome, earning him the patronage of choirboys, church soloists, and church musicians.

Chant in churches evolved from the singing that the earliest Christians heard in their synagogues and in the Temple in Jerusalem. By the time Gregory was born, distinctive styles of chant had developed in various parts of the Roman Empire. The Greeks in Constantinople, the Chaldeans in what is now Iraq and Iran, the Copts in Egypt, and the Christians in Spain, France, and the archdiocese of Milan—each had their own musical repertoire. Gregorian chant was the style of music heard in Rome. The monks, bishops, and kings who visited that city on pilgrimage were so taken with the beauty of the chanting that they introduced it into monasteries and cathedrals throughout western Europe. Sometimes they even managed to convince trained singers from Roman choirs to make the journey over the Alps to teach the Germans or the Franks or the English how to chant properly.

Fine church music was only one of Pope Gregory's interests. He had been a Benedictine monk and always looked back on his years in the monastery as the happiest time of his life. As a result, he encouraged the Benedictines to expand throughout Europe.

As pope, he governed Rome, making peace with barbarian chiefs who threatened the city, appointing generals for its defense, and ordering the stewards of Church-owned lands as far away as North Africa, Sicily, and Croatia to send the lion's share of their harvests to ease chronic food shortages. He took the same practical approach to governing the Church, even writing a small book, *Pastoral Care*, in which he outlined the duties of a good bishop.

After Gregorian chant, St. Gregory's most famous accomplishment is the Benedictine mission to England. According to the story, before becoming pope, he was walking through the market one day and saw a group of teenage boys being auctioned off as slaves. The boys had golden hair, blue eyes, and creamy complexions. "Who are they?" Gregory asked a man in the market. "They are Angles," the man replied. "They are not Angles," Gregory said, "they're angels." Years later, as pope, Gregory sent forty Benedictine monks to convert the English.

See holy card, page 122

ST. JULIANA FALCONIERI

1270–1341 • FEAST DAY: JUNE 19

Juliana Falconieri grew up among saints. Her uncle, St. Alexis Falconieri, was one of the seven founders of the Servite order. The priest who taught her as a child and acted as her spiritual director was St. Philip Benizi, one of the early superiors of the Servites. Inspired by the holiness around her, Juliana decided to affiliate herself with the Servites as a nun.

Through what we would call parish missions, the Servite priests and brothers sought to promote devotion to the Blessed Virgin Mary and to encourage Catholics to repent their sins and increase their commitment to the faith. Juliana added works of charity to the Servite way of life by going out into the streets of Florence to help the sick, the helpless, and the abandoned. The work was hard and dirty; to keep their hands and arms unencumbered, Juliana and the women who joined her modified their religious clothing, or habits, by shortening the sleeves.

Because of her own struggle with sickness, St. Juliana became the patron of people suffering from any type of chronic illness. During the last years of her life, she was plagued by an undiagnosed stomach ailment. She never knew when an attack of nausea or severe cramps would incapacitate her. Even-tually the illness proved fatal. As she lay dying, she was seized by such a severe bout of vomiting that the attending priest deemed her unable to receive Holy Communion. Instead, at Juliana's request, he covered her chest with a square linen cloth known as a corporal and laid the consecrated host over her heart. According to the story, the Eucharist vanished a few moments later.

See holy card, page 122

ST. SCHOLASTICA

ABOUT 480–547 • FEAST DAY: FEBRUARY 10

St. Scholastica and her twin brother, St. Benedict, were the founders of monastic and convent life in the West. In the East, especially in the desert regions, bands of hermits and loosely organized communities of monks practiced extreme penances, depriving themselves of food, water, sleep, and even clothes—to the point that many became physical wrecks, and some went mad.

Scholastica and Benedict designed an orderly, sane, yet spiritually concentrated way of life for men and women seeking God. The Benedictine monks and nuns ate healthy meals that included bread, fresh fruit and vegetables, meat and fish, and even a little wine or beer. They wore religious clothing, or habits, suitable to the local climate. They divided their days into regular periods of work, study, prayer, and recreation. And when their disciples performed acts of penance, they were acts of self-control rather than self-torture.

Brother and sister each founded communities on Monte Cassino south of Rome. Since men were not permitted in Scholastica's convent and women could not enter Benedict's monastery, to visit each other the twins met at a small house halfway between their establishments. On one such visit, Scholastica brought a few of her nuns, and Benedict came accompanied by a few monks. They all spent the afternoon in pleasant conversation, ate dinner together, and were chatting so happily afterward that they forgot the time. Realizing the late hour Benedict rose to go, but Scholastica begged him to stay and talk with her until morning. Benedict refused. His own rule forbade his monks from staying away all night from the monastery. As the men headed out the door, Scholastica bowed her head and began to pray. Immediately a violent storm broke over the mountain, with tornado-force winds and torrential rain. Benedict and his monks retreated back into the house.

"What have you done?" Benedict asked his sister.

"I asked you to grant me a favor and you refused. So I asked the same favor of God and he heard my prayer. Go back to your monastery, if you can."

Unable to fight both Scholastica and God, Benedict resigned himself to spending the night away from home. They talked until dawn, when the storm stopped as suddenly as it had begun. Then Scholastica returned to her nuns and Benedict to his monks.

Three days later Benedict was gazing out his window when he saw his sister's soul, in the form of a white dove, ascending to heaven. Benedict buried Scholastica's body in the tomb he had prepared for himself in the abbey crypt. When he died three years later, he was buried beside her. Sister and brother still lie together in the crypt at Monte Cassino. As for the rule of life they created together, it has become the basis for the rule of every religious order of nuns and monks in the Catholic world.

See holy card, page 123

ST. STEPHEN THE YOUNGER

714–764 • FEAST DAY: NOVEMBER 28

Eastern churches are so rich in sacred imagery that it's hard to imagine a time when such icons were outlawed. The iconoclast movement began in 726, when Emperor Leo III was persuaded by a handful of extremist bishops that the veneration of sacred images was hindering the conversion of Jews and Muslims to Christianity. Leo ordered the destruction of all icons throughout the empire. His successor, Constantine V, took it a step further, persecuting anyone who opposed the policy.

Stephen was abbot of a mountaintop monastery in Bithynia, in north-central Turkey. He lived quietly with his monks, copying books for the monastery's library and supporting himself by making and selling fishing nets. Nothing about his life would attract attention, except one thing: In Stephen's monastery, sacred images were still venerated.

Eventually Stephen and his monks were betrayed, and imperial troops stormed the monastery. When ordered to destroy the icons, Stephen steadfastly refused. He was thrown in prison, where he remained for two years until being tried before the emperor in Constantinople.

It was actually more of a debate than a trial. Emperor and abbot argued until Stephen pulled out a coin bearing Constantine's image. "Is it a crime," he asked, "to trample on the image of the emperor?" For emphasis he dropped the coin and stamped on it.

Livid, Constantine replied: "It is a *great* crime to mistreat the emperor's image." "If it is a crime to tread on a coin that bears the face of the emperor," retorted Stephen, "then why is it permissible to burn an image of Christ?"

Furious at having been made to look foolish, Constantine commanded his guards to whip Stephen and then "get rid of him." After scourging the abbot, the soldiers dragged him into the streets and beat him to death.

See holy card, page 123

ST. THOMAS AQUINAS

1224/5–1274 • FEAST DAY: JANUARY 28

A lifelong teacher and undisputed genius in the disciplines of philosophy and theology, St. Thomas Aquinas is the natural choice as patron of colleges and universities.

Thomas was a man of astonishing intellect who believed that one could arrive at the doctrines of the church by reason as well as by faith. Whether to prove the existence of God, the necessity of Christ's death on the cross, or the role of the sacraments in the lives of Christians, Thomas laid out his arguments in a logical, step-by-step manner. Readers may dispute his conclusions, but it's hard not to admire his method.

But Thomas was not all intellect. He had a profoundly religious temperament and a touch of the mystic, which revealed itself in the hymns and prayers he wrote in honor of the Blessed Sacrament, almost all of which are still prayed and sung today. Nor did he think that theology was only for theologians. He wrote *Summa contra Gentiles* (Summary Against the Gentiles) as a practical handbook for teachers and missionaries to help them explain the Catholic faith to nonbelievers and defend it against heretics.

During the last eight hundred years, enthusiasm for St. Thomas Aquinas has waxed and waned—theologians and philosophers are as susceptible as anyone to the latest academic fashions. But because of his lucid arguments and brilliant, logical method, St. Thomas remains the eternal touchstone of Catholic theology and philosophy.

See holy card, page 123

ST. NORBERT

ABOUT 1080–1134 • FEAST DAY: JUNE 6

Rival popes plagued the Church throughout the Middle Ages; there were twenty-two antipopes between 1058 and 1449, and all were a source of discord, seriously harming both the church's spiritual life and its day-to-day operations.

The papacy owned income-generating properties throughout Europe, and the antipopes tried to spend that money. They appointed their own cardinals, bishops, and abbots, which meant that sometimes two rivals claimed authority over a cathedral or monastery. And, since the pope is the final authority in theological debates, an antipope who supported unorthodox opinions caused tremendous confusion among the people in the pews.

On St. Valentine's Day in 1130, the cardinals in Rome elected Innocent II as the new pope. Three hours later a band of disgruntled cardinals elected an antipope who took the name Anacletus II. Immediately the men started jockeying for the support of various kings and powerful noblemen. In Germany St. Norbert persuaded the king and the aristocracy to acknowledge what they all knew to be true: that Innocent II was the legitimate pope. After this initial success, with the help of St. Bernard of Clairvaux, Norbert kept England, Spain, and France from siding with the antipope. By persuading the most powerful men in Europe to follow their consciences rather than selfish political interests, Norbert helped keep peace in the Church and effectively isolate Anacletus.

Norbert died before Pope Innocent's ultimate triumph. However, in the last three years of his life, Norbert succeeded in keeping the peace between church and state and prevented a self-serving antipope from tearing Europe apart.

See holy card, page 123

ST. JAMES THE GREATER

FIRST CENTURY • FEAST DAY: JULY 25

𝕴 t took the Christians of Spain seven hundred years to drive out the Moorish invaders. The final victory came in 1492, when the famous monarchs Ferdinand and Isabella conquered Granada, the Moors' last stronghold.

During the long years of the *reconquista*, or reconquest, the Spanish adopted as their battle cry "Santiago!" Translated as "St. James," it is the invocation of Spain's patron saint. According to an ancient tradition, the apostle St. James the Greater was the first to preach the gospel in Spain; his relics are said to be enshrined in the magnificent basilica of Compostela.

In one of the earliest wars against the Moors, at the Battle of Clavijo in 844, the Spanish Christians were losing ground when St. James suddenly appeared on the battlefield, riding a white charger. Dressed in armor and brandishing a sword, the saint charged the Moors, cutting them down and trampling them under his horse's hooves. Crying, "Santiago!" the Spanish forces regrouped, charged, and crushed their enemies. This miraculous saintly intervention is commemorated in almost every Spanish cathedral by a sculpture or painting of St. James as a knight riding over panic-stricken Moors. The image is known as Santiago Matamoros, St. James the Moor-slayer.

When the Spanish conquistadors carved out an empire in the New World, their battle cry against the Aztecs, the Incas, and other Indian nations remained "Santiago!" They even named a city in Mexico "Matamoros" in honor of their all-conquering patron saint.

See holy card, page 124

Conscientious Objectors

ST. MARCELLUS
THE CENTURION

DIED 298 • FEAST DAY: OCTOBER 30

Incredibly, a handful of authentic transcripts from the trials of early Christian martyrs has survived, including that of St. Marcellus. Marcellus was a centurion in the Roman army stationed in Tangier, in North Africa.

At a celebration of the emperor's birthday, Marcellus refused to participate because the festivities included pagan sacrifices. He then went a step further: Standing in front of his legion's standards, he cast aside his sword and staff of office, declaring that, as a Christian, he could no longer keep his sworn oath to serve the emperor.

Marcellus was arrested and examined by the *praeses*, the camp's chief officer. "I cannot conceal your rash behavior," the officer told Marcellus; he would have to send Marcellus to a magistrate for trial. Marcellus replied that he would retract nothing.

At the arraignment, Agricolanus, the region's magistrate, asked the prisoner, "Did you say those things recorded in the chief officer's record?"

Marcellus replied, "I did."

Then Agricolanus asked, "Were you serving as a centurion?"

Marcellus answered, "I was."

"What madness possessed you," Agricolanus asked, "to cast aside your oath and say such things?"

Marcellus said, "No madness possesses he who fears God."

Finally Agricolanus asked, "Did you hurl down your weapons?"

"I did," Marcellus replied. "It is not proper for a Christian man to engage in earthly military service."

And, with that, Agricolanus sentenced Marcellus to be beheaded.

Military saints abound, but St. Marcellus is one of the rare few who refused to serve in the army based on religious grounds. For this reason, he is venerated as the patron of conscientious objectors to military service.

See holy card, page 124

ST. THOMAS THE APOSTLE

FIRST CENTURY • FEAST DAY: JULY 3

S t. Thomas the Apostle became the patron of construction workers thanks to a tale recorded in *The Golden Legend*, medieval Europe's best-selling collection of stories about the saints.

One day Thomas met a stranger in the marketplace, a servant of King Gundofor of India who was seeking a skilled builder to construct a Roman-style palace for his master. Thomas took the job.

Thomas's plans for a magnificent palace delighted the king, who gave him a huge sum and then set out on a two-year journey. Once the king was gone, Thomas distributed the money to the poor, the sick, and the helpless.

When Gundofor returned to find no palace waiting for him and all his money given away, he threw Thomas into a dungeon and made plans to skin him alive and then burn him. Thomas's execution was delayed, however, by the unexpected death of the king's brother Gad.

For four days Gad's body lay in state while Gundofor and his court mourned. On the fourth day, to the king's terror, Gad came back to life. Gundofor ran away but Gad pursued and caught his brother, beseeching him to listen.

"Brother," Gad said, "the man you are planning to flay and burn is beloved by God. When I was dead the angels led me to heaven, where they showed me a magnificent palace built of gold and silver and studded with precious stones. 'This,' the angels said, 'is the palace Thomas built for your brother.'"

Realizing that by prayer and good works he could build an eternal palace for himself in paradise, Gundofor released Thomas from prison and asked to be baptized as a Christian.

See holy card, page 124

H. Gertrud.

B.K.   Commissariat of the Holy Land Washington, D.C.

Hle. Perpetua und Felicitas
(6. März)

Nr. 364   VLA

14 Ottobre
S. CALLISTO PAPA

Chi non ama nulla nel mondo nulla dal mondo può temere.
S. Gregorio Magno

Distano dal mondo
Prega pel mondani

Milano presso A.Vallardi Gia C. Mazy 40.

1. Catholic Schools in the United States • St. Elizabeth Ann Seton   2. Cats • St. Gertrude of Nivelles
3. Cattle • SS. Perpetua and Felicity   4. Cemetery Workers • St. Callixtus

ST. VINCENTIUS A PAULO.

S. Nicolaus.

Sanctus Gregorius. - Saint Grégoire.

B. Juliana von Lüttich.

1. Charitable Organizations • St. Vincent de Paul 2. Children • St. Nicholas
3. Choirboys • St. Gregory the Great 4. Chronic Illness • St. Juliana Falconieri

S. SCHOLASTICA V. SOROR S. BENEDICTI O.S.B.

S. STEFANO JUNIORE
SALICE DI MESSINA

SAINT THOMAS D'AQUIN
DOCTEUR DE L'EGLISE

Sint Norbrecht,
Aartsbisschop van Maagdenburg en stichter der
Kloosterorde van Premonstreit.

1. Cloistered Nuns • St. Scholastica 2. Coin Collectors • St. Stephen the Younger
3. Colleges and Universities • St. Thomas Aquinas 4. Concord • St. Norbert

1.

S. GIACOMO APOSTOLO

2.

3.

S. Thomas Ap.

1. Conquistadors • St. James the Greater 2. Conscientious Objectors • St. Marcellus the Centurion
3. Construction Workers • St. Thomas the Apostle

ST. AFRA

DIED 304 • FEAST DAY: AUGUST 7

The life of St. Afra has formed the subject of several legends. The most reliable says that she was a pagan prostitute in a temple dedicated to the goddess Venus that was located in present-day Augsburg, Germany. In the early fourth century, the city was an important Roman colony, and Christianity was gaining strength there as well as throughout the empire. To combat the spread of the religion, the emperor Diocletian began large-scale persecutions, which eventually reached Afra's hometown. After her conversion to the Christian faith, Afra was arrested and hauled before a judge in the German city of Augsburg. The judge commanded her to sacrifice to the gods. Afra refused. "You were a prostitute," the judge reminded her. "The God of the Christians will reject you."

"Not so," Afra replied. "Jesus Christ forgave the adulterous woman because her repentance was sincere. And he will forgive me, too."

The judged sentenced Afra to be suffocated. The guards took her to a small island in the middle of the Lech River, which runs through Augsburg. There they tied her to a stake, built a smoky fire around her, and then left her to be asphyxiated by the fumes.

A later legend provides the story's ending: Afra's mother and three of her female servants—all former prostitutes who had converted to Christianity—took Afra's body away and buried it. The same judge then condemned them and had them burned at the martyr's grave.

St. Afra is the patron of converts to Christianity and of sinners who turn their lives around. She is also one of the patron saints of Augsburg. Her relics are venerated in the city's Church of St. Ulrich and St. Afra, where they were first displayed in 1012.

See holy card, page 141

ST. LAWRENCE

DIED 258 • FEAST DAY: AUGUST 10

In 258 the emperor Valerian began a fresh round of religious persecution. Just days after he'd published his edict outlawing Christianity, Roman soldiers raided the catacomb of Praetextatus on the Appian Way, arresting Pope St. Sixtus II just as he finished saying Mass. The Roman troops also seized four of the pope's deacons, but one named Lawrence escaped. While the soldiers led the prisoners to execution, Lawrence hurried back to Rome. Fearful that the Romans would confiscate the Church's sacred vessels, Lawrence sold them and distributed the proceeds to the poor. He had barely finished when he received his own summons to appear before the city's prefect.

By now Pope Sixtus and his four deacons were already dead. But the prefect promised to spare Lawrence's life—if he surrendered the Church's treasures to the state. Lawrence agreed, and the prefect gave him three days to collect the valuables and deliver them to the tribunal.

Lawrence returned to court three days later with a large crowd of the poor, the blind, the lame, and the helpless. "These," he told the prefect, "are the treasures of the Church." The deacon's ruse put the prefect in a foul mood, and what happened next explains St. Lawrence's position as the patron of cooks, chefs, restaurateurs, and anyone else who works in a kitchen: The prefect called for a large gridiron, commanded his executioners to build a slow fire beneath it, and had Lawrence stripped naked and bound to the grill. According to an account written in the fourth-century *Acts of St. Lawrence*, just before he died, St. Lawrence called to his executioners and said, "Turn me over. I'm done on this side."

See holy card, page 141

ST. QUENTIN

DIED 287 • FEAST DAY: OCTOBER 31

Most of the Christians martyred by the Romans died gruesome deaths. Yet over the centuries storytellers have embellished such tortures, St. Quentin's being just one example.

History confirms that a Christian named Quentin was martyred in the third century, but the details of his death remain uncertain. One especially grisly tale claims that two iron roasting spits were driven through his body before he was beheaded. Another says that he was flogged, stretched on a rack, had sharp wooden pegs driven under his fingernails, and then was tossed into the Somme River to drown. Yet another version alleges that Quentin's executioners poured a mixture of lime, vinegar, and mustard down his throat, which explains why he is invoked against coughs (but makes one wonder why he isn't also invoked against gagging).

We know that St. Quentin was a Roman who preached the gospel in and around the town of Amiens, France. Some legends say he was a bishop; others claim that he was a young man, a Roman soldier, the son of a senator. It is also said that after St. Quentin was martyred, a blind Christian woman named Eusebia was directed by an angel to find his body and give it an honorable burial. With a small crowd of family, friends, and servants, Eusebia went in search of the martyr's relics. When she found them, her sight was restored.

Sometime in the fourth century, the monument over St. Quentin's grave was destroyed, and in the decades that followed, the location of the martyr's tomb was forgotten. It was rediscovered about the year 600, and Eligius (the patron saint of jewelers) was commissioned to build a splendid shrine for St. Quentin's relics. The French were careful never to lose them again; in the ninth century, when the Vikings rampaged through the countryside around Amiens, clergy and laity carried St. Quentin's bones to a safe location.

See holy card, page 141

ST. DEMETRIUS

EARLY FOURTH CENTURY • FEAST DAY: OCTOBER 8

On June 28, 1098, the knights and fighting men of the First Crusade marched out of Antioch to meet a massive Turkish army surrounding the city. The fighting was intense. Turkish archers poured down arrows on the crusaders; another Turkish detachment surprised the Christian soldiers by attacking their undefended left flank; and then, at the frontlines, the Turks set fire to dry grass to incinerate the Christians. As the crusaders' courage wavered, they saw charging down a neighboring hill an immense company of angels, all dressed as knights, mounted on white horses, and bearing snow-white banners. Leading the charge were the three great soldier-martyrs, St. Demetrius, St. Theodore, and St. George. From that day the crusaders regarded St. Demetrius and his companions as their particular patrons.

Although some accounts describe St. Demetrius as a deacon, in most stories and in almost every icon he is portrayed as a soldier. He was mar-tyred in what is now Mitrovic, Serbia, and a church was built over his tomb. Not long afterward a second large church dedicated to St. Demetrius was consecrated in Thessalonica, Greece. The Huns destroyed the Serbian church in 441, and the focus of devotion to St. Demetrius shifted to Thessalonica. Some of his relics may have been sent there before the Huns invaded, or perhaps they were rescued from the desecrated church and moved to Greece. Whatever the case may be, St. Demetrius became a favorite saint among Greek Christians, who gave him the title "Megalomartyr," or Great Martyr.

See holy card, page 141

ST. BRIGID

ABOUT 454–525 • FEAST DAY: FEBRUARY 1

The Irish love miracle stories and lavished them on the lives of all their saints. Countless miracles are attributed to St. Brigid and, in classic Irish style, they are an agreeable blend of piety and whimsy.

On the day Brigid was born, three angels dressed liked priests descended from heaven to baptize her. Once, when the nurse who tended Brigid was thirsty, the holy baby changed water into the finest ale. A few years later Brigid was cooking bacon for some houseguests when a starving dog came to the kitchen door. Pitying the poor animal, Brigid fed him the bacon, piece after piece, until it was all gone. Yet, a moment later, when her father came in to see if the food was ready, he found the cooking pan brimming with perfectly fried bacon.

As abbess of Kildare, Brigid healed lepers, madmen, the blind, and the mute. A single cask of Brigid's convent ale never ran dry, supplying the monks at seventeen neighboring churches for the entire eight-day Easter festival. And, when an unmarried woman falsely accused one of St. Patrick's disciples of fathering her child, Brigid made the sign of the cross over the infant, causing the baby to speak up and name his real father.

St. Brigid is the patron of dairy workers because the cows she raised at her convent produced a lake of milk every day. It's an old custom in rural Ireland to hang a cross made of straw—called St. Brigid's cross—over a barn door to drive away evil and ensure that cows produce a prodigious amount of milk.

See holy card, page 142

Dancers

ST. VITUS

DIED ABOUT 303 • FEAST DAY: JUNE 15

People afflicted with the condition formerly known as "St. Vitus dance" were not dancing. They suffered from Sydenham's chorea, a neurological disorder that causes sudden, rapid, involuntary movement of the body, arms, and legs. During the Middle Ages a pilgrimage to the shrine of St. Vitus, or a novena of prayers offered to him, was believed to cure the affliction. Because the saint's intercession healed many of these cases, the illness became known as St. Vitus's dance and St. Vitus became the patron saint of dancers.

Vitus appears on the list of martyrs compiled by St. Jerome in the fourth century. Yet, the story that has grown around the saint can't be trusted.

The legend says that Vitus was born in Sicily, the son of a pagan senator. Modestus, the slave appointed by the family to be Vitus's tutor, and Crescentia, his nurse (or nanny), were Christians. Unknown to Vitus's father, they taught the boy the Christian faith and had him baptized.

Vitus was about thirteen years old when his secret was revealed. The senator had his son and servants flogged; but before he could punish them further all three escaped, took a boat to southern Italy, and continued on to Rome. There, Vitus exorcized a demon that had possessed the son of the emperor Diocletian. Suspecting that Vitus and his companions were sorcerers, Diocletian condemned them to death. He threw all three to the lions, but the beasts only played like kittens and licked the prisoners' feet. Next the emperor had them thrown into a cauldron of boiling oil, but Vitus, Modestus, and Crescentia emerged unharmed from that, too. Finally they were beheaded.

See holy card, page 142

ST. STEPHEN

DIED ABOUT 34 • FEAST DAY: DECEMBER 26

The Acts of the Apostles, a book from the New Testament, is our only source about St. Stephen. One of the Church's first seven deacons, Stephen was chosen and ordained by the apostles themselves to serve needy Christians and teach the faith. Acts tells us that he was striking in appearance, with "the face of an angel . . . full of grace and fortitude." He came from a family of Jewish Greeks, and after his ordination he debated members of four of Jerusalem's Greek synagogues. When they could not out-argue or silence this zealous young deacon, the Greek Jews hauled Stephen before the Sanhedrin (the Jews' supreme tribunal), accusing him of blasphemy for ridiculing the Temple and the Law of Moses.

Asked to defend himself, Stephen launched into a long speech. He highlighted moments in Jewish history when the people of Israel had turned away from God, implying that, by not recognizing Jesus Christ as the Messiah, they had been stubborn, proud, and faithless once again. Then he exclaimed, "Behold, I see the heavens opened, and the Son of Man standing at the right hand of God." It was the last straw. With a roar of indignation the men in the court rushed at Stephen, dragged him outside the city walls, and stoned him to death. As he fell to the ground, he prayed, "Lord, do not hold this sin against them." A man who witnessed and approved of Stephen's execution—he watched the coats of the men hurling the rocks—was a virulent Christian hater named Saul, later the great apostle St. Paul.

St. Stephen is venerated not only as a model for deacons but also as the Church's first martyr.

See holy card, page 142

Difficult Choices

ST. EUSTACE OR EUSTACHIUS

DIED 118 • FEAST DAY: SEPTEMBER 20

The story of St. Eustace was wildly popular during the Middle Ages. It was the equivalent of the cliffhanger serials of the 1930s or one of Hollywood's blockbuster melodramas—think *Gladiator*—with plenty of tragic reversals, unexpected coincidences, and a grand finale.

Eustace was a wealthy man and a respected general in the emperor Trajan's army. He and his wife, Theopistes, and their sons, Agapitus and Theopistus, were pagans. After converting to Christianity, however, the family was besieged by one disaster after another: Trajan stripped Eustace of his rank. A plague took the lives of all their servants as well as their flocks and herds. Robbers broke into the house and stole all their valuables. Pirates kidnapped Theopistes.

Destitute and distraught from the loss of his wife, Eustace took his two little boys and headed into the wilderness outside Rome. They stopped at a raging river. Since the current was too strong for Eustace to carry both boys simultaneously, he decided to take one across at a time. He had gotten his first son safely to the opposite shore and was midway in the river to retrieve the other when a wolf darted out of the brush and seized the child he'd just carried over. Seconds later a lion leapt out of the forest and seized the child Eustace was on his way to get. As the wild beasts dragged his sons in opposite directions, Eustace stood in the middle of the river howling with rage and grief. It was this dilemma that makes St. Eustace the patron of all those confronted with difficult choices.

But the story doesn't end there, of course. Eustace dragged himself out of the river and wandered aimlessly until he came upon a peasant village. There he stayed for fifteen years, guarding the villagers' fields and livestock. Eustace's sons, meanwhile, had been rescued by shepherds and grew up in a neighboring village. Even Theopistes was spared—the lecherous pirate kidnapper died before laying a hand on her.

Meanwhile, Rome's enemies were forming an alliance to destroy the empire. Trajan missed his old general, and he dispatched scouts in every direction to find him. Eventually two old comrades found Eustace at his new village. Moved by the danger facing Rome, Eustace agreed to command the legions once again. He called for fresh conscripts, and among them were his long-lost sons. The men didn't recognize one another, but the two young soldiers were so strong and intelligent that Eustace placed them on his staff.

After defeating the barbarians, Eustace and his staff were returning to Rome to celebrate when they stopped at a country inn. The woman who ran the inn was Eustace's wife. Recognizing one another, the family was at last reunited.

They all traveled to Rome together, but, by the time they arrived, Trajan had died and Hadrian had succeeded him as the new emperor. Surprised that Eustace and his family did not participate in sacrifices of thanks-giving to the gods, Hadrian confronted Eustace, who replied, "We worship Christ alone."

Alarmed that such an influential man was a Christian, Hadrian had an enormous hollow bronze bull brought out, ordered Eustace and his family to be bound, and stuffed them inside. Then the executioners lit a fire beneath the bull and roasted the four martyrs alive.

See holy card, page 142

ST. THOMAS BECKET

ABOUT 1120-1170 • FEAST DAY: DECEMBER 29

Nothing in St. Thomas Becket's early life suggested that he would become a defender of the liberty of the Church, let alone a martyr. Ambition, not godliness, led him to choose a career as a cleric. He was a shrewd administrator with a special talent for making money. He was handsome and could be charming when necessary. He proved to be the ideal royal servant—whatever King Henry II wanted done, Becket accomplished.

When the old archbishop of Canterbury died, Henry asserted a royal privilege claimed by many European kings: He took it upon himself to name the successor rather than waiting for the pope to do so. Henry named Becket. In the king's mind, Becket was the perfect choice. With one of his closest friends as archbishop of Canterbury, Henry felt he could extend his royal authority over the Church in England. He was wrong.

Once Thomas Becket was consecrated archbishop of Canterbury, grace touched his heart and he became a changed man. He was as careful about his prayers and saying Mass as once he had been about the king's business. He did penance to make up for years of careless living. The man who'd refused to clothe one freezing beggar now gave lavishly to the poor. We don't know if Henry noticed the change that had come over his friend. When the king made his first move against the Church, however, it became clear that Becket was not the puppet archbishop he was supposed to be.

In their first squabble, Henry argued that priests who committed crimes were treated too leniently by Church courts and they should submit to the courts of England. Becket replied that laymen did not have jurisdiction over clergymen. Stung by Becket's opposition, Henry brought a host of false charges against his one-time friend. He had Becket indicted for squandering royal funds and even accused the archbishop of treason.

Death threats from the king's men followed. Fearing for his life, Becket fled to France.

For the next six years Henry and Becket jockeyed for position, each trying to win the pope's support. In the end arbitrators for each side worked out a truce that permitted Becket to return home to Canterbury, although the central issue of the liberty of the Church remained unresolved. When Becket excommunicated bishops who had supported Henry and infringed on the prerogatives of the archbishops of Canterbury, Henry threw one of his notorious tantrums that ended with him crying, "Will no one relieve me of this troublesome priest?"

Four of the king's knights, all bitter enemies of the archbishop, set out at once for Canterbury. There they confronted Becket in his own cathedral, demanding that he give in to all of Henry's demands. When the archbishop refused, the knights attacked, hacking him to death at the foot of the altar.

The shock of Becket's murder reverberated across Europe. Henry submitted to public penance, letting the Canterbury monks flog him as he knelt at his friend's tomb. In two years the pope declared Thomas Becket a saint. Soon pilgrims from every shire of England and every corner of Christendom were making the journey to St. Thomas's shrine in Canterbury.

St. Thomas Becket quarreled with his king over the liberty of the Church, but it was the diocesan clergy whose rights would be lost if the king won. As a result, they look upon the archbishop as their particular champion.

See holy card, page 143

BLESSED MARGARET OF CASTELLO

1287–1320 • FEAST DAY: APRIL 13

Blessed Margaret's life is one of the most heart-wrenching stories in the roster of saints. She was born blind and with severe curvature of the spine; her right leg was an inch and a half shorter than her left, and her left arm was malformed. She never grew taller than four feet.

Her parents kept little Margaret hidden away in their house in Metola, in the Italian province of Umbria. When Margaret was six years old, the family traveled to a shrine at Castello, hoping for a miracle. When none took place, her mother and father abandoned her.

Some women of Castello found the terrified child and took care of her until they could arrange for her adoption. A husband and wife, Venfarino and Grigia, adopted Margaret and treated her with love and kindness as their own daughter. She appears to have spent the rest of her life with them.

Margaret's disabilities did not make her bitter; rather, she became one of the most generous, sympathetic people in Castello. She nursed the sick, consoled the dying, and visited prisoners. She regarded her own disabilities as a means to unite her pain with the suffering that Christ endured on the cross. Her courage, patience, and deep religious devotion won her the affection of everyone in town.

At Margaret's funeral, the crowd was immense. The parish priest planned to bury Margaret in the churchyard, but the mourners insisted that she have a tomb inside the church, alongside the other distinguished dead of Castello. The priest was still arguing the point when a girl whose legs were crippled dragged herself to Margaret's coffin. She touched the casket and then stood up and began to walk. The priest gave Margaret a tomb inside the church.

See holy card, page 143

ST. GENEVIEVE

ABOUT 422–ABOUT 500 • FEAST DAY: JANUARY 3

Devotion to St. Genevieve has always been strongest in Paris, the city she saved from disaster time and again.

At age fifteen she took the vows of a nun but didn't enter a cloister or even live quietly at home. Like St. Joan of Arc, Genevieve felt drawn to an active life. The Franks—the barbarian pagan tribe that would eventually conquer Roman-held Gaul and give their name to the country—captured Paris after a long siege that brought the city to the brink of starvation. After the surrender Genevieve led a flotilla of ships up the Seine to Troyes to bring back food for her famished neighbors.

The Huns attacked next, led by Attila himself. The Parisians wanted to flee, but Genevieve convinced them to defend their city, pray intensely, and trust in God. Inexplicably, the Huns soon turned away from the city and headed off in another direction. Later, when the Frankish kings Childeric and then Clovis captured Paris and seized many distinguished citizens, it was Genevieve who persuaded the conquerors to spare the lives of their prisoners.

Even after Genevieve's death, Parisian citizens turned to her in times of calamity. In 834, when the Seine River threatened to drown the city, they invoked St. Genevieve and the floodwater subsided. In 1129, when thousands were dying in an epidemic of ergotism, a fatal condition brought about by eating rye bread made from fungus-infected grain, the archbishop of Paris organized a solemn procession and carried the relics of St. Genevieve from her shrine through the streets of the city to the cathedral of Notre Dame. The epidemic subsided shortly thereafter.

See holy card, page 143

Discretion

ST. JOHN NEPOMUK

ABOUT 1340–1393 • FEAST DAY: MAY 16

Like the more famous St. Thomas Becket, St. John Nepomuk was a high-ranking clergyman who ran afoul of his king.

Wenceslaus IV, king of Bohemia, wanted to make one of his cronies a bishop. When the abbot of an important monastery died, Wenceslaus seized his chance. He insisted that the Church declare the abbey to be a new cathedral, with his own candidate installed as the first bishop. As vicar general of Prague, John replied on behalf of the Church: The region around the monastery already had a bishop, and canon law did not permit gerrymandering a diocese to accommodate the whims of a king.

It was unfortunate that John Nepomuk was the one to respond, for the king already held a grudge against him. Wenceslaus suspected his wife of cheating on him and had ordered John to reveal whether she had confessed to adultery. But the seal of the confessional is absolute, and John refused to disclose the queen's sins.

Now that John Nepomuk had gotten in his way again, Wenceslaus was furious. He had John and three other church officials arrested and tortured. In their agony the officials swore to uphold the king's "right" to create new dioceses and bishops, but John held firm. The torturers racked him, whipped him, slashed him with knives, and held flaming torches against his sides—still he would not submit. Wenceslaus ordered John gagged with a wooden block, led in chains through the streets of Prague, and then thrown into the Moldau River to drown.

Since his death, John's defense of canon law has been almost forgotten in favor of his protection of the confidentiality of the confessional. For that reason he has become the patron saint of discretion, which encompasses confessors, penitents, and anyone obliged to keep a secret.

See holy card, page 143

ST. CHAD

ABOUT 630–672 • FEAST DAY: MARCH 2

C had. The very word summons unhappy memories of the pandemonium following the 2000 U.S. presidential race. That St. Chad has recently come to be considered the patron of disputed elections, because of not just his name but also his own involvement in a conflict over an office, makes for an interesting, if ironic, story.

Chad grew up in Northumbria, near the Scottish border in far northern England. After rigorous training with the austere monks at Mellifont Abbey in Ireland, Chad returned to England and was ordained as a priest. Within a few years, his reputation for holiness and wisdom had spread throughout the land, so, when the city of York needed a bishop, King Oswy appointed Chad. And that's when the trouble started.

Technically, York already had a bishop. In 664 St. Wilfrid had been appointed and sent to France to be consecrated a bishop. But months had gone by and Wilfrid was still on

the continent, showing no sign that he ever intended to return to his diocese. Although Wilfrid had never submitted a formal resignation nor stated flat-out that he would not be returning to England, Chad was persuaded that the post had been abandoned, and he consented to become bishop in Wilfrid's place.

Chad made a splendid bishop. He spent much of his time on the road, visiting his diocese, resolving disputes, and teaching the faith. No village was too small, no hut too miserable for Chad to visit. But five years after Chad had assumed office, Wilfrid returned. Embarrassed by his long absence and Chad's superb leadership, Wilfrid kept quiet and retired to a monastery at Ripon.

Wilfrid's retirement was tactful but, under church law, not strictly legal—a technicality that the new archbishop of Canterbury, St. Theodore, pointed out to both men when he made a pastoral visit to York. Though Chad was the sentimental favorite, he didn't take advantage of people's goodwill to keep his job. "I gladly resign," he told Theodore. "I never thought myself worthy of the office and agreed to undertake it . . . only under obedience." Chad's gracious departure from York confirmed everyone's good opinion of him. He had been living in a monastery near his family's home for just a short time when Archbishop Theodore wrote saying that Lichfield needed a bishop, and he had decided to appoint Chad.

Although devotion to St. Chad is fourteen hundred years old, his reputation as the patron of disputed elections is recent. During the upheaval after the 2000 elections, when hanging and dimpled ballot chads became a national obsession, an unnamed reporter recalled St. Chad's story and its similarities to recent events. And, just as has happened with so many saints invoked for particular causes, the people, not the pope, acclaimed St. Chad as the patron of disputed elections.

See holy card, page 144

S. Afra.

S. LORENZO MARTIRE

Saint Quentin.

Sanctus Quintinus

St. DEMETRIUS

1. Converts • St. Afra 2. Cooks • St. Lawrence
3. Coughs • St. Quentin 4. Crusaders • St. Demetrius

S. Brigida.

B.K. Carl Poellath, Schrobenhausen

Svatý Vít.

S. Stephanus.

S. Eustachius.

Sumptibus Fr. Pustet, Ratisbonæ

1. Dairy Workers • St. Brigid 2. Dancers • St. Vitus
3. Deacons • St. Stephen 4. Difficult Choices • St. Eustace or Eustachius

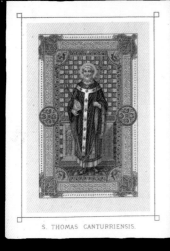

S. THOMAS CANTURRIENSIS.

B. Margarita de Castello DOP

S. Genovefa.

POD OCHRANU TVOU UTÍKÁME SE,
SVATÁ BOŽÍ RODIČKO !

1. Diocesan Priests • St. Thomas Becket 2. Disabilities • Blessed Margaret of Castello
3. Disasters • St. Genevieve 4. Discretion • St. John Nepomuk

S. CHAD. B.C.

Die heilige Helena, Kaiserin.

Benziger & Co.   Dépenl.   1870.   Einsiedeln, Schweiz.

S. S. Cosme y Damian

ST. ROCHUS.

1. Disputed Elections • St. Chad 2. Divorced or Divorcing Couples • St. Helen
3. Doctors • SS. Cosmas and Damian 4. Dogs • St. Rocco

144

ST. HELEN

249–329 • FEAST DAY: AUGUST 18

Helen's marriage to Constantius Chlorus was a love match. She was at her parents' home in northern Turkey when she met her future husband, a goat herder's son making a career for himself in the Roman army. They were wed in 270 and, two years later, Helen gave birth to their son Constantine.

Constantius's career prospered, and in 288 he was appointed governor of Dalmatia (present-day Croatia). Impressed by Constantius's administration of the territory, the Roman co-emperors Diocletian and Maximian promoted him to rule over a vast stretch of Roman provinces in Gaul, Spain, and Britain. Then Maximian paid the new governor a high compliment—he offered Constantius the hand of his stepdaughter Flavia. Of course, for Constantius to accept the emperor's offer, Helen would have to go. Constantius did not hesitate. He divorced his wife of twenty-two years and married into the imperial family.

No account survives of what Helen did between her divorce in 292 and 312, when her son Constantine became sole emperor of Rome. We know that Constantius died in 305, and in 309 Helen became a Christian. Helen likely influenced her son's decision to end Rome's anti-Christian policy.

Perhaps as a consolation to his mother for the pain and humiliation of being cast off by Constantius, Constantine bestowed a string of honors on her. He renamed her birthplace Helenopolis; he gave her the Sessorian Palace in Rome as her residence; he had coins struck bearing her image; and he granted her the titles of Empress and Augusta.

Constantius had hoped that by divorcing Helen he could marry up. But, in the end, Helen outranked him as both an empress and a saint.

See holy card, page 144

SS. COSMAS & DAMIAN

DIED ABOUT 287 • FEAST DAY: SEPTEMBER 26

Twin brothers Cosmas and Damian were physicians in life, but that's not the only reason they became the patron saints of medical doctors. After their death, the dramatic cures wrought in the church containing their tombs contributed to their reputation.

The sick and infirm traveled from miles around to the church, located outside Antioch in present-day Syria, to spend the night sleeping as close as possible to the saints' burial place. The saints would appear to them in a dream, administer medicine or perform a surgical procedure, and in the morning the pilgrims would wake up perfectly healthy.

Cosmas and Damian's most famous miracle involved a man whose leg bone was ravaged by cancer. One night the saints appeared to him in a dream, amputated his diseased leg, and replaced it with the leg of a Moor who had died earlier that day. In the morning the man awoke to find his cancerous limb replaced by a healthy black one.

Cosmas and Damian practiced medicine in what is now Iskendrun, Turkey. They never charged for their services, but while examining patients they took the opportunity to discuss their Christian faith. Such indiscretion led to their arrest, along with that of their three younger brothers. The region's governor condemned all five brothers to be drowned in the sea, but they simply floated on the surface. He ordered them to be burned alive, but the flames wouldn't touch them. He had them tied to crosses so that soldiers could shoot them with arrows and bystanders could stone them, but the arrows and stones struck the soldiers and bystanders instead. Finally, the governor condemned the brothers to be beheaded, and this time the execution was successful.

See holy card, page 144

ST. ROCCO

DIED 1378 • FEAST DAY: AUGUST 16

St. Rocco's story dates from the time when the Black Death first ravaged Europe. The epidemic arrived on the continent in October 1347, when a ship full of sick and dying sailors docked in Messina, Italy. Physicians were mystified by the sailors' symptoms: They sweated profusely, coughed up blood, and had large black swellings in their armpits and groins. All the sailors died, and the mysterious illness passed to the townspeople. From Messina the plague spread to every part of Europe—even to remote Iceland—taking the lives of 20 million people within four years.

In 1372 St. Rocco was on his way home from a pilgrimage to Rome when he stopped in the Italian city of Piacenza. Plague had just broken out there, and the inhabitants who weren't dying were in a state of panic. Moved by the suffering, Rocco began volunteering as a nurse in one of the city's hospitals. It is said that he cured hundreds of plague victims by making the sign of the cross on their feverish foreheads.

But then one morning Rocco woke up very ill. In his armpits and groin he found the telltale dark swellings of the Black Death. Rather than infect anyone else, he dragged himself outside the city to die alone in the woods. Rocco had just made himself a bed of leaves when a dog trotted up, carrying a large loaf of bread in its mouth. Every day the dog returned with another fresh loaf. Incredibly, Rocco recovered. He returned to Piacenza and resumed his work in the hospital.

Thanks to the friendly canine that kept Rocco from starvation, all dogs have St. Rocco as their patron. His emblem, which appears beside the saint in virtually every picture or statue, is the dog with the loaf of bread in its mouth.

See holy card, page 144

ST. ANTHONY OF PADUA

1195–1231 • FEAST DAY: JUNE 13

St. Anthony of Padua was an eloquent preacher. He was so good, and so well known, that cities and towns across Europe competed for his presence. He once traveled to Italy's Adriatic coast, to the small town of Rimini, as a guest preacher. One of the town's most outspoken and obnoxious citizens was a merchant named Bonillo, a man who was notorious for mocking his neighbors' faith in the Church's doctrine of the Real Presence, which states that the consecrated Host is truly the body and blood, soul and divinity of Jesus Christ. During his stay in Rimini, Anthony tried to persuade Bonillo that the Real Presence was not "a fable," as the scoffer insisted. But the saint's arguments fell on deaf ears.

A few days later, Anthony carried the Blessed Sacrament in a solemn procession through the city streets. As the Host passed, all the spectators knelt—all but Bonillo the merchant. He was feeding his donkey, and he kept right on feeding it as the procession came his way. But, as St. Anthony and the Blessed Sacrament approached, Bonillo's donkey turned away from its fodder, went down on its knees, and bowed its head to the ground. Bonillo, who could not be convinced by any human argument, was converted by a donkey's miraculous act of adoration.

Because of this miracle, St. Anthony of Padua is regarded as the protector of donkeys, mules, and asses.

St. Anthony of Padua was born Fernando de Bulhões to a wealthy, noble family in Lisbon, Portugal. Young Fernando received a traditional education at the nearby cathedral school and then went on to enter the Augustinian Abbey just outside the city. Fernando soon proved himself to be gifted for understanding and synthesizing complex theological matters. He longed for the simple life of the Franciscans and, in 1220, joined their order, taking the name Anthony in honor of St. Anthony the Great.

See holy card, page 161

ST. THOMAS THE APOSTLE

FIRST CENTURY • FEAST DAY: JULY 3

The story of the apostle known as Doubting Thomas begins after the first Easter. Fearing for their lives after Jesus's crucifixion, the eleven surviving apostles (Judas had hanged himself) locked themselves in the room they'd used for the Last Supper.

On Easter evening, Jesus—whom they'd all seen die on the cross—suddenly appeared among them. St. Thomas wasn't there, but when he returned the other apostles were still joyous and excited. But Thomas refused to believe that Jesus had risen from the dead, and no amount of assurance from his friends would convince him. "Unless I see in his hands the print of the nails," he said, "and place my finger in the mark of the nails, and place my hand in his side, I will not believe."

Eight days later Christ returned, and this time Thomas was in the room. Turning to his skeptical apostle, Jesus said, "Put your finger here, and see my hands; and put out your hand, and place it in my side; do not be faithless, but believing."

Overwhelmed by the sight of Jesus, Thomas exclaimed, "My Lord and my God!" Catholics still pray this exclamation silently at Mass, at the moment the priest raises the Host after consecrating it in preparation for Communion.

Addressing St. Thomas and all doubters through the ages, Jesus said, "Have you believed because you have seen me? Blessed are those who have not seen and yet believe."

Because of his period of disbelief, St. Thomas has become the patron saint who resolves the qualms, misgivings, and reservations of doubters, skeptics, and cynics.

See holy card, page 161

ST. RADEGUNDE

518–587 • FEAST DAY: AUGUST 13

Radegunde lived in the first years after the Roman empire's collapse, when the barbarian tribes were gaining power. Like many Christians of the time, she identified with Roman civilization, but in fact Radegunde had been born a pagan princess in the Thurginian tribe, who settled in eastern Germany around present-day Erfurt. Radegunde had a tumultuous childhood. When she was young her uncle murdered her father, and then the Franks conquered Thurginia and took her with them as a prize. In France she became a Christian, but she was still a captive.

When Radegunde was eighteen, Clothaire, the king of the Franks, forced her to marry him. Although ostensibly a Christian, by this time the king had wed at least five times and was probably still married to a few of the women (it's unlikely they all died or that he had been granted five annulments).

The marriage was wretched. No matter how many wives he had, Clothaire climbed into bed with any woman who attracted him. He was violent and beat Radegunde, blaming her for their lack of children. The antagonism between the royal couple came to a head in 550, when Clothaire murdered Radegunde's brother. She ran away, took vows as a nun, and sent Germanus, the bishop of Paris, to convince Clothaire to leave her in peace. Clothaire, who had always complained he was married to a nun rather than a queen, was happy to let Radegunde go. He even sent parting gifts to her convent in Poitiers, France.

Radegunde made her Convent of the Holy Cross an island of piety, beauty, education, and refinement amid a sea of ignorance and violence. Her chaplain, St. Venantius Fortunatus, was a Roman gentleman, a priest who wrote Latin poetry in the classical style. Women looking for a secure, serene escape from the violence of their time flocked to the convent. Many were from noble families, and a significant number were royalty.

Radegunde designed a routine of prayer, contemplation, study, silence, austerity, and works of charity.

As her convent's name suggests, Radegunde was deeply devoted to the cross upon which Jesus was crucified and longed to have a fragment of the True Cross to venerate in her church. In 569 Emperor Justin II sent her a piece of the cross set in a jewel-studded gold reliquary. To commemorate the arrival of such an important relic, Venantius wrote a poem, *Vexilla regis prodeunt* (The Banners of the King Go Forth). The poem was set to music and is one of the loveliest hymns in the repertoire of Gregorian chant.

Not long after Radegunde died, one of her servants was deep-sea fishing. A storm came up suddenly and giant waves swamped the boat. Before the poor man had a chance to start bailing, his boat filled with water and sank. As he went under, the terrified fisherman invoked St. Radegunde. A moment later he and his boat bobbed to the surface, the storm vanished, the sky cleared, and the sea calmed. Ever after, St. Radegunde has been the patron saint of those who fear drowning.

See holy card, page 161

ST. EUGENE DE MAZENOD

1782–1861 • FEAST DAY: MAY 21

The Mazenod family was doomed from the beginning. Charles-Antoine de Mazenod was a member of the French aristocracy, a man of genteel breeding who had received a superb classical education. Unfortunately, his distinguished title and good manners were all he possessed—the once-respectable Mazenod fortune had been squandered by Charles-Antoine's father and grandfather.

Marie-Rose Joannis, on the other hand, came from a family that was solidly bourgeois and very rich. When Charles-Antoine and Marie-Rose announced their engagement, the bride's family insisted that the dowry remain in Marie-Rose's name, out of Charles-Antoine's reach. That was just the first in a constant stream of the Joannis clan's interference in the couple's marriage.

Nonetheless, for Marie-Rose's sake, the Joannis family kept money flowing steadily into the couple's bank account. But such generosity came at a price. Marie-Rose's mother meddled in the couple's every decision; her emotionally unbalanced aunt demanded constant attention; and the Joannis women took every opportunity to humiliate Charles-Antoine by reminding him that he'd joined their family penniless.

On August 1, 1782, in Provence, St. Eugene de Mazenod was born into this wretched family. While he was still a little boy, his family's dysfunction was further complicated by the French Revolution, which claimed the lives of thousands of aristocratic families. To escape the guillotine, in 1791 the Mazenods fled to Venice, Italy. Four years later Marie-Rose walked out on her husband and her son, returned to France, and filed for divorce. When the divorce was final, she wrote to her ex-husband, "Now you have nothing."

Eugene found refuge in the Church, where has was able to escape from his miserable home life. In 1808 he entered the seminary in

Paris, and in 1811 he was ordained a priest; he asked to be assigned to work among the poor country people in the south of France. His superiors granted the request, in part because Eugene had grown up in the district and spoke the local dialect.

The French Revolution had caused tremendous disruption to religious life throughout the country. Bishops, priests, monks, and nuns who had not been killed were living in exile or had disgraced their vocation. Churches and schools stood abandoned; convents and monasteries lay in ruins. An entire generation had grown up with virtually no religious instruction.

By 1815 Eugene had assembled a band of dedicated priests who worked with him as missionaries in the rural areas of Provence, bringing people who were nominally Christian back to the ancient faith. In recognition of the group's success, the pope organized them into a new religious order and gave them their name, the Oblates of Mary Immaculate. An oblate is one who offers his life and all his efforts to God (or in this case the Virgin Mary) for the good of others. As for Eugene, his reward was being named bishop of Marseilles, a position he held from 1837 until his death, in 1861.

St. Eugene may not have been able to reconcile his parents or bring peace to his family, but he and his fellow priests did draw countless thousands back to the Church.

See holy card, page 162

ST. EMIDIUS

DIED 304 • FEAST DAY: AUGUST 5

Joseph Sadoc Alemany, a Spanish Dominican, was only thirty-nine years old in 1853 when the pope named him the first archbishop of San Francisco. The title was misleading because Alemany's archdiocese covered the entire state of California. On top of too few parishes, hardly any priests, and no nuns, schools, or hospitals to speak of, Archbishop Alemany couldn't help noticing another difficulty that plagued California: The state was rocked by earthquakes. He could build churches, schools, and hospitals and recruit priests and nuns to staff them, but a force of nature was a different beast altogether. In 1869, at the request of Archbishop Alemany, Blessed Pope Pius IX established the feast of St. Emidius as a special day of prayer in California.

We know a bishop named Emidius was martyred in 304 in the town of Ascoli Piceno, in eastern Italy. The rest of the saint's story is legend. After being baptized in Germany he supposedly traveled to Rome, where, in his zeal for the Christian faith, he entered a Roman temple to the god Asclepius and knocked over a statue. Pope Marcellus quickly made Emidius a bishop and, for his safety, shipped him out of town to Ascoli Piceno. But Bishop Emidius was only marginally more discreet there: He didn't smash any more idols, but he did preach boldly in the streets. The Roman authorities arrested and beheaded him.

Like California, Ascoli Piceno is susceptible to earthquakes. The people of the region credit St. Emidius with saving them from disaster many times over the centuries. In art St. Emidius is usually depicted holding up a building on the verge of collapse.

See holy card, page 162

ST. FRANCIS OF ASSISI

1182–1226 • FEAST DAY: OCTOBER 4

Statues of St. Francis standing amid a flowerbed or perched on the edge of a birdbath are a garden cliché. But if sentimentalizing St. Francis is bad, turning him into some sun-and-moon worshipping pantheist is worse. The man was deeply, unshakably committed to the Catholic faith. When he contemplated the natural world, he saw a gloriously complex, interrelated system that reflected the splendor, goodness, and generosity of God. His famous "Canticle of the Sun" is a hymn of praise and thanksgiving to God for all the wonders of creation.

Francis began composing the canticle in 1225. He wrote in the style of the troubadours, the romantic poets he'd tried to imitate as a teenager running in the streets of Assisi. So that his hymn would reach the widest audience possible, he wrote it in Italian rather than Latin. From time to time he added new verses; some of these were likely lost because Francis appears to have added verses spontaneously to fit a particular moment. He composed some lines on the virtue of forgiveness (this verse has come down to us) after he'd arbitrated a dispute between the bishop and governor of Assisi. He made his final addition to the canticle while lying on his deathbed. "Praised be my Lord for our Sister mortal death," Francis sang, "from whom no man alive will escape."

Because St. Francis loved and cherished the universe God made and all the creatures in it, in 1980 Pope John Paul II officially proclaimed Francis the patron of ecology and the environmental movement.

See holy card, page 162

ST. JOHN BOSCO

1815–1888 • FEAST DAY: JANUARY 31

In 1884 Italy held one of those national expositions, beloved in the nineteenth century, to show off its progress in science, industry, and the arts. St. John Bosco was one of the exhibitors. His display was listed in the program as "Don Bosco: Salesian Paper Mill, Printing Works, Bindery, and Bookshop." ("Don" is the preferred title of respect for a priest in Italy.) At that time, the mood in Italy was decidedly anticlerical, and many considered it a joke that a priest was participating in an exhibition showcasing the latest technological advances. Yet visitors to Don Bosco's booth were surprised to find a man who understood every facet of the book-publishing industry, from making paper to getting his books to the marketplace. That's how Don Bosco became the patron of editors.

Book publishing was only one of Don Bosco's areas of expertise. He dedicated his life to saving orphaned and abandoned children from a life of degradation, violence, and crime.

He opened homes where these street kids were sheltered, loved, and cared for—where they were given an education and taught a useful trade. Each of Don Bosco's homes had fully outfitted shoemaker and tailor shops, a foundry, a carpenter shop for building furniture and cabinetry, and, of course, a publishing company.

Unfortunately, Don Bosco had started his religious community at the moment when the Italian government was trying to expel the Church's religious orders from the country. But Don Bosco received help from an unexpected quarter—Urban Rattazzi, Italy's minister of the interior and the author of the legislation that shut down the religious orders in Italy. Though Rattazzi loathed priests in general, he liked and admired Don Bosco. It may have been Rattazzi's sense of pragmatism that convinced him of Don Bosco's worthiness; after all, by transforming troubled boys into productive members of society, Don Bosco was doing the Italian state a great service. Whatever his reasons, Rattazzi helped the priest word the official paperwork required to register the Salesians with the government so that they appeared to be a civil society rather than a religious order. Once his original establishment in Turin managed to fly under the government's radar, St. John expanded into other cities and countries. By the time of his death, Don Bosco had opened thirty-eight complexes for boys in Europe and another twenty-six in the Americas.

Nonetheless, not everyone approved of Don Bosco's work. Social conservatives complained that he was wasting resources on the dregs of the world, and political radicals criticized Bosco for removing disenchanted youths from the proletarian class and making them permanent members of the bourgeoisie. Whether from the right or the left, the criticism didn't faze him. "Denunciation and political action we leave to others," Don Bosco said. "We go straight to the poor."

See holy card, page 162

ST. DYMPHNA

SEVENTH CENTURY • FEAST DAY: MAY 15

In the ninth century the bones of the martyr St. Dymphna were discovered outside the town of Gheel, in present-day Belgium. Large crowds turned out for the transfer of the saint's relics to a shrine in the town's church, believing that at such a momentous event, the saint would manifest her power. St. Dymphna didn't disappoint. During the procession of her relics, so many emotionally disturbed and mentally ill people were healed that the town's Christians took it as a sign of Dymphna's wish to be invoked against such afflictions. In her honor, they built a hospital in Gheel for people with emotional problems or mental illness, which still operates today.

The first "biography" of St. Dymphna was written six hundred years after her death, so what we know of her life is probably more legend than fact. According to the story, Dymphna was the daughter of Damon, a pagan Irish king. She converted to Christianity in her teens,

and soon thereafter her mother died. The loss of his beloved wife drove Damon mad, so much so that, since Dymphna strongly resembled her mother, he decided to marry his daughter.

To escape her unbalanced father and the threat of incest, Dymphna set sail for the continent with her chaplain, Gerebernus. They went ashore in present-day Belgium and settled in Gheel, but to no avail. Damon followed them and beheaded his daughter while his bodyguard murdered Gerebernus. The people of Gheel placed the saints' bodies in two plain stone sarcophagi and buried them inside a cave, where they remained until they were discovered several hundred years later. Portions of the sarcophagi have survived and are still displayed in Gheel.

See holy card, page 163

OUR LADY OF GOOD COUNSEL

FEAST DAY: APRIL 26

St. Augustine said that the Blessed Virgin Mary was "the counsel of the Apostles," and she is still the counsel of all nations. In other words, just as she directed and guided the apostles after Christ returned to heaven, she still directs and guides people toward her son. One thousand years later, Augustine's concept would be assigned in a tangible way to a particular portrait of Mary.

The image known as Our Lady of Good Counsel is preserved in the church of the same name in the town of Genazzano, about thirty miles south of Rome. It's a small picture, only about seventeen inches wide by fifteen inches tall, painted on a thin fragment of plaster no thicker than a postcard. The first record of the image dates to April 25, 1467, when it was discovered during the church's renovation. A record compiled by a local notary testifies that during the four months after its discovery, 171 miracles in Genazzano were attributed to the intercession of Our Lady of Good Counsel.

At some point this holy picture of the Virgin and Child shifted slightly from a wonder-working icon into a focus of a particular devotion—that Mary would enlighten and direct all who called upon her under her title of Good Counsel. Many popes especially have looked for guidance to the Mother of Good Counsel. In 1680 Urban VIII made a pilgrimage to the shrine, as did Blessed Pius IX in 1864 and Blessed John XXIII in 1959. In 1939 Pope Pius XII placed his entire pontificate under the protection of Our Lady of Good Counsel.

During World War II a bomb crashed through the church roof, destroying the sanctuary and high altar. Although the fragile image was only a few feet away, it survived unscathed.

See holy card, page 163

ST. WILLIBRORD

ABOUT 658–739 • FEAST DAY: NOVEMBER 7

Odd folk customs sometimes get tangled up with devotion to the saints, and Willibrord is a classic example. A legend dating from the fourteenth century tells how a strange epidemic infected the cattle of the region around Echternach Abbey in Luxemburg, where St. Willibrord lies buried. The main symptom of the illness was uncontrollable trembling, followed by a quick death. The peasants invoked St. Willibrord, and, in a procession to his shrine, some in the crowd began to do an impromptu dance that resembled the convulsions of the cattle.

The veracity of the story is questionable. However, we do know that by the fifteenth century an annual dancing procession ended at the shrine, where the saint was invoked against epilepsy and other nervous disorders afflicting humans rather than cattle. The dancing procession still takes place every year in Echternach on the Tuesday after Pentecost Sunday. The dancers move through the streets into the abbey church and circle around St. Willibrord's shrine before settling down for a religious ceremony.

As for St. Willibrord, he was an English missionary who crossed the channel to preach the gospel in the Netherlands. His mission got off to a good start, with so many locals asking to be baptized that he built many churches and founded the Abbey of Echternach. In 716 a pagan chieftain named Radbod conquered the region and destroyed the churches. Willibrord escaped, and after Radbod's death he began his work once again.

At the end of his long life, Willibrod retired to Echternach, where he died. He was venerated as a saint from the moment of his death, and devotion to him remains strong in Luxemburg.

See holy card, page 163

Sanctus Antonius de Padua

3.

Sainte Radegonde

[Sancta Radegundis.Reg. Franc.]

1. Donkeys, Asses, and Mules • St. Anthony of Padua 2. Doubters • St. Thomas the Apostle
3. Drowning • St. Radegunde

BLESSED

EUGENE DE MAZENOD

BISHOP OF MARSEILLES

Founder of the Congregation
of the Missionary Oblates of Mary Immaculate

SANT'EMIDIO V. e M.

PROTETTORE CONTRO IL FLAGELLO DEL TERREMOTO

SAINT FRANCIS OF ASSISI

pray for us

MAISON BOUASSE-LEBEL, 29 RUE St. SULPICE, PARIS — 6520 — MADE IN FRANCE

DON BOSCO

1. Dysfunctional Families • St. Eugene de Mazenod 2. Earthquakes • St. Emidius
3. Ecology • St. Francis of Assisi 4. Editors • St. John Bosco

St. Dymphna Virgo et Martyr, O.P.N.

Mater Boni Consilii

S. Willibrord.

Die hl. Rosa von Viterbo, Jungfrau.

1. **Emotionally Disturbed** • St. Dymphna 2. **Enlightenment** • Our Lady of Good Counsel
3. **Epilepsy and Nervous Disorders** • St. Willibrord 4. **Exiles** • St. Rose of Viterbo

S.ta BARBARA

S.te Lucie V. M.

S.ta MARIA EGYPTIANA.

Édition de la CHOCOLATERIE D'AIGUEBELLE (Drôme)

S.te BLANDINE ÉPARGNÉE PAR LES LIONS

1. Explosives • St. Barbara 2. Eye Ailments • St. Lucy
3. Fallen Women • St. Mary of Egypt 4. Falsely Accused • St. Blandina

164

ST. ROSE OF VITERBO

1235–1252 • FEAST DAY: SEPTEMBER 4

The stories of the saints are full of legends of precocious sanctity, but St. Rose of Viterbo was the real thing. Rose was only twelve years old when the Blessed Virgin appeared to her, instructing her to go into the streets of Viterbo and urge her neighbors to defend the pope. The Holy Roman Emperor Frederick II was trying to become the dominant power in Europe, at the expense of the papacy. Although Viterbo was an Italian town and only 150 miles north of Rome, it aligned itself with the emperor—that is, until Rose started collecting crowds in piazzas and on street corners.

Since the emperor had begun vying for supreme power, Rose argued, Italy and all nations under his control had been plagued by civil strife, political upheaval, and heresy. God rules above all, she said. Therefore, the pope, who acts as God's representative on earth, stands as the ultimate authority in Christendom. Rose stuck to her argument for three years, making such headway that the prefect, the emperor's man in Viterbo, banished her and her parents. Rose was fifteen years old.

The exiled family found refuge in papal territory. Less than one year later, on December 5, 1250, Rose prophesied that Frederick II was about to die. On December 13 the emperor did just that, and the people of Viterbo needed no further proof of Rose's sanctity. They invited her and her parents to return home.

Despite being famous and respected, Rose and her family remained poor. When Rose tried to enter a convent, the mother superior turned her away because Rose had no dowry, the traditional gift a family offered when their daughter became a novice. Rose went home and tried to live like a nun in her parents' house until she died there at the age of seventeen.

See holy card, page 163

ST. BARBARA

DIED ABOUT 235 • FEAST DAY: DECEMBER 4

A fairy-tale quality characterizes the legend of St. Barbara. According to the story, her father locked her up in a tower with only one window, hoping to keep her away from unsuitable men. One day, as she sat at her window, a man passed by singing a song she'd never heard. The strange music was a Christian hymn, and the man was a priest. The young woman in the tower and the man in the road started talking, and by the time they finished Barbara had converted to Christianity.

Not long afterward, Barbara's father sent architects to his daughter's tower to install a second window. Barbara instructed them to install three, in honor of the Holy Trinity. When the workers reported what Barbara said, her father flew into a rage. He hurried to the tower, dragged Barbara out by her hair, and denounced his own child to the local magistrate. (That was during one of the periods of anti-Christian persecution raging throughout the the Roman Empire.)

The magistrate condemned Barbara to death, and her father carried out the sentence himself. But an instant after he had lopped off his daughter's head, fire from heaven consumed him.

St. Barbara is an early example of patron saints keeping up with the times. Although her popularity in the Christian world was centuries old, the widespread use of gunpowder across Europe in the fifteenth century brought her a new level of fame. The new art of artillery warfare reminded soldiers of the fire from heaven that struck down St. Barbara's impious father, so they made her the patron saint of artillery soldiers. By extension she became the patron of bomb makers and munitions workers as well as fireworks and explosives of all kinds.

See holy card, page 164

ST. LUCY

DIED ABOUT 304 • FEAST DAY: DECEMBER 13

How St. Lucy came to be the patron of eye ailments depends on which story you prefer. One version says that the executioner tore out Lucy's eyes during her martyrdom. Another tradition tells of a pagan suitor who complimented Lucy on the beauty of her eyes, so she plucked them out and handed them to him. A less grisly rationale is the name Lucy itself, which comes from the Latin word *lux*, meaning "light."

St. Lucy ranks with Saints Agnes, Agatha, and Cecilia as one of the early Church's four great virgin martyrs. Devotion to her has remained strong for more than seventeen hundred years, not only in her native Sicily but throughout the Christian world. Even the overwhelmingly Protestant countries of Scandinavia celebrate the feast day of Santa Lucia. Nonetheless, as is true of many ancient martyrs, few facts about St. Lucy's life are known. All that's certain is that her martyrdom occurred during the persecution of Christians by the Roman emperor Diocletian; she probably died in Syracuse, the city that has always been the center of devotion to her.

By the fifth century, an unknown author had recorded a legendary biography filling in the details. The story says that Lucy came from a Christian family and that, by the time she was about twenty years old, her father was dead and her mother, Eutychia, was dying from a chronic hemorrhage. In hope of a cure, mother and daughter traveled to Catania, to the tomb of St. Agatha. The women spent the night beside the martyr's tomb, and while they slept, St. Agatha appeared to Lucy in a dream. Calling Lucy "sister," St. Agatha assured her that her mother had been healed. Then the saint said that just as she was famous and revered in her native Catania, Lucy would be famous and revered in her home, Syracuse.

The next morning Eutychia was overjoyed to find that she was perfectly well. Lucy took this opportunity to ask her mother to let her break off her betrothal to a young pagan and consecrate her virginity to Christ. Eutychia agreed, and, upon returning to Syracuse, they distributed Lucy's dowry to the poor.

Angry at having been jilted, Lucy's fiancé denounced her as a Christian to the local magistrate. Operating on the principle of "let the punishment fit the crime," he sentenced the virginal Lucy to serve in a brothel. When guards tried to lead her away, Lucy did not move; she was supernaturally rooted to the spot. No amount of pulling or pushing—not even a team of oxen—could dislodge her. The magistrate commanded his servants to pile wood around Lucy and burn her where she stood, but the flames billowed away from her. Finally one of the judge's henchmen plunged a dagger into Lucy's throat, yet even then she lingered until a priest came to give her Holy Communion for the last time. Then she died.

See holy card, page 164

ST. MARY OF EGYPT

ABOUT 344–ABOUT 421 • FEAST DAY: APRIL 2

Mary began her sexual adventures when she was twelve years old. Some collections of saints' lives call her a prostitute, but, in a sixth-century text supposedly based on her own memoirs, Mary is quoted as saying she never asked her lovers for money but delighted in "doing free of charge what gave me pleasure." Her specialty was corrupting naïve young men. "There is no mentionable or unmentionable depravity," she said, "of which I was not their teacher."

After years of trolling for new sexual conquests on the streets of Alexandria, Egypt, Mary one day saw a group of men boarding a ship. A sailor told her they were pilgrims traveling to Jerusalem. Impulsively, Mary joined the party. By the time the ship arrived in the Holy Land, Mary had seduced every man on board.

She then decided to practice her special talents in Jerusalem. Led again by her whims, she joined the crowd heading for the Church of the Holy Sepulcher on the Feast of the Holy Cross. As she arrived at the door, an invisible force prevented her from entering the holy place. Time and again she tried to cross the threshold, but it was as if strong hands were holding her back. Then it struck her: Her lifetime of sinful living made her unworthy of getting any closer to Christ's tomb. Overcome with shame she began to weep, but through her tears she saw an image of the Virgin Mary. Calling on the Mother of God and promising to do penance for all her sins, Mary prayed, "Help me, for I have no other help!" At once the unseen power released her.

Mary fulfilled her promise. She confessed her sins and then traveled far into the desert, where she spent the rest of her life as a hermit dedicated to prayer and penance.

See holy card, page 164

ST. BLANDINA

DIED 177 • FEAST DAY: JUNE 2

mperor Marcus Aurelius's persecution of Christians began as a legal process, but in Lyon and Vienne, in Gaul (present-day France), it degenerated into mass hysteria. Howling pagan mobs rampaged through the cities, looting Christian houses and businesses and dragging Christians to the tribunal, where they accused them of cannibalism, incest, and other crimes so foul that an authentic document from the period describing the persecution refuses to name them.

No Christian was spared. A fifteen-year-old Christian boy named Ponticus was tortured to death in the Lyon amphitheater before a cheering crowd. Pothinus, Lyon's ninety-plus-year-old bishop, was attacked by spectators at his trial and beaten to death.

Blandina was a slave. In prison her torturers tried to get her to confess that Christians murdered children and ate their flesh, but all Blandina would say was, "I am a Christian, and nothing wicked happens among us." Because she refused to admit to the imagined crimes, Blandina was sentenced to a long death. On the first day she was tortured in the arena with whips and hot irons. On the second day she was suspended from a stake so lions could maul her. On the third day they brought her out again to watch the martyrdom of St. Ponticus. And on the fourth and final day she was wrapped in a net and exposed to a wild bull, which gored her and tossed her about the amphitheater. Seeing that she was still alive after all these ordeals, an executioner slit Blandina's throat.

Although St. Blandina was just one of many martyrs killed in Lyon, her courage and steadfast assertion that the charges made against Christians were entirely false captured the imagination of her fellow Christians. They venerated all the Lyon martyrs as saints, but devotion to St. Blandina remains especially strong to this day.

See holy card, page 164

ST. WALBURGA

ABOUT 710–779 • FEAST DAY: FEBRUARY 25

In the Middle Ages saints often had several feast days, the primary one being the day of the saint's death. Local churches also celebrated the day a saint's relics were translated, or moved, to a new shrine. On May 1, 780, St. Walburga's relics were moved from her convent at Heidenheim to the one at Eichstatt, both in present-day Germany, so that she would be buried with her brother St. Winnibald. Because May 1 is the beginning of the planting season, German peasants prayed to St. Walburga on that day to give them a good harvest and save them from famine.

Walburga was an English nun, the niece of St. Boniface, the great missionary to the pagan tribes of Germany. He had taken with him Walburga's two brothers, Saints Winnibald and Willibald. The three English monks converted so many people that they wrote to the convents of England for nuns who could help by instructing women and children especially. Hence, St. Walburga became one of the first missionary nuns in Germany. She settled at a convent on the Tauber River, south of Wurzburg, where she taught the faith and opened a clinic. Through her teaching and medical skills, she brought even more converts into the Church.

At Heidenheim, Walburga became abbess of a convent of English and German nuns, while her brother Winnibald was abbot of the monks nearby. When Winnibald became too ill to govern, Walburga became the superior of both the convent and the monastery—an unusual situation but a tribute to her wisdom and holiness.

Since her death St. Walburga's sanctity has been confirmed by a remarkable oil that trickles from her tomb. The oil still flows and is said to work miraculous cures. Although she is invoked against famine, Walburga is famous for the holy oil. In art she is almost always shown carrying a little bottle of it.

See holy card, page 181

ST. ISIDORE THE FARMER

ABOUT 1080–1130 • FEAST DAY: MAY 15

Isidore and his wife, Maria de la Cabeza (also a saint), never owned any land but worked as tenant farmers on an estate outside Madrid. The couple was devout, and Isidore carried his religious devotion into his work. He left the house early every morning to attend Mass before arriving at the fields. As he plowed or harvested grain, he prayed. His neighbors said they saw angels guiding his plow, which explained why Isidore did three times as much work as any other tenant farmer.

After Isidore's death, his neighbors began to invoke him as they would any other saint. Forty years later, as part of an informal investigation of Isidore's life, local church authorities opened his grave: His body was incorrupt, a marvel that everyone took as proof that Isidore was truly a saint.

But it took five hundred years for the church to make his sainthood official. For centuries in Spain everyone from the king down to the poorest tenant farmer regarded Isidore as a saint (such informal canonizations by popular acclaim were common in the Middle Ages). Then, in 1615, Philip III recovered from a fatal illness through Isidore's intercession. In gratitude the king petitioned the pope to formally canonize Isidore. The pope acquiesced, and Isidore was officially declared a saint.

Devotion to St. Isidore and St. Maria spread to the Americas. In the United States, the National Catholic Rural Life Conference encourages farmers to pray to St. Isidore and his wife, St. Maria. Every year the conference presents the Isidore and Maria Award to a husband and wife who demonstrate integrity, religious faith, and good stewardship of the land.

See holy card, page 181

ST. JULIANA OF CORNILLON

1192–1258 • FEAST DAY: APRIL 6

One of the essentials of the Catholic faith is the belief that at Mass—when the priest recites, "This is my body. . . . This is my blood"—the bread and wine truly become the body and blood of Jesus Christ, thus making the Lord physically present in the church. Catholic devotion to this miracle, popularly known as the Blessed Sacrament, has always been strong.

Early in the thirteenth century, in the Augustinian convent of Mont Cornillion in present-day Belgium, there lived a young nun named Juliana. She was especially devoted to the Blessed Sacrament, and, while praying in front of the tabernacle (the receptacle where the consecrated bread is kept), she had a vision. In it, Christ pointed out to Juliana that, in the Church's calendar, there was no feast day dedicated to the Blessed Sacrament, and he wanted her to have one established.

It was an intimidating request, yet Juliana went about it in a systematic way, first consulting a wise priest for his opinion, then asking him to lay the idea before some local theologians. With their support, Juliana appealed to the local bishop, who also approved. In 1246 the Feast of Corpus Christi (Latin for "the Body of Christ") was celebrated for the first time in Liège, Belgium, complete with a solemn Mass and an elaborate procession. It might have remained a local holy day except for one unexpected accident of fate. In 1261 James Panteleon, one of the theologians Juliana had consulted, was elected pope. As Urban IV, he directed the Catholic world to celebrate the Feast of Corpus Christi on the first Thursday after Trinity Sunday. The feast has been an important religious celebration ever since.

See holy card, page 181

Fever

ST. DOMITIAN OF HUY

DIED 560 • FEAST DAY: MAY 7

St. Domitian is one of those tireless missionary bishops of the sixth and seventh centuries who brought countless new converts into the Church and were models of charity. At this time in the Church's history bishops acted more as missionaries than administrators. They had no other option, really—they had no cathedral, no diocesan bureaucracy, and often not even a congregation. Bishops like St. Domitian took the Christian faith, as well as Roman civilization, into lands where both were virtually unknown.

Domitian traveled throughout the Meuse Valley in south-central Belgium, baptizing pagans, building churches, and urging new Christians to be generous to the poor, the sick, and the helpless. He set the example by building hospitals and giving away all his money. Once, when he noticed that charitable giving had declined, he prophesied a record harvest. Reassured by their bishop, the congregation gave generously again.

In art St. Domitian is sometimes pictured with a dragon, a reference to a legend that he killed a dragon that had poisoned the drinking water. Once the monster was dead, Domitian's prayers purified the water supply.

After St. Domitian's death, the pilgrims who flocked to his tomb noticed that although many of their ailments were cured during the visit, the prayers of those sick with fever were always answered. Therefore, Domitian became the patron saint invoked against fevers. The Belgian towns of Huy (where he is buried), Liege, and Tongres all venerate St. Domitian, as does Maastricht, in the Netherlands.

See holy card, page 181

ST. NOTBURGA

ABOUT 1265–1313 • FEAST DAY: SEPTEMBER 14

The daughter of peasants, Notburga was born in the village of Rattenberg, in the Tyrol region of Austria. At age eighteen she hired herself out as a servant in the household of Count Henry of Rattenberg; the countess, Ottilia, assigned Notburga to the kitchen.

As in every great house at the time, much of the food prepared went to waste. Notburga took it upon herself to distribute the leftovers to the poor. The family knew about her acts of charity—the crowds of hungry folk waiting for Notburga outside the castle's kitchen door were a dead giveaway. Countess Ottilia chafed but kept silent because her husband's mother regarded Notburga's work as saintly. But, after the elderly countess died and Ottilia took over management of the castle, one of her first commands was that Notburga feed the leftovers to the pigs.

Notburga tried to compromise by feeding table scraps to the swine and sharing her own rations with the poor. As a kitchen maid she just didn't get enough food, so she resumed her distribution of the leftovers as surreptitiously as she could. Ottilia found out soon enough and fired her.

Notburga then found work as a field hand for a farmer in the nearby village of Eben. Her employer agreed to allow her to leave work early on Saturdays and the evenings before holy days to attend the evening prayers known as vespers. One Saturday during harvest, Notburga heard the vespers bell, stopped working, and headed for church. Her employer told her to get back to work because he wanted the harvest in before the weather turned bad. Notburga reminded the farmer of their arrangement, but he wouldn't back down. Neither would Notburga. She suggested they let God decide, and she flung her sickle into the air. As it hung suspended in midair, Notburga continued on her way to church.

See holy card, page 182

ST. FLORIAN

DIED 304 • FEAST DAY: MAY 4

Courage is the firefighters' hallmark, so it makes sense that they have as their patron saint a man who was both a soldier and a martyr. Florian was a high-ranking Roman officer during the emperor Diocletian's persecution of the Church. He was stationed near modern-day Lorch, Austria, where Aquilinus, the local magistrate, was especially scrupulous about finding Christians to persecute. One day while crossing a bridge over the Emms River, Florian ran into a band of soldiers setting out to round up Christians. Some of the legionnaires were old comrades, so Florian stopped to greet them.

"Where are you going, friends?" he asked.

"We're hunting for Christians," one of the soldiers replied.

"Brothers," Florian said, "I am a Christian."

The legionnaires did not like arresting one of their own, but they were obliged by oath to execute the emperor's edicts. They bound Florian and led him to the tribunal. Aquilinus offered to spare Florian's life if he sacrificed to the Roman gods, but Florian refused and Aquilinus threatened to burn him alive. "I will rise to heaven in a burst of flames," Florian replied.

Instead, Aquilinus sentenced Florian to be flogged, then drowned. The executioners beat him until he could barely walk, and then they dragged him to the bridge over the Emms, tied a millstone to his neck, and pushed him into the water.

As a saint who was threatened with fire but whose life was finally extinguished by water, Florian is the natural patron of firefighters. In the Middle Ages, another legend sprang up that affirms his position even further; that story tells how Florian rescued an entire town from destruction by putting out a raging fire with a single bucket of water.

See holy card, page 182

ST. TARSICIUS & BLESSED IMELDA LAMBERTINI

THIRD CENTURY • FEAST DAY: AUGUST 26
1322–1333 • FEAST DAY: MAY 13

St. Tarsicius was a Roman acolyte, or altar boy, during the age of persecution.

Our primary source about his life comes from Pope Damasus I (reigned 366–384), who told his story in the inscription for the boy-martyr's tomb. After Mass had been said in one of the catacombs outside Rome, the priests gave the consecrated Host to Tarsicius to deliver to imprisoned Christians awaiting martyrdom. They assumed the guards would be less suspicious of a boy than a man visiting the prisoners.

On the Appian Way, Tarsicius encountered a group of pagan boys and men. From the way Tarsicius kept his hands under his clothes, they could tell he was hiding something. They asked to see what he was guarding so carefully, but the boy said no, or, as St. Damasus put it, he refused to "surrender the Sacred Body [of Christ] to rabid dogs."

The first blow may have been playful, a way to persuade Tarsicius to show them what he had. But when the boy continued to refuse, the little mob got angry. They beat him with clubs and pounded him with stones. When Tarsicius collapsed, he fell facedown to protect the Blessed Sacrament, and even then the mob kept beating him. Within a few minutes, Tarsicius was dead.

The men surged forward to see what Tarsicius wanted to keep from them. They rolled his body over and searched his hands and clothes, but they found nothing. The Host that Tarsicius had given his life to protect had vanished.

The Christians of Rome retrieved the martyr's body and buried it in the catacomb of St. Callixtus on the Appian Way, not far from the place where he had been killed. Today the relics of St. Tarsicius, the martyr of the Blessed Sacrament, are enshrined in Rome's Church of San Silvestro in Capite.

The second saint who is the patron of First Communicants is Blessed Imelda Lambertini. Until 1910 Catholic children made their First Communion when they were about fourteen years old. For Blessed Imelda Lambertini, a little girl with an intense love for the Blessed Sacrament, that was too long a wait.

Imelda was the daughter of the Count and Countess Lambertini, whose estates lay in the region around Bologna, Italy. When Imelda was nine years old, her parents sent her to the town's convent school, which was run by the Dominican nuns. Seeing the older girls make their First Communion filled Imelda with a kind of holy envy. It wasn't the fancy dress or the party or the gifts that always attend such an event; Imelda yearned for the supernatural communion with Christ that comes when one receives the Host. She tried to persuade the convent's chaplain to let her make her Communion early, but the priest stuck to the rules—Imelda would have to wait until age fourteen.

Disappointment only intensified Imelda's devotion to the Eucharist. On the Feast of Christ's Ascension into heaven, after Mass had been said in the convent chapel, Imelda went up to the altar rail to pray before the tabernacle while the nuns remained in their places making their thanksgiving. Suddenly, all the nuns saw a radiant Host appear above Imelda. Hearing the commotion in the chapel, the priest came out of the sacristy; he saw the Host, too. Immediately he went to the tabernacle, removed the sacred vessel that holds the consecrated Hosts, and gave Imelda her First Communion.

Filled with inexpressible joy, eleven-year-old Imelda died that same day.

See holy cards, page 182

ST. ANDREW

FIRST CENTURY • FEAST DAY: NOVEMBER 30

Andrew and his brother Peter were sitting in their fishing boat on the Sea of Galilee, repairing their nets, when Christ called to them, saying, "Come follow me, and I will make you fishers of men." Although the brothers did leave their boat to follow the Lord, they never stopped catching fish—it was how they supported themselves and their families.

Time and again the gospels take us back to the Sea of Galilee: On one occasion, Jesus climbed into Peter and Andrew's boat to preach to a crowd on the shore; on another, while the brothers and some of the other disciples were out fishing, they saw Christ advancing toward them, walking on the water. After a long night of fishing and catching nothing, Christ urged the brothers to go out to the deepest part of the sea and lower their nets one more time. This time the catch was so great that the fishing nets broke and Peter and Andrew had to signal to their fellow apostles and business partners, James and John, to come help them haul in the fish. And, when there was nothing for the crowd of five thousand to eat, it was Andrew who brought forward a boy who had five barley loaves and two fish, which Christ multiplied to feed the multitude.

Tradition says that St. Andrew carried the gospel to Greece. At the town of Patras he was arrested and tied to an X-shaped cross. The legend claims it took him three days to die, and the entire time he hung on the cross St. Andrew preached to all who passed by.

See holy card, page 183

ST. GREGORY THAUMATURGUS

ABOUT 213–ABOUT 270 • FEAST DAY: NOVEMBER 17

Thaumaturgus is Greek for "wonder-worker," and, true to his name, St. Gregory is said to have performed many miracles in his day. The Lycus River, which flowed through his diocese in what is now Turkey, often flooded the region, ruining crops and sweeping away entire villages. Gregory walked to the banks of the river, drove his staff into the ground, and asked God never to let the river rise beyond that point. The legend goes on to say that Gregory's staff took root and grew into a massive tree, an impressive sign of his favor with God. Ever since, St. Gregory has been invoked against floods.

Gregory was the son of a wealthy pagan family in Asia Minor. As a teenager he decided to study law, but on his way to the university he met the Christian theologian Origen. A few conversations with Origen were all it took for Gregory to abandon his plans of becoming a lawyer. He converted to Christianity and spent the next seven years studying philosophy and theology under Origen.

Gregory's learning impressed the bishops and clergy of Asia Minor, and though he was still a young man, they named him bishop of Caesarea. It's said that when Gregory arrived in his diocese there were only seventeen Christians, and that when he died, there were only seventeen pagans left. He was a tireless and innovative bishop. One of his favorite methods of getting pagans interested in Christianity was to include secular music, dancing, and public banquets in the celebration of the feast days of the martyrs. Many pagans who came initially for the entertainment stayed to learn more about the faith.

See holy card, page 183

S. Walburga

Saint Isidore

B^{ta} Juliana Cornelionensis.

Sanctvs : Domitianvs.

Verlag von Rudolf Vaeth in Aachen.

1. Famine • St. Walburga 2. Farmers and Their Crops • St. Isidore the Farmer
3. Feast of Corpus Christi • St. Juliana of Cornillon 4. Fever • St. Domitian of Huy

S. Nothburga

St. Florian

Les Saints Modèles de l'Enfance

St. Tarsicius.

B. IMELDA LAMBERTINI
DOMENICANA

1. Field Hands • St. Nothburga 2. Firefighters • St. Florian
3. First Communicants • St. Tarsicius 4. First Communicants • Blessed Imelda Lambertini

S. Andrea. – S. Andrés.

Sanctus Andreas, Apostolus

S. Andrew. – H. Andreas.

Święta
Teresa od Dzieciątka Jezus

"Ufność w Bogu tak dobrym,
potężnym i miłosiernym nie
jest nigdy zbyt wielką".

Fait en France

1. Fishermen • St. Andrew 2. Floods • St. Gregory Thaumaturgus
3. Florists • St. Therese the Little Flower

S. Ægidius.

Serie VIII.   B. Kühlen, M.Gladbach.

Grablegung Christi.

Verlag von G.J.Manz in Regensburg

Ste. Rose de Lima.

1. Forests • St. Giles 2. Funeral Directors • St. Joseph of Arimathea
3. Gamblers • St. Cajetan 4. Gardeners • St. Rose of Lima

Florists

ST. THÉRÈSE
THE LITTLE FLOWER

1873–1897 • FEAST DAY: OCTOBER 1

*I*t's only natural that a saint who bears the affectionate pet name "the Little Flower" would be the patron of florists. It's a nickname St. Thérèse adopted for herself, in keeping with her modesty and humility as well as her belief that even the smallest task, when performed for love of God, has merit.

In her autobiography, *Story of a Soul,* she wrote, "The splendor of the rose and the whiteness of the lily do not rob the little violet of its scent nor the daisy of its simple charm. . . . It is just the same in the world of souls. . . . He has created the great saints who are like the lilies and the roses, but he has also created much lesser saints, and they must be content to be the daisies or the violets that rejoice his eyes whenever he glances down."

Thérèse lived a quiet obscure life, first among her tightly knit family in Lisieux, France, and then in her hometown's Carmelite cloister. During her brief life—she died of tuberculosis at age twenty-four—no one outside her community had heard of her. Her autobiography, published after her death, first won her attention.

And then came the miracles. On her deathbed Thérèse had promised, "I will spend my heaven doing good on earth" and that the prayers she answered would fall "like a shower of roses." So many miracles were attributed to Thérèse's intercession that in 1914 the Vatican waived the usual fifty-year waiting period and began investigating her life and virtues. Eleven years later she was declared a saint.

One final floral aspect marks the devotion to St. Thérèse: It is said you can always tell if St. Thérèse has heard your prayer, because out of the blue someone will present you with a rose.

See holy card, page 183

ST. GILES

ABOUT 650–ABOUT 710 • FEAST DAY: SEPTEMBER 1

Like St. Roch and his dog and St. Christopher with the Christ Child on his shoulder, St. Giles is almost always shown with a deer. The deer, along with St. Giles's association with forests, originates with a medieval legend.

According to the story, Giles was born to a wealthy, noble family in Athens. In his homeland, he became so admired for his piety that he was eagerly sought out by disciples in need of a teacher. But Giles longed for peace and a life of isolation. He traveled to southern France and began living as a hermit in a forest outside Nîmes. He made his home in a cave whose entrance was camouflaged by a large briar bush. He spent several years in peaceful meditation and conversation with God. Because there was not enough to eat in this forest, every day God sent a hind, or female deer, to the cave so that Giles could milk her.

One day the local king, Wamba, led a hunting party into Giles's woods.

They saw the hermit's deer and took off in pursuit. The frightened animal ran straight for Giles's cave, leapt over the briar bush, and took refuge in the hermit's arms. A moment later the hunters crashed into the clearing, and one of them shot an arrow into the bush to kill the deer hiding there. When Wamba pulled back the briar, he saw the hind in Giles's arms and the hunter's arrow lodged in Giles's leg.

Mortified at having wounded a man of God, Wamba offered to call for physicians, but Giles refused, saying he did not want his solitude disturbed. Nonetheless, Wamba came back often to visit Giles. Together they planned to build a monastery, and Giles agreed to serve as the first abbot. The monastery was built near Arles, and after St. Giles's death his tomb became a destination for pilgrims from all over Europe.

Christians during the Middle Ages loved the story of Giles and the hind. In the British Isles, no fewer than 162 parishes were dedicated to him, and in German-speaking lands St. Giles was listed among the Fourteen Holy Helpers, the saints believed to be especially prompt in answering prayers. Perhaps that explains why St. Giles is called upon for so many things: In addition to acting as the patron of forests, for his love of his home in the woods, he is also the patron of nursing mothers (because he was fed by a hind's milk), the patron of anyone who has trouble walking (because of his wounded leg), a patron of beggars (because he was poor), and a patron of cancer patients (again, because of his wounded leg).

See holy card, page 184

Funeral Directors

ST. JOSEPH OF ARIMATHEA

FIRST CENTURY • FEAST DAY: MARCH 17

St. Patrick has a lock on March 17. Who could compete with all the parades, music, and corned beef and cabbage? Alas, certainly not the dozen or so other saints who share Patrick's feast day. But that's a shame because one saint who has gotten lost in the March 17 hoopla is St. Joseph of Arimathea.

All four gospels mention Joseph as a wealthy man and a secret disciple of Christ. That first dreadful Good Friday when the apostles were hiding and scattered, Joseph found the courage to go to Pontius Pilate and request Jesus's body. Along with Nicodemus, another clandestine disciple, Joseph took Christ's body from the cross, wrapped it in linen, and carried it to a cave tomb he'd prepared for his own use. That act of kindness has made him remembered and honored throughout the Christian world, and it is the reason funeral directors regard St. Joseph of Arimathea as their patron saint.

The gospels mention no more about Joseph, so the rest of his story is legend. Eventually Joseph became linked with the Holy Grail. In this legend Joseph was the uncle of the Blessed Virgin Mary, and a merchant whose business interests took him far from the Holy Land to the island of Britain. Once, when Jesus was a boy, Joseph took him along on a voyage to England. The eighteenth-century poet William Blake immortalized this tale is his poem "Jerusalem":

And did those feet in ancient time
Walk on England's mountains
green?
And was the holy Lamb of God
On England's pleasant pastures
seen?

Fast-forward to the crucifixion, where the legend places Joseph at the foot of the cross. As Christ's blood dripped from his wounds, Joseph caught it in the cup Christ had used at the Last Supper. Later he transferred the blood to two cruets.

After Christ's ascension into heaven, Joseph gathered the cruets and the cup, known as the Holy Grail and, accompanied by twelve priests, took the gospel to England.

The missionaries are said to have settled at Glastonbury, where they built a chapel dedicated to the Blessed Virgin. A persistent tradition in England claims that Joseph's chapel, known as "the Old Church," survived at Glastonbury until 1184, when it was destroyed by a great fire. In 1186 the current Lady Chapel was consecrated on the site of Joseph's church.

In 1965, amid the ruins of the Glastonbury Abbey, Queen Elizabeth II erected a large wooden cross with an inscription that alludes to the legend of St. Joseph of Arimathea. It reads: "The cross. The symbol of our faith. The gift of Queen Elizabeth II marks a Christian sanctuary so ancient that only legend can record its origin."

See holy card, page 184

ST. CAJETAN

1480–1547 • FEAST DAY: AUGUST 7

St. Cajetan (also known as Gaetano) and his parishioners liked to play a little game. If he found out that one of them was having difficulty, he would bet the person he could solve the problem. If he fulfilled his side of the bargain, the parishioner would have to "pay up" by attending Mass, saying rosaries, or lighting holy candles. If he failed, Cajetan would have to take care of the Masses, rosaries, or candles himself. The scam was an innocent one since everybody knew Cajetan was sure to fix whatever needed fixing, but the losers never seemed to mind. And it did establish St. Cajetan as the patron of gamblers, both the compulsive sort who want to quit and the occasional but unlucky kind who could use a winning streak.

Cajetan's life spanned the period when the dissolute, corrupt lives of too many priests, bishops, and even popes finally led to the revolt known as the Reformation. In an effort to correct the flagrant abuses around him, Cajetan started a new order of priests with an ambitious set of goals—to teach sound doctrine to the laity and bring the clergy back to a holy way of life, including improved preaching, renewed dedication to their parishioners, and true reverence when saying Mass.

As if all that weren't enough, Cajetan was devoted to caring for the sick as well. One of his earliest supporters was Giovanni Caraffa, the bishop of Theate who gave Cajetan's priests their name, the Theatines. The Theatines set the example of what Catholic clergy ought to be, and in the Counter-Reformation, when the Church set out to reform itself and bring Protestants back to the faith, they were among the new orders at the forefront of the work.

Sadly, the Theatines died out by the beginning of the twentieth century, but the memory of their founder, St. Cajetan, endures.

See holy card, page 184

ST. ROSE OF LIMA

1586–1617 • FEAST DAY: AUGUST 23

Her parents named her Isabel, but the family's Incan housemaid said the baby girl was lovely "as a rose," and that was the name that stuck, the one under which Rose of Lima was canonized.

Rose grew up in a fine villa in Lima, Peru. Behind the house was a spacious garden that she especially loved. Given Rose's wealth, rank, and beauty, her parents expected her to make a brilliant marriage. Rose, however, wanted to be a nun. After a period of bickering they reached a compromise: Rose did not have to marry, but she could not enter a convent. She could, however, join the Dominican Third Order, which permitted her to take religious vows and wear a nun's habit while still living at home.

Aided by one of her brothers, Rose built a small cottage for herself in the family garden. She had not been living in her "hermitage" very long when her family's fortunes collapsed. To help, Rose took on lace-making and embroidery work and became a professional gardener, selling her flowers in the market of Lima.

Her family's distress made Rose more sensitive to the misfortunes of others. With her parents' permission, she turned one room of their house into an informal clinic, where she tended sick children and elderly people. Soon the townspeople were telling one another stories of the miracles wrought by Rose—her prayers saved Lima from an attack by pirates; her touch healed the sick in her hospital.

Upon being canonized by Pope Clement X in 1671, Rose of Lima became the first saint of the New World. Because of Rose's love for her garden and her work growing flowers to help her family, gardeners revere her as their patron, the saint who helps them produce glorious blooms and keep insects at bay.

See holy card, page 184

ST. AGNES

DIED ABOUT 305 • FEAST DAY: JANUARY 21

These days, invoking God when reciting the "Girl Scout Promise" is optional. Nonetheless, for Catholics and perhaps members of other Christian churches, St. Agnes is still on the books as the Girl Scouts' patron saint. St. Agnes was chosen because not only was she martyred when she was barely in her teens, she also possessed many of the qualities Girl Scouts try to cultivate in themselves: courage, honesty, respect for self and for others, and service to God and neighbor.

Agnes came from a Christian family in Rome. She was about thirteen years old when she was arrested and hauled before a judge for the crime of professing Christianity. He threatened to burn her alive, but Agnes would not deny her faith. Next he tried to force her to join the virgins who served the goddess Vesta, but Agnes refused to perform any function in a pagan temple. Finally the judge had the poor girl exposed naked in a brothel and then beheaded.

Although Agnes was just one among the tens of thousands of Christians martyred during the emperor Diocletian's persecution of the Church, devotion to her began almost instantly after her death. By 350 Constantia, the sister of Constantine, the first Christian emperor, had built a basilica over St. Agnes's grave as well as a mausoleum for herself so that she would lie near her favorite saint. From Rome, devotion to St. Agnes spread throughout the world.

In art Agnes is always portrayed with a lamb. It is a symbol of her innocence and purity as well as a pun on her name—in Latin, the word for "lamb" is *agnus*.

See holy card, page 201

ST. JOHN THE EVANGELIST

DIED ABOUT 100 • FEAST DAY: DECEMBER 27

Among the twelve apostles, Christ's three closest friends were St. Peter, St. James the Greater, and St. John. Within this inner circle, John was the Lord's favorite, the one referred to as "the beloved disciple" in St. John's gospel. By tradition John is also believed to have been the youngest of the apostles, perhaps barely out of his teens when he followed Christ. To emphasize his youth, artists tend to depict St. John as beardless, with long hair and fresh, boyish good looks.

After Jesus was arrested, St. John was the only one of the apostles who remained with him. He witnessed Christ's trial before Pontius Pilate, followed him as he carried the cross through the streets of Jerusalem, stood at the foot of the cross with the Blessed Virgin Mary, and helped take Christ's body off the cross and lay it in the tomb. Before Christ died, he rewarded his most loyal friend by placing Mary in John's care. "Woman," Christ said to his mother, "behold your son." Then addressing John he said, "Son, behold your mother."

Initially John preached in Jerusalem but then moved to Ephesus, the greatest city in the Eastern Roman Empire. A tradition that dates to at least the second century says that John took Mary with him. Amid the ruins of Ephesus stands a little stone house believed to have been Mary's home.

St. John died peacefully at age ninety-four, the only one of the apostles who was not martyred. Sparing him a violent death may have been Christ's last gift to his best friend.

See holy card, page 201

Grandparents

SS. ANNE & JOACHIM

FIRST CENTURY • FEAST DAY: JULY 26

The New Testament never mentions the parents of the Blessed Virgin Mary. She obviously had a mother and a father, but the only source for their names and their story is a book known as the *Protoevangelium of James*, an apocryphal work written about AD 150. This "gospel" tells us that Mary's parents were named Anne and Joachim, that they lived in Jerusalem, and that after many years of being childless they each received a visit from an angel announcing they would have a daughter who would be "spoken of in all the world."

It's possible that the first Christians in Judea passed down the names of Mary's parents, who, of course, were Christ's grandparents. More certain is a desire among early Christians to know more about the family of Jesus and Mary. By 550, devotion to St. Anne was so well established that the emperor Justinian built a church in her honor in Constantinople. Devotion to St. Joachim developed more slowly, but by the eighth century he was venerated in both the East and the West. As Jesus's grandparents, their popularity was assured.

During the late Middle Ages, more legends sprang up in German-speaking lands, giving Mary a large extended family of aunts, uncles, and cousins collectively known as the "Holy Kindred." During the Counter-Reformation the Church suppressed this devotion as too much of a good thing.

Today in Jerusalem the Church of St. Anne stands near St. Stephen's Gate. Archaeologists have excavated beneath the medieval church and found the remains of what appears to be a house. Whether it was the home of St. Anne, St. Joachim, and their holy child Mary, we'll never know.

See holy cards, page 201

ST. BARNABAS

FIRST CENTURY • FEAST DAY: JUNE 11

In the New Testament, the Acts of the Apostles tells how St. Paul and St. Barnabas were the first Christians to preach in the city of Lystra, in what is now Turkey. Paul healed a lame man, and the pagans took the miracle as a sign that Paul and Barnabas were the gods Mercury and Jupiter. Although they insisted they were only men, pagan priests brought out a bull to sacrifice to them. The two disciples kept protesting until finally the people of Lystra understood. The crowd's euphoria turned quickly into rage, and they stoned Paul and Barnabas out of the city.

In art, St. Barnabas is often depicted with a pile of small stones at his feet. Take that iconographic detail and combine it with the saint's feast day, June 11, the beginning of the growing season in most of Europe. Farmers shaky on the details of the story assumed that the stones were hail and invoked St. Barnabas to protect their young crops from being battered into the ground by hailstorms.

Barnabas was born into a Jewish family on the island of Cyprus. He was a Levite, a hereditary class responsible for serving in the Temple in Jerusalem. In fact, he was living in Jerusalem at the same time Christ was preaching in Galilee and Judea. After the initial Pentecost, Barnabas was among the first Jews to convert to Christianity.

Barnabas had a gift for oratory, so the apostles sent him to preach in Antioch, where he enjoyed tremendous success in bringing new converts into the fledgling Church. The Church in Jerusalem came to regard him as one of their greatest assets, and Barnabas took advantage of his standing when he acted as sponsor for the newly converted Saul, now known as St. Paul, introducing him personally to the apostles.

Paul and Barnabas became close friends and collaborators on missionary journeys throughout Asia Minor. To assist them, Barnabas invited along his young cousin John

Mark. They baptized thousands and shared many adventures together, but John Mark put a strain on the friendship when Paul came to the conclusion that the boy was unreliable and inconstant. When the two friends began planning a second missionary venture in Asia Minor, Barnabas again suggested they bring John Mark with them, but Paul was adamant—he would not travel with the kid. Barnabas was offended, Paul was exasperated, and they agreed to split up. Paul and another disciple, St. Silas, traveled to Asia Minor; Barnabas and John Mark went to Cyprus.

No one knows what happened to St. Barnabas after his break with St. Paul. Tradition says that he was martyred on Cyprus. The story is impossible to verify; nonetheless, Cyprus regards Barnabas as its first bishop and patron saint.

See holy card, page 202

ST. MARY MAGDALENE

FIRST CENTURY • FEAST DAY: JULY 22

In his gospel, St. Luke tells how one day a woman who was a notorious sinner entered a house where Jesus was dining with friends, and, to everyone's astonishment, knelt, bathed his feet with her tears, and then dried them with her hair. Luke does not give the penitent's name, but a tradition that dates back as least as far as Pope St. Gregory the Great (reigned 590–604) asserts that she is Mary Magdalene. Ever since, artists have shown St. Mary with a luxurious head of hair, usually red or auburn. That is why hairstylists have taken Mary Magdalene as their patron.

Mary Magdalene was not a prostitute. According to the gospels, although Christ drove seven demons out of her, it doesn't follow that she was promiscuous. Christ drove demons out of men, too, yet no tradition says that they were lechers. It was St. Gregory who tried to simplify things by conflating into a single character Mary the sister of Martha and Lazarus; Mary Magdalene; and St. Luke's anonymous sinner. Instead of clarifying the situation, Pope Gregory only made things worse—thanks to him, for the next fifteen hundred years Christians held a distorted idea about the character of three distinct women mentioned in the gospels.

A medieval legend claims that after Christ ascended into heaven, Mary Magdalene, her sister Martha, and her brother Lazarus sailed to southern France to preach. Mary then retired to a cave east of Marseille, where she lived as a hermit. In time, her clothes became rags that fell off her body, but by a miracle her hair grew so thick and so long that it covered her completely, preserving her modesty and reinforcing her patronage of hairstylists.

See holy card, page 202

ST. BIBIANA

DIED ABOUT 361 • FEAST DAY: DECEMBER 2

In 313 the emperor Constantine issued an edict that put an end to almost three hundred years of anti-Christian persecution in the Roman Empire. He proved to be generous as well as tolerant in the years that followed: He showered gifts of land and money on the pope and the bishops, and he built several Christian basilicas, including Old St. Peter's in Rome (the predecessor of the current church).

Constantine was succeeded by his nephew Julian. Although he had been raised a Christian, Julian wanted to turn back the clock. He outlawed Christianity again, restored the worship of the pagan gods, and arrested and executed any Christian who opposed him. For all these reasons, he is known as Julian the Apostate. Among Julian's victims was an entire family of Roman Christians, Flavian and Dafrosa and their two daughters, Bibiana and Demetria.

St. Bibiana's name appears in the medieval text known as the *Liber Pontificalis* (Book of the Popes), which states that the fifth-century pope Simplicius "consecrated a basilica of the holy martyr Bibiana, which contained her body, near the 'palatium Licinianum.'" Aside from this brief mention and a few dubious later legends, few additional facts are known about her life.

It took time for Bibiana to be honored as the patron saint of hangovers. Displayed in the church built over her tomb was an ancient Roman column—tradition says that Bibiana had been bound to this pillar and scourged to death. During the Middle Ages, visitors to the church believed that a little dust scraped off St. Bibiana's column could cure headaches when mixed with mint growing in the church's garden. It's also possible that a pun on St. Bibiana's name led her to being associated with hangovers—in Latin, the word *bibulus* means "to be fond of drinking."

See holy card, page 202

ST. JOSEPH

FIRST CENTURY • FEAST DAY: MARCH 19

St. Joseph as the patron of a happy death comes from a fifth-century apocryphal work called *The History of Joseph the Carpenter*. The most dramatic (and lengthy) part of the narrative is St. Joseph's deathbed scene. In this version, Joseph is terrified of dying, despite his stature as a holy man chosen by God to guard the Blessed Virgin Mary and act as a father to Jesus Christ. Jesus and Mary try to comfort him, but poor Joseph is convinced that he has led a sinful life.

As his final moments draw near, Joseph can no longer speak. During the good old man's final hours, Jesus, who is eighteen years old in this story, sits at his bedside holding Joseph's hands while Mary sits on the other side, weeping. As the frightful figure of Death personified comes to claim St. Joseph, Jesus calls the archangels St. Michael and St. Gabriel down from heaven to escort Joseph's soul into God's presence. Joseph dies peacefully in Christ's arms, with Mary at his side and with the two greatest angels waiting to receive his soul.

The details of the story are undoubtedly pure fiction, but that St. Joseph died in the presence of Jesus and Mary is entirely plausible. The last time we hear of Joseph in the New Testament is in St. Luke's account of twelve-year-old Jesus wandering off to spend three days debating with the priests and wise men in the Temple of Jerusalem. Both scholarship and tradition agree that if Joseph were still alive at the time of Christ's crucifixion, he would have been standing at the foot of the cross with Mary.

The point of devotion to St. Joseph as the patron of a happy death is the hope among the devout that at the moment of death, St. Joseph will bring Jesus and Mary to console us and lead us to heaven.

See holy card, page 203

ST. JAMES THE LESS

DIED 61 • FEAST DAY: MAY 3

Two apostles were named James. The James whose brother was St. John the Evangelist and part of the inner circle of Peter, James, and John is known as St. James the Greater. The James whom the gospels describe as the son of Alphaeus and brother of St. Jude Thaddeus is the saint under discussion here—St. James the Less.

This St. James is probably the author of the New Testament Epistle of James, the document that, among other things, asserts the essential role of good works in reaching salvation. "Faith without works," writes James, "is dead."

St. Paul knew James very well; he was the first bishop of Jerusalem, the champion of the idea that Jewish converts to Christianity ought to still keep the Law of Moses regarding circumcision and eating only kosher food. St. Paul tells us that St. James was one of the few apostles to whom Christ appeared privately after his resurrection.

The first-century Jewish historian Josephus tells us that James was arrested, tried before the Sanhedrin, and sentenced to death by stoning. A later tradition says that James was first thrown off the pinnacle of the temple, then stoned, and finally finished off by a blow to the head with a fuller's club.

A fuller uses a wooden club to beat layers of cloth together to make a thicker fabric, such as felt, either for clothes or more often for hats. That is why hatmakers, who beat cloth into felt, have chosen St. James the Less as their patron.

See holy card, page 203

3-203. PRINTED IN ITALY 1b

Si quelqu'un mange ce pain, il vivra éternellement. (S. Jean VI.)

Wie mijn vleesch eet, Zal eeuwig leven.

(S.t Jan. VI.)

O Bonne Sainte Anne, de Beaupré P.P.N.

Laat ons Joachim loven, roemrijk in zijn nageslacht.

1. Girl Scouts • St. Agnes 2. Good Friendships • St. John the Evangelist
3. Grandparents • St. Anne 4. Grandparents • St. Joachim

1.

Les Grands Martyrs : St BARNABÉ

Edité par la CHOCOLATERIE D'AIGUEBELLE Monastère de la Trappe (Drôme)

2.

S.te Marie Madeleine

S. BIBIANA
VERGINE E MARTIRE

Scultura in marmo di G.L. Bernini,
venerata nella Chiesa di S. Bibiana
Via G. Giolitti, 154 - 00185 ROMA

1. Hailstorms • St. Barnabas 2. Hairstylists • St. Mary Magdalene
3. Hangover • St. Bibiana

Wer den Herrn fürchtet, wird
gesegnet am Tage seines Hin-
scheidens. (Sir. 1, 13.)
Verl.-Anst. Benziger & Co. A. G. Dep. 3726 Einsiedeln.

Sanctus Jacobus min.

Mühlbauer & Behrle, Chicago.

S. ACACIO MARTIRE
CROCIFISSO SUL MONTE ARARAT CON ALTRI 10000 CRISTIANI

Waakt,   gedraagt
staat   u
in   manhaftig,
het   en wordt
geloof,   versterkt!
Cor. XVI. 13.

St. Cornelius.

1. Happy Death • St. Joseph   2. Hatmakers • St. James the Less
3. Headaches • St. Acacius   4. Hearing Ailments • St. Cornelius

1. Hermits • St. Paul the Hermit 2. Highway Construction Workers • St. John the Baptist
3. Homeless • St. Benedict Joseph Labre 4. Horseback Riders • St. Martin of Tours

ST. ACACIUS

DIED 303 • FEAST DAY: MAY 8

The Roman emperor Diocletian commanded all members of the Roman legions to prove their loyalty to the state by sacrificing to the Roman gods. Acacius, a centurion and a Christian, refused. The local magistrate where Acacius was stationed, in what is now northern Turkey, ordered him arrested and handed over to torturers. Among the agonies inflicted on Acacius, the torturers took thorn branches and twisted them tightly around his head. Then Acacius was taken to the town of Byzantium, known today as Istanbul, where, after a public scourging, he was beheaded.

Devotion to St. Acacius began in the East. In the sixth century, the emperor Justinian built a church over his grave. In the church's courtyard stood an old walnut tree, and believers said St. Acasius had been whipped as he hung from one of the tree's branches.

But because of the thorn branches the executioners had twisted around the martyr's head, western European Christians venerated St. Acacius as the patron of headaches. During the Middle Ages, he was listed among the Fourteen Holy Helpers, a group of saints who were patrons of common troubles and ailments. The Holy Helpers were especially popular in German-speaking lands, and even today it's not unusual to see in old Catholic churches a shrine with images of all fourteen saints. St. Acacius's statue is easy to recognize because he's always either bearing or wearing a crown of thorns.

See holy card, page 203

ST. CORNELIUS

DIED 253 • FEAST DAY: SEPTEMBER 16

Cornelius is an example of a saint whose patronage is based on his name, combined with some confused iconography. The name Cornelius comes from the Latin word for "horn," such as a bull or ram's horn. In art, St. Cornelius is usually shown holding a horn, although more often than not it's a curved brass horn, the type used in the Middle Ages to rally troops in battle. As it happens, these war horns look almost exactly like the ear trumpets or ear horns that hard-of-hearing people once used to amplify sounds. And so St. Cornelius has become the patron of those with hearing trouble.

Cornelius belonged to one of the most distinguished patrician families in Rome. In 251, when he was elected pope, the Church in Rome was in disarray. Christians had just endured an especially violent period of persecution under the late emperor Decius. Across the realm were Christians who had abandoned their faith and sacrificed to the pagan gods, because of either torture or fear of a terrible death. A faction within the Church insisted the lapsed Christians should never be permitted to return, but Pope Cornelius took a more lenient view. Arguing that for sincere penitents God's forgiveness had no limit, Cornelius declared that those who wished to return to the faith would be welcomed back after performing a proper penance.

Cornelius's pontificate was short. In 252 a plague broke out in Rome, and the pagans blamed the Christians. Cornelius was seized and exiled to Civitavecchia, where he was so badly mistreated that he died in 253. Although his death was not violent, the Roman Christians venerated him as a martyr because of the sufferings he'd endured in exile. St. Cornelius's original tombstone can still be found in the catacomb of San Callisto, outside Rome. It reads simply, "Cornelius, Martyr."

See holy card, page 203

ST. PAUL THE HERMIT

ABOUT 230–342 • FEAST DAY: JANUARY 15

St. Paul was the first Christian hermit, choosing to renounce family, society, riches, and all comforts for a solitary life of prayer and penance in the desert.

Paul came from a well-to-do Christian family who lived near Thebes, in Egypt. His parents died the year he turned fifteen; four years later Emperor Decius began his ferocious persecution of Christians. Paul hid in the home of a friend and then fled into the desert. In a year or two Decius was dead and the persecution faded, but Paul had grown to love the seclusion and silence of wilderness life. He found a cave, lived on water and wild fruit, and wove for himself a loincloth of palm leaves. Tradition says that every day God sent a raven to bring Paul a loaf of bread.

After ninety years of solitude, Paul had a visitor. St. Anthony of the Desert thought he was the first Christian hermit and took some pride in it until he had a dream in which a voice told him another man had been living alone much longer, a man holier than Anthony. So Anthony set out to find this saintly hermit. Legend says that he got lost, but a centaur gave him directions to Paul's cave.

Upon meeting, the two hermits became instant friends. At dinner, since Paul had a guest, the raven brought twice as much bread. Anthony set out for home the next morning. He had not traveled far when he saw angels bearing Paul's soul to heaven. Hurrying back to the cave, Anthony found Paul dead, with two lions digging a grave for him with their paws. When the lions had finished the job, Anthony buried the saint's body and then took Paul's only possession—a mantle of woven palm leaves—as a remembrance. Ever after, St. Anthony wore St. Paul's mantle at Mass on the most solemn holy days.

See holy card, page 204

207

ST. JOHN THE BAPTIST

FIRST CENTURY • FEAST DAYS: JUNE 24 AND AUGUST 29

The prophet Isaiah foretold that before the Messiah manifested himself, his precursor, or herald, would appear in the wilderness crying, "Prepare the way of the Lord! Make straight in the desert a highway for our God." That precursor was St. John the Baptist, and the reference to making straight roads through wild places has led highway construction workers to invoke him as their patron.

St. John was related to Christ—their mothers, Elizabeth and Mary, were cousins. Before Christ began his public ministry, John went out to the Jordan River and announced to all who would listen that the Messiah was coming and they must prepare by repenting their sins. John baptized those who repented, using the river as the baptismal font.

But John got himself into trouble when he publicly denounced Judea's king, Herod Antipas, one of the most brazen sinners in the land. Herod had violated Jewish law by marrying Herodias, his own niece and the ex-wife of his half brother. John challenged Herod to rid himself of Herodias and do penance for his sin, an appeal that filled Herod with superstitious dread and enraged Herodias. She badgered the king until he threw John into prison, and then she waited for an opportunity to have the holy man killed.

On Herod's birthday Herodias had her daughter Salome dance for the king and all his guests. Full of wine and lascivious thoughts, Herod swore to Salome she could have anything she wanted. She demanded the head of John the Baptist on a platter. Herod was distraught by the girl's request but too ashamed to back down. He gave the order, and a few minutes later the executioner presented the grisly prize to Salome, who passed it along to her mother.

See holy card, page 204

ST. BENEDICT JOSEPH LABRE

1748–1783 • FEAST DAY: APRIL 16

Christ once said of himself, "Foxes have holes, and birds of the air have nests, but the Son of man has nowhere to lay his head." Those words struck Benedict Joseph Labre with such force that he decided to imitate Christ by becoming a permanent pilgrim, wandering from one holy place to the next, with no belongings but the clothes he wore and no food except what he could beg from strangers.

Initially he traveled all over Europe, from the shrine of St. James at Compostela in Spain to the tombs of Saints Francis and Clare in Assisi. In 1774 he decided to settle in Rome, where he camped out amid the ruins of the Colosseum, went to Mass every morning at the church of Santa Maria dei Monti, and then spent the rest of the day visiting other Roman churches.

He was dirty. He smelled bad. Because he never washed his clothes, they became infested with lice. It was not unusual for a parish sexton to drive Benedict Joseph out of the church after one look (or one whiff).

About the year 1782 Benedict Joseph moved into a homeless shelter. His health had been ruined from years of subsisting on a meager diet and sleeping outdoors in all weather. He was at Mass in Santa Maria dei Monti on Wednesday of Holy Week in 1783 when he collapsed. A few hours later he died.

Immediately, Romans who had regarded Benedict Joseph as an eccentric (if not a pest) when he was alive began hailing him as a saint in death. The priests at Santa Maria had a death mask made and preserved Benedict Joseph's filthy clothes as relics. In 1883, after an especially rigorous investigation, Blessed Pope Pius IX concluded that Benedict Joseph Labre was neither mentally ill nor a pious fraud, and he canonized him as a true saint.

See holy card, page 204

ST. MARTIN OF TOURS

ABOUT 336–397 • FEAST DAY: NOVEMBER 11

St. Martin is the patron of equestrians because he is almost always pictured on horseback. His story is set in Amiens, in Gaul (present-day France), on a bitterly cold night in midwinter. Martin, an officer in the Roman army, was riding back to his quarters, looking quite dashing in a magnificent red wool cloak given to him by the men in his cohort. As he rode along, Martin saw a poor man dressed in rags, shivering violently and begging passersby to give him something warm to wear to protect him from the frigid weather. Everyone ignored the poor man—except Martin. He stopped his horse, drew his sword, cut his fine cloak in half, and gave it to the half-frozen beggar. Then he spurred his horse and continued on his way.

That night Martin awoke to find his room filled with dazzling light. Christ stood at the foot of the bed, surrounded by angels. The piece of cloak Martin had given the poor man was wrapped around the Lord's shoulders. "Look," Christ said to the angels. "Martin, who is not even baptized yet, has wrapped me in his own cloak." Then the vision vanished.

Martin, the son of a pagan family, had begun studying the Christian faith only when he was called up to serve in the army. No Christian chaplains traveled with the legions, so Martin's religious formation was put on hold. He had learned some Christian prayers, however, and understood the concept of good works. Even before he met the beggar he kept from his pay only what he and his servant needed, giving the rest to the poor. Once his term of military service was done, Martin traveled to Poitiers, where the famous bishop St. Hilary completed his religious instruction and baptized him at last.

See holy card, page 204

ST. MEINRAD

DIED 861 • FEAST DAY: JANUARY 21

St. Meinrad's hospitable instincts were ultimately his undoing. A Benedictine priest, he had been living for thirty years in his hermitage deep in the forest outside Zurich when two strangers knocked on his door. Meinrad invited them in, fed them, gave them a bed for the night, and treated them like old friends. But these were not travelers lost in the woods—they were robbers who had purposely sought out Meinrad's hut after hearing a rumor that he was a wealthy miser living in the forest to safeguard his gold. The two men demanded that Meinrad hand over his treasure. It took some time, but the holy man succeeded in convincing the robbers that he truly was a poor hermit, just as it appeared, and that he had no gold stashed away in a secret hiding place. Angry with themselves for having been duped by gossip, the robbers turned on Meinrad and beat him to death. Legend says that ravens attacked the killers as they left Meinrad's hut, pecking at their heads and driving them through the forest back to Zurich, where they confessed their crime and were executed.

After Meinrad's death the Benedictine monks built an abbey at the site of his hut. Called Einsiedeln (German for "hermitage"), it's still a great pilgrimage site, not only as the tomb of St. Meinrad but also as the shrine of Our Lady of Einsiedeln, a small wooden statue of the Virgin and Child that may have been Meinrad's one treasure.

See holy card, page 221

ST. JULIAN THE HOSPITALLER

FEAST DAY: FEBRUARY 12

A touch of Greek mythology enhances the story of St. Julian the Hospitaller, also known as St. Julian the Poor. Julian, a wealthy young nobleman, was hunting a splendid stag when the animal spoke to him. "Why are you trying to kill me," the animal asked, "when you will kill your own parents?" Horrified by the stag's prediction, Julian never returned home. Instead, he ran to a distant country, where he offered his services to the prince. Julian proved to be a valiant, heroic knight. In gratitude, the prince gave Julian a wealthy, widowed noblewoman as his wife.

While Julian was making a new life for himself, his distraught parents wandered across Europe looking for him. One day they arrived at Julian's castle. Julian was away, but his wife welcomed the strangers, and when she heard their story, she recognized it as Julian's own. Realizing that the travel-worn couple must be his parents, she was even more gracious to her guests, even insisting that they

sleep in the best bed in the house—the bed she shared with Julian.

Julian returned home very late that night, entered his bedroom, and found a man and woman asleep in his bed. Thinking his wife had taken a lover, he drew his sword and killed the sleepers, only to meet his wife as he rushed out of the room.

"Who are the man and woman in our bed?" he asked.

"They are your parents," his wife replied. "They have been searching for you everywhere, and now you are all reunited!"

Overcome with anguish, Julian cried, "I have killed them! I thought you had betrayed me. I thought they were you and a lover."

To atone for his terrible sin, Julian resolved to walk all the way to Rome to beg for absolution from the pope. His wife said she would go, too.

In Rome the pope heard Julian's confession and absolved him, but as penance he commanded Julian to find a way to help strangers and travelers such as his mother and father had been. Julian and his wife built a hospice beside a wide, raging river and acquired a boat that Julian used to carry travelers safely from one side to the other.

One bitter winter night a beggar, half frozen and very ill, came to the hospice door. Julian took the poor man in and seated him beside the fire. Still the beggar shivered, so Julian carried the stranger to his own room, placed him in his own bed, and covered him with the warmest blankets in the house. He had made the beggar as comfortable as he could when the poor man was transfigured into an angel. "Julian," the angel said, "Christ our Lord has sent me to tell you that he has accepted your penance and that a place is prepared for you and your wife in heaven." Then the angel vanished. Soon thereafter Julian and his wife died and went to claim their eternal reward.

See holy card, page 221

ST. ZITA

1212–1272 • FEAST DAY: APRIL 27

ousework ranks high on the list of tedious, time-consuming tasks. At first glance, washing and dusting don't seem like an opportunity to grow in holiness—yet the life of St. Zita shows that isn't always the case.

Zita was only twelve years old when she went to work as a servant for the Fatinellis, a family of well-to-do silk merchants in Lucca, Italy. Other servants worked in the house, of course, and within days of her arrival Zita knew that none of them liked her. They interpreted her piety as posturing, her submissiveness as stupidity, and her diligence as a mean-spirited way to make them look like slackers.

As the new girl, Zita was given all the dirtiest and most monotonous household tasks. She did them all well, but when she felt the drudgery getting to her she would say a very short prayer to remind herself that she was doing this unpleasant job for love of God rather than to win praise from her employers.

Prayer sustained Zita. She went to Mass daily, and if she had any spare time during her workday she would slip away to a corner of the attic to pray. Once Zita found she had some free time after putting bread in the oven, so she hurried to her "chapel" in the attic. Her prayers became so intense and the sweetness of being in conversation with God so delightful that Zita lost all track of time. When she came to her senses, she rushed back to the kitchen, certain that the loaves of bread must be burned. But instead of a kitchen filled with acrid smoke, she found beautiful, fragrant loaves laid out on the table. While Zita talked with God, angels had attended to her baking.

In time, the Fatinellis and Zita's fellow servants all came to realize that her faith and good works were genuine. After several years, the family made her mistress of the household and governess of the Fatinelli children.

In terms of charity, Zita was a

soft touch, and the beggars and the poor in and around Lucca knew it. She shared her own food with anyone who came to her door, and when she had given away her portion she dipped into the Fatinellis' pantry. During a famine, an endless procession of hungry people came to Zita for help and in response she gave away the Fatinellis' entire store of dried beans—the one thing the household was counting on to get them through the food shortage. It was too much for Signor Fatinelli—he dragged Zita into the storeroom to impress upon her what she had done. But when Zita and the elder Fatinelli arrived in the pantry, they found to their surprise (and Zita's relief) that the supply of dried beans was undiminished.

And so the years passed, with Zita exasperating Signor Fatinelli with her works of charity, only to be bailed out at the last moment by divine intervention. St. Zita died peacefully in the Fatinelli house on April 27, 1272. She was sixty years old and had served and edified the family for forty-eight years.

See holy card, page 221

ST. HUBERT

DIED 727 • FEAST DAY: NOVEMBER 3

Although born into a Christian family in what is now Belgium, Hubert had no love for God. He cared only about hunting, placing it above all other things.

In those days the Ardennes forest was filled with enough wild boar, deer, and wolves to keep happy even so ardent a hunter as Hubert. One Good Friday, while his family was in church, Hubert rode into the forest for yet another hunt. Suddenly he came upon a magnificent stag, the finest he had ever seen. Killing it would be the achievement of his lifetime. Hubert spurred his horse and gave chase as the stag bounded into the forest. It was a wild ride, and the animal led Hubert deeper into the Ardennes than he had ever been before. Then, in a large clearing, the stag came to halt and turned to face Hubert. To the huntsman's astonishment, he saw a crucifix between the stag's massive antlers. Then the stag spoke. "Hubert," he said, "unless you return to the Lord, you will fall into Hell."

Hubert dismounted and knelt on the ground. "What should I do, Lord?" he asked.

"Go find Lambert, the bishop of Maastricht," the stag replied. "He will guide you."

Hubert did go to Bishop Lambert. He gave up his frivolous life, became a priest and eventually a bishop, and spent the rest of his years pursuing souls for God rather than hunting wild animals. When he died in 727, he was buried in the Ardennes forest, where he had seen the vision that changed his life.

See holy card, page 221

ST. FRANCES XAVIER CABRINI

1850–1917 • FEAST DAY: NOVEMBER 13

As a child in Italy, Francesca Cabrini was enthralled by the Asian adventures of St. Francis Xavier, the sixteenth-century Jesuit missionary. When she made her vows as a nun, she took Xavier's name in the hopes of following in his footsteps as a missionary in China or Japan. She even told Pope Leo XIII of her desire, but he responded that her mission lay "not in the East, but to the West." He meant the United States, where millions of poor Italian immigrants were pouring into America's cities.

As often happens with immigrant groups, the Italians were simultaneously accepted and despised in the United States. They were welcome to the extent that America needed cheap, willing laborers—women and girls to toil in mills and factories, and men and boys to work on docks and construction sites. But they were rejected by polite society because, as foreigners, they spoke little or no English, and many were desperately poor. And there were so many of them—between 1899 and 1910, two million Italians disembarked in the United States.

Even the country's Catholic Church felt ambivalent about them. Most priests and bishops in America were Irish born or of Irish descent, unable to speak Italian and unsure of what to make of emotional Italian piety or the Italian custom of celebrating saints' days with exuberant street festivals. The American bishops deluged the Vatican with appeals for Italian priests, and the pope complied, sending Franciscans and Scalabrini Fathers to serve as missionaries.

In spring 1889 New York's archbishop Michael Corrigan was waiting for a new flock of priests from Italy when an Italian nun knocked on his door. She introduced herself as Mother Cabrini and said that she and six sisters had come to do what they could for the city's Italian immigrants. Archbishop Corrigan was not happy—he felt that slums were no place for nuns. He told Mother

Cabrini to take the next ship back to Italy. Mother Cabrini stood up—she was barely five feet tall—and said, "I have letters from the pope. I'm staying." And stay she did.

Archbishop Corrigan's apprehensions were not without merit. Mother Cabrini's first "convent" in America was a cockroach- and bedbug-infested apartment in a tenement in Little Italy. From the day they arrived the sisters were besieged by children who were orphaned or abandoned by their parents; women whose husbands had died or deserted them; sick folk who couldn't afford a doctor; and unemployed people who couldn't buy a meal. But the Sisters of Charity and the Bon Secours Sisters in New York City helped Mother Cabrini and her sisters establish themselves, and eventually Archbishop Corrigan, impressed by the determination of the Italian nuns, became their chief benefactor.

For twenty-nine years Mother Cabrini worked virtually nonstop in America to improve the life of all immigrants—Italian and non-Italian. She founded sixty-seven hospitals and named all of them for her favorite Italian hero, Christopher Columbus. In 1916, ill and exhausted, she retired to the convent attached to Columbus Hospital in Chicago. There, three days before Christmas 1917, she died quietly in her rocking chair. She was officially declared a saint in 1946, and her charitable work earned her formal recognition from Pope Pius XII as the patron of immigrants.

See holy card, page 222

ST. JUDE

FIRST CENTURY • FEAST DAY: OCTOBER 28

St. Jude's role as the patron saint of the impossible is an American phenomenon; European Catholics in desperate straits pray to St. Rita of Cascia to fix the unfixable. Although the story of how St. Jude came to be associated with impossible cases is itself impossible to pin down, we do know how devotion to St. Jude first began to spread in the United States.

In the 1920s the Claretian Fathers staffed Our Lady of Guadalupe parish on the South Side of Chicago, a neighborhood surrounded by steel mills where many of the parishioners worked. Business slowed toward the end of the decade, and the mills started laying off workers. Jobs became scarce and unemployment insurance did not exist yet. Sadly Father James Tort, the pastor of Our of Lady of Guadalupe, began to see many of his parishioners standing on breadlines.

Father Tort had a deep devotion to St. Jude, a saint who was not widely revered at the time. At first he prayed to his favorite saint in private, but as conditions for his unemployed parishioners worsened, Father Tort announced a public novena, nine days of solemn prayer to St. Jude to begin on February 17, 1929. So many parishioners attended that first novena that Father Tort repeated it again and again. Several months later, on October 28, the saint's feast day, the parish concluded a solemn novena to St. Jude that was so packed that loudspeakers were hauled in to broadcast the service to a crowd of a thousand who stood outside.

The next day the stock market crashed, a catastrophe that made the St. Jude novena a regular part of parish life at Our Lady of Guadalupe for years to come. As stories of answered prayers spread across Chicago and the nation, other parishes began novenas to St. Jude as well. Throughout the Great Depression and World War II, and every day since, the priests and people of Our Lady of Guadalupe have gathered to ask St. Jude to help them in every temporal and spiritual necessity. Today Our Lady of Guadalupe is recognized as the National Shrine of St. Jude, and every day the mail brings stories from grateful people who testify that St. Jude helped them at the moment when they had despaired of finding any help.

Who was St. Jude? St. Luke's gospel tells us that he was the brother of the apostle St. James the Less and that they were both related to Jesus. St. Jude is also credited as the author of one of the New Testament epistles. Tradition says that he and his fellow apostle St. Simon carried the gospel to Persia, where both were martyred. St. Simon was sawn in half; St. Jude was clubbed to death.

In art St. Jude is almost always shown wearing or holding a medal bearing the image of a man, which refers to the ancient legend of Abgar, king of Edessa. According to the story, Abgar sent a letter to Jesus asking to be healed of leprosy; Jesus wrote back that, although he couldn't come himself, he would send one of his apostles. To console the king over his absence, Jesus pressed a cloth to his face and left a perfect picture of himself on the fabric. St. Jude later took this portrait of Christ to Edessa and healed Abgar. Over time, the miraculous image of the Lord's face on cloth has evolved into the portrait medallion that appears in almost every picture and statue of St. Jude.

See holy card, page 222

S. MEINRADE, O. P. N.

S. JULIEN L'HOSPITALIER

© Ars sacra   9933   eccl. appr.

St. Zita

1. Hospitality • St. Meinrad 2. Hotelkeepers • St. Julian the Hospitaller
3. Housekeepers • St. Zita 4. Hunters • St. Hubert

NOVENA
SAINT FRANCES XAVIER CABRINI
HEAVENLY PATRON OF THE IMMIGRANTS

*May Saint Jude, the apostle of hopeless
cases, obtain for you the graces
which you desire.*

BOUASSE-JEUNE   1515 A.   MADE IN FRANCE

Sv. Anna.

DIE HEILIGE ELISABETH
in der Franziskushauskapelle in Altötting

1. **Immigrants** • St. Frances Xavier Cabrini 2. **Impossible Situations** • St. Jude
3. **Infertility** • St. Anne 4. **In-law Problems** • St. Elizabeth of Hungary

S. Pietro Martire.

QUEEN · AND · PEACE · MAKER
ST · ELIZABETH · OF · PORTUGAL
PRAY FOR US

Sanctus Eligius.

1. Inquisitors • St. Peter of Verona 2. Internet • St. Isidore of Seville
3. Jealousy • St. Elizabeth of Portugal 4. Jewelers • St. Eligius

1. **Juvenile Delinquents** • St. Dominic Savio 2. **Kings** • St. Henry
3. **Lace Makers** • St. John Francis Regis 4. **Lapsed Catholics** • St. Monica

ST. ANNE

FIRST CENTURY • FEAST DAY: JULY 26

According to a second-century apocryphal work called *The Protoevangelium of James*, Anne lived with her husband, Joachim, for many years without bearing a child. But, as with Hannah, the mother of the Old Testament prophet Samuel, and Elizabeth and Zachary, the parents of St. John the Baptist, at long last God sent an angel to announce to Anne that she would become pregnant and give birth to a daughter. As if that good news weren't enough, the angel also promised Anne that her child would be spoken of around the world. "Now I know the Lord God has blessed me exceedingly," Anne said to Joachim. "I, the childless, shall conceive." Anne and Joachim's daughter was, of course, the Blessed Virgin Mary.

Though Anne's primary feast day is July 26, she is associated with a whole string of church holidays: The day Anne conceived Mary is celebrated on December 8 as the Immaculate Conception; the day Anne gave birth to her daughter is honored on September 8 as the Nativity of Mary; and even the day Anne named her daughter is commemorated on September 11, the feast of the Holy Name of Mary.

Since St. Anne is the mother of Mary and the grandmother of Jesus, Christians have always believed that her prayers must have great influence in heaven. Housekeepers, lace makers, seamstresses, broom makers, and even second-hand clothes dealers have taken her as their patron. But, because of her special situation, devotion to St. Anne is especially strong among women who long for children but have a hard time becoming pregnant.

See holy card, page 222

ST. ELIZABETH OF HUNGARY

1207–1231 • FEAST DAY: NOVEMBER 17

The hypercritical mother-in-law and boorish brother-in-law are stock characters in television sitcoms, but there was nothing comical about the trouble St. Elizabeth of Hungary experienced at the hands of her in-laws. As the daughter of Hungary's king and queen, four-year-old Elizabeth was offered as a symbol of political alliance when she was betrothed to the eleven-year-old German prince Ludwig of Thuringia. They married ten years later.

Elizabeth's in-laws took an immediate dislike to her. First, she was Hungarian, a fact that could not be overlooked by her brother-in-law, Henry, who was the leader of an anti-Hungarian faction within the Thuringian court. Her sister-in-law Agnes was put off by Elizabeth's humble demeanor, which Agnes found entirely unbecoming in a princess. And finally, Elizabeth was not circumspect in her acts of piety or charity, which aroused the ire of many at court. Once, when Elizabeth prostrated herself be-fore a large crucifix, her mother-in-law commanded, "Get up! Bent over like that you look like a tired old mule."

But cutting remarks were nothing compared to Elizabeth's trials under her brother-in-law Henry. Tragically, Ludwig died just as Elizabeth was in labor with their third child. Moving quickly, her brother-in-law Henry and his anti-Hungarian faction declared Elizabeth's five-year-old son Hermann the heir to the throne and appointed Henry regent until his nephew came of age. Then he banished Elizabeth and her two daughters, three-year-old Sophia and the hours-old Gertrude.

Elizabeth and her little family of exiles were taken in by her aunt, the abbess of the Kitzingen convent. Eventually, Elizabeth settled in Marburg, Germany, where she opened a hospital and worked in the wards for the last four years of her life, free from criticism of her piety or her humility.

See holy card, page 222

ST. PETER OF VERONA

1205–1253 • FEAST DAY: APRIL 6 OR APRIL 29

In the twelfth century, merchants from Eastern Europe introduced the Cathar heresy to southern France and northern Italy. The Cathars (also known as Albigensians) rejected all the sacraments and the authority of the Church, believed in reincarnation, and taught that the Christian God was in fact Satan. To orthodox Christians this last teaching was blasphemy.

St. Peter of Verona's mother and father were Cathars, and they raised their son as one. As he grew up, however, Peter felt drawn to the Catholic faith, and he converted to Catholicism after hearing St. Dominic preach. He joined the Dominican order, was ordained a priest, and almost immediately began preaching to Cathar congregations in northern Italy. Given his Cathar upbringing, Peter's preaching was especially effective, and soon the pope named him inquisitor for northern Italy, giving him the authority to reform and correct Catholic clergy in addition to converting Cathars.

Peter preached all over Italy, defending and explaining Catholic doctrine, calling on Catholic laymen and laywomen to repent their sins, and insisting that priests and monks live holy lives. He almost single-handedly revived religious life throughout the country, converting so many Cathars that some came to see him as a threat.

On April 6, 1253, Peter was ambushed by a band of Cathars who split his skull and drove a knife through his heart. Catholics recovered his body and buried it in a church in Milan. So many miracles were reported at his tomb that, just one year later, the pope declared Peter a saint.

After his death Peter the inquisitor made one last convert: Carino, one of his murderers, repented his role in the crime and joined the Dominican order. In the region around Forli, the penitent saint killer is still venerated as Blessed Carino.

See holy card, page 223

ST. ISIDORE OF SEVILLE

560–636 • FEAST DAY: APRIL 4

Back in 1999, some Catholics in the emerging dot-com industry petitioned Pope John Paul II for their own patron saint. They had someone in mind: the learned Spanish bishop St. Isidore of Seville.

Why choose an obscure Spanish bishop as patron of the most exciting advance in information technology since the printing press? St. Isidore died in 636, so obviously he never surfed the Web. But, in his time, he did something that can be regarded as just as amazing—he compiled a twenty-volume encyclopedia of all existing knowledge. This encyclopedia, the dot-com Catholics said, could be regarded as the world's first database.

Such a compendium was the labor of a lifetime, and Bishop Isidore felt it was worth the effort. More than a century before his birth, Rome had fallen to the barbarians. One by one the Roman legions withdrew from the empire's provinces; as they retreated the barbarian tribes advanced, burning libraries, smashing artworks, damaging aqueducts and public baths beyond repair, and leaving cities and towns depopulated and in ruins. For men such as Isidore, the destruction of Roman civilization was unspeakably painful. And so, like monks and bishops in other corners of the old Roman world, he decided to act before the glories and accomplishments of Rome were forgotten forever.

In his encyclopedia, Isidore recorded the essentials of Roman law, government, medicine, architecture, and agriculture; he even noted how to build roads and make furniture. It was a breathtaking achievement, a tribute not only to his own wide-ranging intellect but also to his hopes for the future. The Web is about collecting, preserving, and disseminating information—precisely what Isidore accomplished in his life. So until a webmaster or blogger is cannonized, St. Isidore of Seville seems to be the right patron for the Internet.

See holy card, page 223

ST. ELIZABETH OF PORTUGAL

1271–1336 • FEAST DAY: JULY 4

Like her great-aunt St. Elizabeth of Hungary, Elizabeth of Portugal married at a young age. At twelve she became the bride of Portugal's twenty-year-old king, Dinis. Of course, Dinis had little interest in his child bride, and probably several years passed before the marriage was consummated. (Elizabeth was nineteen when she gave birth to her first child.) In the meantime, Dinis was hardly lonely. He had a string of mistresses by whom he fathered at least seven, and perhaps as many as nine, children.

Dinis was very fond of his illegitimate children; he brought them all to live in the palace and insisted that Elizabeth raise them. This kind of heartless demand could easily wreck a marriage, yet whatever emotions Elizabeth may have felt, she kept them to herself and proved to be a loving foster mother.

As callous as Dinis was to his wife, he compounded the problem by favoring one of his illegitimate sons over his eldest son and heir, Alfonso.

Unlike his saintly mother, Prince Alfonso did not suppress his feelings of jealousy and resentment. Four times Alfonso schemed to overthrow his father and seize the crown; once he even contrived to murder his half-brother, the son Dinis loved best. Each time Elizabeth made peace in the family, although with each of Alfonso's plots the task became increasingly difficult. Once, when Alfonso's army was arrayed at one end of the battlefield and King Dinis's on the other, Elizabeth rode between them and refused to leave until father and son had reconciled.

We don't know if Dinis ever asked Elizabeth to forgive him for all the pain he had caused her. After the king died, his will named her as executor of all he possessed. Although Dinis couldn't respect Elizabeth during his life, at least he showed her a token of his esteem after his death.

See holy card, page 223

ST. ELIGIUS

588–660 • FEAST DAY: DECEMBER 1

As a boy, Eligius was apprenticed to a goldsmith who was also master of France's royal mint. The boy had a flair for designing and crafting splendid jewelry. Once his apprenticeship was complete, Eligius took advantage of his master's royal connections and traveled to Paris, where he offered his services to King Clotaire II. To see what the young genius could do, Clotaire gave Eligius a mass of gold and a bag of precious stones and ordered him to make a throne. Using these materials, the clever metalsmith fashioned two thrones. Impressed by the beauty of the workmanship, the honesty of the artist, and the unexpected pleasure of getting two thrones for the price of one, Clotaire made Eligius his court goldsmith.

Other important commissions soon followed. Eligius created reliquaries for the shrines of St. Martin in Tours, St. Denis and St. Genevieve in Paris, and Saints Crispin and Crispinian in Soissons. Between royal patronage and working for some of the wealthiest monasteries in France, Eligius became a very rich man. His clothes were made of silk, embellished with gold threads and studded with jewels. But if he was a flashy dresser, he was also a man with a soft heart. He gave alms so lavishly that he could hardly set foot outside his house without being besieged by needy people.

Even after becoming first a monk and then the bishop of Noyon, Eligius continued to make glorious gold and silver artworks for the Church. Tragically, most of his major works were destroyed during the French Revolution. The few that have survived reveal that St. Eligius was a man of deep faith and unparalleled skill.

See holy card, page 223

ST. DOMINIC SAVIO

1842–1857 • FEAST DAY: MARCH 9

In Turin, Italy, St. John Bosco operated a large complex that was part trade school, part seminary, part shelter for orphaned and abandoned street kids. Twelve-year-old Dominic Savio entered the school with the hope of someday becoming a priest. He was precociously and genuinely devout. After his entrance interview with the boy, Don Bosco recorded, "I marveled at the work of divine grace in one so young."

Dominic must have been aware that his religious life was much more intense than that of almost everyone else he knew. His reaction to this knowledge was to imagine he was cut out for some kind of heroic life of prolonged periods of prayer and harsh penances. Don Bosco refused to permit it. He knew that Dominic was emotionally and spiritually immature and that such a life would probably lead to Dominic keeping himself aloof from the other students—maybe even imagining himself to be some type of superior being. Don Bosco reminded Dominic that, in terms of penances, it would be enough if he patiently endured heat, cold, sickness, the drudgery of schoolwork, and "other people's tiresome ways." And, to keep him grounded, he channeled Dominic's energies into a religious volunteer organization whose members tried to befriend boys who had trouble fitting in at the school.

For Dominic, this assignment was tough. He felt awkward around the juvenile delinquents Don Bosco took in, and the rough boys dismissed Dominic as priggish. The barrier between them broke down a bit thanks to Dominic's sharp wit, which he couldn't resist using, even against the school's teachers. It got Dominic in trouble, to be sure, but also made him more "normal" in the eyes of the street kids. When he managed to defuse a playground quarrel that had turned ugly, with the two boys arming themselves with sharp rocks, Dominic's reputation in the school soared.

In winter 1857, just before Dominic turned fifteen, he suffered an inflammation of the lungs. Don Bosco sent him home to be with his parents. The local doctor came and prescribed bleeding, but then bled the boy too much. As Dominic's condition deteriorated, the family sent for the priest. The boy lived just long enough to receive the Last Rites; he died murmuring good-bye to his father.

Initially some Vatican bureaucrats rejected the possibility of canonizing a fourteen-year-old boy, but Pope Pius X considered Dominic Savio's youth and innocence as a plus and brushed aside all objections. In 1950 Pope Pius XII declared Dominic "Blessed" and, four years later, proclaimed him a saint.

See holy card, page 224

ST. HENRY

972–1024 • FEAST DAY: JULY 13

It's hard to be an absolute monarch and a saint. The demands of royal office, the easy access to every kind of vice, the plots, betrayals, and wars—all get in the way of cultivating a holy life. Yet St. Henry, together with his queen, St. Cunegundis, managed to sidestep the dangers and lead a virtuous life.

Henry always tried to strike a balance between what was expected of him as a king and what he was obliged to do as a Christian. When his brother led a revolt against him, Henry crushed the uprising that would have brought chaos and perhaps civil war to his people. But he also forgave his brother and reconciled with him. Henry secured his kingdom's borders, made peace with his neighbors, and developed a strong defense to protect his people against attacks from barbarian tribes. He also founded schools, made the city of Bamberg the launching point for missions to the pagan Slavic nations, actively supported reform in the Church, and gave generously to abbeys that set the example of what a monastery ought to be. In recognition of Henry's wisdom, strength, and goodness, in 1014 the pope crowned him Holy Roman Emperor.

Henry and Cunegundis had no children. Later, a legend sprang up that the royal couple were so holy that they lived as brother and sister. No evidence supports this story. It is true that, after Cunegundis died, Henry told a Benedictine abbot that he planned to abdicate and become a monk, but the abbot convinced him that his responsibilities lay outside the monastery, where he could do a great deal of good.

See holy card, page 224

ST. JOHN FRANCIS REGIS

1597–1640 • FEAST DAY: DECEMBER 31

St. John Francis Regis always said that there was never a shortage of priests to serve the rich, so instead he lived his life as a priest among peasants, laborers, and prostitutes. He preached straightforward sermons that uneducated people could understand; he ate simple food and wore plain clothes; and he was happiest saying Mass, hearing confessions, and teaching children the fundamentals of the faith.

Father Regis's temperament hid an aggressive side, too. He felt no qualms about instructing physicians that they must treat his sick parishioners free of charge, for they were too poor to pay doctors' fees. To keep funds streaming regularly to the neediest families and individuals, Father Regis founded Confraternities of the Blessed Sacrament. Membership was limited to well-to-do women, each of whom received a list of poor people who became her personal responsibility.

Father Regis's sanctity, simple life, and direct method of preaching proved to be especially effective with the French Protestants known as the Huguenots. Catholic bishops whose dioceses included large Huguenot populations were eager to have Father Regis participate in public debates or deliver sermons on Catholic doctrine. His gift for bringing Huguenots back to the Church made him a minor celebrity in France, but he never abandoned his dedication to the poor.

During Christmas 1640, Father Regis was visiting mountain villages when the weather turned ugly. Another man might have waited out the storm in a parish rectory, but as one priest who knew Father Regis recalled, "No cold, no snow-blocked path, no rain-swollen torrent could stop him." He was expected at a little town called La Louvesc; by the time he arrived he was stricken with pneumonia. He tried to keep to a schedule of preaching three times a day and hearing confessions between sermons, but he collapsed while sitting in the confessional. Men who had been waiting to confess carried Father Regis to the parish priest's house, where he died.

Father Regis is buried in La Louvesc, a fact that has made the remote village a goal for hordes of pilgrims. The idyllic rural region is a fitting final resting place since he'd always been wary of cities. In fact, to help poor country girls resist the allure of urban life, Father Regis had set up a lace-making and embroidery business so that the women could earn a living without leaving their families and friends. And that's how St. John Francis Regis became the patron of lace makers and embroiderers.

See holy card, page 224

ST. MONICA

331–387 • FEAST DAY: AUGUST 27

Lapsed Catholics are not a modern phenomenon—the life of St. Monica teaches us that. Her own son Augustine rejected the faith she had taught him and joined the peculiar Manichean sect.

Monica was born into a Christian family in the town of Thagaste, now Souk Ahras, in Algeria. Her husband, Patricius, appears to have been religiously indifferent, but he did not interfere with Monica's faith and permitted her to raise their children as Catholics.

When Augustine was born, Monica didn't have him baptized. During the first centuries of Christianity, many believers put off baptism until they were on their deathbed. Nonetheless, Monica did ask her priest to mark the infant Augustine with holy oil in the sign of the cross and sprinkle blessed salt, a sign of exorcism, on his tongue. This ceremony made him a catechumen, one who was taking instruction in the faith, and Monica was his teacher.

Monica and Patricius had great ambitions for their son. They wanted Augustine to receive a classical education so that he could enter one of the professions. Before Augustine went off to the university at Carthage—the "Harvard" of Roman North Africa—Monica pleaded with him to remain chaste. In his Confessions, Augustine admits he treated her "womanish advice" with contempt. He was, as he says, "in the mood to be seduced." In fact, soon after arriving in Carthage, he found a mistress and they moved in together. A year later, the woman (in none of his writings does Augustine ever mention her name) gave birth to a boy they named Adeodatus, meaning "gift from God."

That news was bad enough. But Augustine compounded it by abandoning the Catholic faith and joining the Manicheans, a sect that considered itself an intellectual and spiritual elite. Manicheans taught that there were two gods—one good, the other evil—who were in constant conflict for control of the universe. Throughout history many "Jesuses" had come to earth to struggle on the side of good, but none had ever triumphed over evil.

That her son joined such a sect broke Monica's heart. She sought out a bishop who had once been a Manichean and begged him to speak to Augustine. The bishop answered that, so early in his conversion, Augustine would be unwilling to listen to any arguments. But Monica refused to take no for an answer. She pleaded and wept and made such a nuisance of herself that the bishop lost his temper. "Go away from me!" he cried. Instantly regretting his bad manners, he added, "Do not worry. It is not possible that the son of so many tears should be lost forever."

Seventeen years passed before Augustine was ready to reevaluate his life. By then he was teaching philosophy in Milan. Monica had moved there, too; there she found an ally in the city's bishop, St. Ambrose, a man as learned and cultivated as Augustine. To please his mother, Augustine accompanied her to church to hear Bishop Ambrose preach. That was all it took. Augustine began attending any Mass where Ambrose was preaching; with Monica's prayers and Ambrose's eloquence, Augustine renounced the Manicheans and entered the Catholic Church. On the night of April 24/25, 387, at the Mass of the Easter Vigil, St. Ambrose baptized Augustine and Adeodatus. The prediction made so many years before by an irritable African bishop had at last been fulfilled, thanks to the tears and prayers of St. Monica.

See holy card, page 224

ST. NICHOLAS OF FLUE

1417–1487 • FEAST DAY: MARCH 21

In Switzerland both Catholics and Protestants revere St. Nicholas of Flue as a man of great holiness and personal integrity, one who had a genius for settling the most acrimonious disputes. He came by his piety honestly: His mother, Emma, was one of the Friends of God, a Catholic religious movement that encouraged members to draw close to God through concentrated prayer, meditation on the sufferings of Christ, self-denial, and service to neighbors. Emma taught this method to her children, but her son Nicholas especially responded to it. The Friends of God tended to be laypeople, so Nicholas felt no pressure to enter a religious order. He would have been rejected if he'd tried—Nicholas couldn't read or write.

Nicholas took up farming, and at age twenty-five he married a devout young woman named Dorothy Wissling. The marriage may have been arranged, but Nicholas and Dorothy were compatible and fell in love. They had ten children, five boys and five girls—which explains how St. Nicholas came to be the patron of large families. He must have been a man of great energy because he managed to run a prosperous farm, serve as a local magistrate, act as an arbitrator when local disputes turned nasty, and still find time to maintain his life of intense prayer.

After twenty-five years of marriage, Nicholas wanted to leave the farm and become a hermit, but he wouldn't go if his family objected. Dorothy gave her consent, and so did the children. He didn't travel far, just to a neighboring valley near the village of Sachseln, Dorothy's hometown. They all must have remained in contact because, as Nicholas lay dying, Dorothy, their children, and some of their grandchildren were at his bedside. After Nicholas's death, one of his grandsons took up the hermit life and moved into his grandfather's cabin.

See holy card, page 241

ST. STANISLAUS KOSTKA

1550–1568 • FEAST DAY: AUGUST 15

Today Poland is a Catholic monolith, but in the sixteenth century it was anything but religiously homogenous. About half the population belonged to the Greek, Russian, or Ukrainian Orthodox church. There was also a large Jewish community. The king was Catholic, but half the members of the country's parliament belonged to one or another of the Protestant denominations. And many members of the Polish nobility who still called themselves Catholic were careless in their practice of the faith.

Jan and Margaret Kostka's attitude toward their Catholicism was decidedly worldly, so they were perplexed about what to do as their son Stanislaus grew to be a seriously devout little boy. If Stanislaus's piety exasperated his parents, his parents' offhanded manner regarding religious matters wounded Stanislaus. After laughing at an irreverent joke, Jan Kostka warned the storyteller not to repeat it in front of Stanislaus.

"He'll faint," his father said.

When Stanislaus was fourteen years old, his parents sent him, along with his sixteen-year-old brother Paul and their private tutor, to the Jesuit college in Vienna. Initially the three lived in a college dormitory. Stanislaus felt at ease in the school's religious atmosphere, but Paul wanted more freedom. He convinced the tutor to let the boys rent rooms off-campus. The house Paul chose belonged to a zealous Lutheran. Stanislaus objected to giving up rooms at a Catholic school to pay rent to a heretic, but Paul bullied him into moving.

For the next two years, Stanislaus led a miserable life. His brother beat him up. His landlord and fellow Catholic students mocked his piety. And the poor boy's tutor did nothing to help. Finally the stress reached the breaking point, and Stanislaus suffered some type of breakdown, the physical symptoms of which felt so bad that he believed he was dying. He asked for a priest to administer the Last Rites, but his Lutheran land-lord refused to permit the Blessed Sacrament in his house. Sick and now close to despair, Stanislaus prayed to one of his favorite saints, St. Barbara. After recovering, he insisted that, at her intercession, an angel carrying the Host had appeared in his room to give him Holy Communion.

St. Stanislaus did not die on that occasion, but his mystical Holy Communion led to his being revered as the patron of all who ask for the Last Sacraments.

See holy card, page 241

1.

B. Nicolaus de Flue.

2.

S. STANISLAUS KOSTKA.

3.

SANCTUS YVO

4.

Sant' Ambrogio, Vescovo

1. Large Families • St. Nicholas of Flue   2. Last Rites • St. Stanislaus Kostka
3. Lawyers • St. Ivo   4. Learning • St. Ambrose

S. LAZARUS

Sᵗᵃ CATHARINA

Sᵗᵃ THOMAS AQUINAS

S. Marco Evangelista

1. Lepers • St. Lazarus   2. Libraries and Librarians • St. Catherine of Alexandria
3. Lightning • St. Thomas Aquinas   4. Lions • St. Mark the Evangelist

S.W. Piotr Apostoł.

S. FELICE MARTIRE
che si venera in Tavernola S. Felice

1. Locksmiths • St. Peter   2. Lost Animals • St. Felix of Nola
3. Lost Objects • St. Anthony of Padua   4. Lovers and Engaged Couples • St. Valentine

Saint Simon.

Sancte Simon Apostole, ora pro nobis.

S. BALTHASAR.

3.

S. GABRIELE DELL'ADDOLORATA, PASSIONISTA

Compatrono della Gioventù Cattolica Italiana

ST. IVO

1253–1303 • FEAST DAY: MAY 19

A Latin ditty popular in the Middle Ages goes, "St. Ivo was a Breton, a lawyer but not a thief, which people say is a wondrous thing."

Ivo trained at the universities in Paris and Orleans, becoming a master of both civil and canon law. He made a name for himself as a compassionate man who defended the poor free of charge, even supplying them with food and warm clothes while they sat in prison awaiting trial. He prosecuted noblemen who demanded excessive taxes from their tenants, and, to spare litigants the time and expense of a trial, he tried to settle cases out of court. Unlike many of his colleagues, St. Ivo refused all bribes.

After about twenty years practicing law, Ivo began studying for the priesthood. His bishop sent him to tend two parishes in Brittany, his home, where Ivo put his old courtroom skills to use settling local disputes. He lived as simply as the poorest members of his parishes,

eating brown bread, vegetables, and beans. As a lawyer, Ivo had never turned away a poor client; now as a priest he never refused help to the needy. On holy days he threw banquets for the poor. He welcomed travelers into the rectory as if they were wandering angels. And it was said that during a famine, when the whole countryside turned to Ivo for help, his own store of grain was miraculously replenished until the famine came to an end.

Ivo became gravely ill during Lent in 1303, lingering on through Easter. On the eve of the feast of the Ascension, he insisted on saying Mass one last time. Too weak to stand and supported by two men, Ivo finished Mass and then was carried back to his rectory, where he died.

See holy card, page 241

ST. AMBROSE

ABOUT 340–397 • FEAST DAY: DECEMBER 7

In St. Ambrose's day, all Roman boys studied the Latin classics. But Ambrose's mother found him a tutor who also taught him Greek so that he could read Plato, Aristotle, and other great authors of Greece's golden age. This mastery of both the Latin and Greek schools of philosophy gave Ambrose an intellectual edge over his contemporaries.

As bishop of Milan, he tailored his sermons to fit the audience. To worshippers at Sunday Mass, he spoke of the joys of living virtuously. But when addressing the emperor or Roman senators or some other highbrow audience, he drew upon his classical education to present sophisticated arguments that his cultured listeners would appreciate.

About 386, a woman named Monica arrived in Milan and began attending Mass at Ambrose's cathedral. The sorrow of Monica's life was that her brilliant son Augustine had rejected Christianity in favor of a pagan sect known as the Manicheans.

Upon hearing Ambrose preach, Monica knew she had found a man whose learning equaled, perhaps even surpassed, that of her son. Monica dragged Augustine to Ambrose's Masses, and her instincts proved to be correct. Augustine was impressed by this bishop, who was as familiar with Plato's philosophy as he was with the four gospels. After listening to a few sermons, he sought out Ambrose for private discussions about Christianity. Unfortunately, no scribe was present to record the conversations of these two great minds; whatever was said, Ambrose convinced Augustine of the truth of the Catholic faith. On the night of April 24/25, 387, at the Mass of the Easter Vigil, Ambrose baptized Augustine. It was a triumph for classical learning and for the faith.

See holy card, page 241

ST. LAZARUS

FIRST CENTURY? • FEAST DAY: JUNE 21

In St. Luke's gospel, Christ tells a parable about poor Lazarus, starving and covered with sores, who lay begging at the door of a nameless rich man. When Lazarus died, the angels carried his soul to heaven; but when the heartless rich man died, his soul was thrown into hell.

This is the only example from the Lord's parables of a fictional character being venerated as a saint. The tradition appears to have originated among Christians in the East, perhaps among the Ethiopians who list St. Lazarus on their calendar. Devotion to Lazarus spread to Europe during the Crusades after a band of knights organized themselves into the Order of St. Lazarus of Jerusalem, a military-and-nursing order dedicated to tending lepers.

Although the gospel does describe Lazarus as suffering from open wounds, it doesn't specifically state that his ailment was leprosy. But because the Knights of St. Lazarus nursed lepers, he became their patron. In Italian and Spanish, Lazarus's name was adapted to *lazaretto*, a synonym for "hospital," and *lazarone*, a term for a poor man who lives in the streets.

Devotion to St. Lazarus is especially strong among Spanish-speaking Catholics, who venerate him as the patron of the poor and the humble. In Hispanic devotional art, St. Lazarus is usually depicted as an old man, nearly naked, supported by a crutch and with dogs licking his sores.

See holy card, page 242

ST. CATHERINE OF ALEXANDRIA

ABOUT 305 • FEAST DAY: NOVEMBER 25

The story of St. Catherine of Alexandria is especially charming, and it made her one of the most popular saints during the Middle Ages. St. Joan of Arc said that St. Catherine's was one of the three heavenly voices that guided her.

The "life" of St. Catherine, as it has come down to us, is almost certainly a legend. But it's so beautiful, it's worth retelling. The daughter of a king who gave her an excellent education, Catherine spent almost all her time reading in the great library of Alexandria, Egypt; while still in her teens, she had mastered philosophy and all the sciences and was a skillful orator.

One day at the library, she fell asleep over her books and dreamed of a beautiful woman, dressed like a queen and holding on her lap the loveliest little boy. Indicating to Catherine, the woman asked the child, "Would you like to marry this young woman?" The little boy replied, "Absolutely not. She is so ugly."

Catherine awoke from her dream sobbing. As she tried to control herself, an elderly man approached to ask if he could help. At his urging, Catherine told him what she had seen.

"I can interpret your dream for you," he said. "The beautiful woman was the Virgin Mary. The little boy was her son, Jesus Christ. It was not your person he finds ugly, but your soul, because you are a pagan."

"How can I make myself beautiful for him?" Catherine asked.

"Baptism will make your soul pure and perfectly pleasing to Christ," the old man answered. Then he revealed that he was a Christian priest and would be willing to instruct her in the faith.

Catherine learned quickly, and in a short time she was ready to be baptized. After receiving the sacrament she fell asleep, and once again Mary and the Child Jesus appeared to her. Mary put the same question to her son, "Would you like to marry this young woman?" This time Christ replied, "Yes! Because now she is truly beautiful." Then the little boy gave Catherine a ring. When she awoke, she found the mystical band on her finger.

Catherine was only eighteen years old when Emperor Maximus began to persecute Christians in Egypt. At her court arraignment, she defended her new faith so well that Maximus assembled fifty of Alexandria's wisest pagan scholars to debate her. In spite of all their learning, the philosophers lost. Furious at being humiliated by a girl, Maximus ordered the hapless philosophers to be burned alive and then sentenced Catherine to be torn apart on a spiked wheel. As soon as she touched the wheel, however, it exploded and the broken shards flew into the crowd who had come to watch her torment.

At that, Maximus ordered Catherine to be beheaded. The moment she died, angels lifted her body and buried it on Mount Sinai. Since the early Middle Ages, her relics have been enshrined in Sinai's Monastery of St. Catherine.

Because of her wisdom, her intelligence, and her love for books, St. Catherine of Alexandria is the patron of libraries and librarians.

See holy card, page 242

ST. THOMAS AQUINAS

1224/5–1274 • FEAST DAY: JANUARY 28

St. Thomas Aquinas seems like an odd choice for the saint to invoke against lightning. He is, of course, the brilliant theologian who systematized all the teachings of the Catholic Church; the ingenious teacher who demonstrated how Aristotle's philosophy could clarify Church doctrine; and the mystical poet whose hymns to the Blessed Sacrament are still sung in churches around the world.

The d'Aquinos (Aquinas is the Latin form of the name) were members of the minor nobility. The family's castle stood at Roccasecca, south of Rome. Thomas's parents had at least nine children—five girls and four boys—and Thomas was the youngest boy.

Within the castle, a chamber in the tower served as the nursery; Thomas, not yet five years old, shared the room with his baby sister. One night, during a violent thunderstorm, a bolt of lightning struck the tower, killing Thomas's sister. He never forgot the terror of that night—the terrible crashing, the blinding flash, the horrified shrieks of his mother clutching her dead child.

One would imagine that a man graced with such a powerful intellect would be able to rationalize his fears, but the memory of his sister's death proved to be too traumatic. For the rest of his life, at the first rumble of thunder, St. Thomas would hurry to a church or chapel, where he would remain, frightened and praying, until the storm passed.

See holy card, page 242

ST. MARK THE EVANGELIST

FIRST CENTURY • FEAST DAY: APRIL 25

In a vision, the Hebrew prophet Ezekiel saw four winged creatures supporting the throne of God: one had the face of a man, the second that of a lion, the third an ox, and the fourth an eagle. Since at least the fourth century, Christians have interpreted these four creatures as representing the authors of the gospels. St. Matthew is shown as a winged man because his gospel begins with the genealogy of Christ; St. Luke's symbol is the winged ox because his gospel begins in the Jerusalem temple where oxen were sacrificed; the eagle is St. John's emblem because the beginning of his gospel is so poetic and theologically sophisticated, it seems to soar to heaven. And because St. Mark's gospel begins in the wilderness where St. John the Baptist is preaching, his emblem is the winged lion.

One could argue that the lion is the most famous of the symbols, thanks to Venice. More than one thousand years ago, two daring Venetian merchants stole St. Mark's relics from a tomb in Alexandria and carried them home—not as a trophy, they asserted, but to protect the relics from desecration at the hands of Egypt's Muslim rulers. Because Mark became Venice's primary patron saint, the lion appeared everywhere—in churches and squares, above doorways and arches, and on flags and banners, gondolas and currency.

We know little about St. Mark, but he may have identified himself indirectly in his own gospel. The night Christ is arrested, a young man wearing only a loincloth follows the apostles to Gethsemane. As the soldiers seize Jesus, the young man turns to flee. One of the soldiers reaches to grab him but finds himself holding nothing but the loincloth. The young man had run naked into the night. This streaker may have been St. Mark.

It's possible that Mark the Evangelist is also the young man known in the Acts of the Apostles as John Mark, the cousin of St. Barnabas, the young boy whom St. Paul couldn't stand to have around. St. Peter, on the other hand, was very fond of Mark, referring to him at the end of his first epistle as "my son." From this passing reference came the tradition that St. Peter was the primary source for St. Mark's gospel.

St. Mark's gospel is written in fluent Greek; it contains a few errors about the geography of Palestine; and the author goes to the trouble of translating certain Aramaic terms and explaining Jewish religious customs. All these clues have led biblical scholars to conclude that St. Mark was a Greek Jew who wrote his gospel for a Gentile audience.

Legend tells us that St. Mark served as the first bishop of Alexandria, Egypt. The Copts, the Christians of Egypt, venerate him as the founder of their church. According to an old legend, Mark was arrested on Easter Sunday in the year 68, during Nero's persecution of the Church. The soldiers who seized him tied a noose around his neck and dragged him around the city. After a day and night of such mistreatment, St. Mark died of strangulation.

See holy card, page 242

ST. PETER

DIED ABOUT 64 • FEAST DAYS: JUNE 29, FEBRUARY 22, NOVEMBER 18

I will give to you the keys of the kingdom of heaven," Christ told St. Peter. "And whatever you bind on earth shall be bound in heaven, and whatever you loose on earth shall be loosed in heaven."

This text from St. Matthew's gospel establishes St. Peter as the first pope—and as the patron of locksmiths. In terms of spiritual authority, Peter holds "the power of the keys." But locksmiths call on him to give them their own version of the power of the keys, opening what was locked up and locking what had been open.

In art, St. Peter is almost always shown clutching a pair of large keys, one gold, the other silver. By tradition, the gold key opens and closes the gates of heaven, whereas the silver one opens and shuts the gates of hell. There is a widely held belief among Christians of all denominations that St. Peter is heaven's gatekeeper, deciding who's allowed in and who gets sent to a decidedly less comfortable destination. It's not doctrine and certainly is not found anywhere in the New Testament—it's just a bit of innocent religious folklore that has been passed through the generations since at least the Middle Ages.

As the heirs of St. Peter, Catholic popes have chosen his keys as their emblem. You can find the text about the saint and his keys, inscribed in golden letters about six feet tall, encircling the great dome of St. Peter's Basilica in Vatican City.

See holy card, page 243

ST. FELIX OF NOLA

DIED 260 • FEAST DAY: JANUARY 14

Usually it's easy to identify who is a martyr. If the saint has suffered torture and imprisonment and given up his life for his faith, then he is clearly a martyr. St. Felix of Nola is one of those rare saints who, although he did not die a violent death, has been revered as a martyr because of all he endured for love of Christ.

Felix was a priest who served as an assistant to Maximus, the elderly bishop of Nola. When the Roman emperor began persecuting local Christians, Felix helped Maximus escape into the mountains. The Romans arrested Felix, scourged him almost to death, and left him chained in a cell. Legend says that an angel broke Felix's chains, shattered the lock on the cell door, and then told him where to find Maximus.

By the time Felix found him, the old bishop was nearly dead from hunger and exposure. Felix fed Maximus, nursed him, and carried him on his back to a remote place, leaving him in the care of an elderly Christian woman.

With Maximus settled safely, Felix looked for his own hiding place. He was still searching when he heard soldiers in the distance. Felix began to run, and by good fortune he came across a ruined building. Rubble blocked the door, but he managed to squeeze in through a window. Meanwhile he could hear the soldiers heading straight for him. Frightened though he was, Felix noticed a spider dangling near the window. As he watched, the spider spun a web that soon covered the opening. A moment later the soldiers arrived, but they didn't bother to search the abandoned structure—after all, the door was blocked and the only other entrance was covered by an unbroken spider web.

Felix lived in the ruin for months until the persecution ended. When Maximus died, the Christians of Nola wanted Felix to be their bishop, but he refused the honor. He remained a humble priest for the rest of his life, supporting himself and feeding the poor by farming three acres on the outskirts of town.

Since St. Felix's death, devotion to him has been intense in the region around Naples, Italy. Paulinus, bishop of Nola in the first decades of the fifth century and also later a saint, was cured of an eye ailment through his intercession. He then set about compiling testimonies of the miracles experienced by visitors to St. Felix's shrine. Among Paulinus's surviving papers is a prayer he overheard a peasant making at the tomb. The man's oxen had been stolen, and he wanted St. Felix to bring them back. "Restore these same animals," he told the saint. "I shall not accept any others." Upon returning to his farm, the peasant found his oxen safely back in their stalls. Ever since, St. Felix of Nola has been venerated as the saint who finds and returns lost animals.

See holy card, page 243

Lost Objects

ST. ANTHONY OF PADUA

1195–1231 • FEAST DAY: JUNE 13

It wasn't so long ago that Catholic school children, upon losing a ball while at recess, would chant, "St. Anthony, St. Anthony, look all around. There's something that's missing and cannot be found." Today those kids are adults who, even if they no longer sing rhymes, still call on St. Anthony when they have mislaid their wallet or misplaced the house keys or lost an earring. When it comes to finding objects that have gone missing, St. Anthony delivers.

One story explains how Anthony came to be the saint who finds stuff, but it's probably apocryphal. According to the tale, a novice in Anthony's friary in Padua concluded that religious life was not for him. Rather than go through the formality of taking leave of his superiors, the young man thought he would just walk out the door. Then it occurred to him that it would be a shame to leave without some memento of his days as a Franciscan. But what to take? In his room, Anthony kept an especially beautiful copy of the psalms; the runaway novice decided he would take that.

Soon after the novice absconded with the book, Anthony returned to his room. As a Franciscan committed to a life of poverty, Anthony didn't have much, so he immediately noticed the book's absence. Distressed by the loss, he prayed for help in finding it. At that moment the thief was hurrying away from Padua. Suddenly a hideous apparition blocked his path, crying, "Return that book to Anthony!" The terrified young man ran all the way back to the friary and returned the cherished volume to its rightful owner.

See holy card, page 243

ST. VALENTINE

DIED ABOUT 270 • FEAST DAY: FEBRUARY 14

The Roman priest and martyr St. Valentine was no one's lover, nor was he ever engaged. So, as far as we know, he never experienced the pangs suffered by the lovelorn. How, then, did he become the patron saint of love, romance, marriage, and even the romantically disadvantaged? The answer is complicated, a grab bag of legends and even odd medieval bird lore.

One legend says that, while Valentine was in prison, he befriended the jailer's daughter. The day he was led away to execution, he left the girl a farewell note signed, "your Valentine." Such is the supposed origin of sending cards to loved ones on St. Valentine's Day.

In medieval Europe, it was widely believed that birds paired up for life on St. Valentine's Day. The poet Geoffrey Chaucer mentioned that on February 14 "every fowl comes . . . to choose his mate." Apparently St. Valentine even plays matchmaker for birds.

As for Valentine himself, he did indeed exist. In fact, there were two Valentines, and both are commemorated on February 14. The first one was a Roman priest beaten and beheaded about the year 270. By 350 a church had been built over his grave outside Rome. Since 820 the relics of this St. Valentine have been enshrined inside the city walls, at the Church of St. Praxedes on Rome's Esquiline Hill.

The second St. Valentine was a bishop martyred in Terni, about sixty miles from Rome. His relics are enshrined in the local basilica. In recent years the town has been trying to boost its tourist trade by encouraging lovers to spend a romantic vacation in the hometown of St. Valentine.

See holy card, page 243

ST. SIMON THE APOSTLE

FIRST CENTURY • FEAST DAY: OCTOBER 28

Each time the New Testament writers list the twelve apostles, Simon's name appears. The gospels of Matthew and Mark call him Simon the Canaanite, which may mean that he came from the Canaan region of Israel, near what is now Gaza. Luke calls him Simon the Zealot, a name that has stirred up almost two thousand years of debate. Some biblical scholars say it refers to St. Simon's zeal in adhering to God's law. Others believe that he had once been a member of the Zealots, a political party that incited rebellions against the Roman occupation. St. Simon never speaks in the gospels, and he wrote no epistles; we aren't even certain where he preached when he and the other apostles went forth to teach all nations.

There are legends about his life, however. One says that Simon teamed up with St. Jude, and together they traveled to Persia, where they preached the gospel and performed an astonishing array of miracles.

They healed a band of sorcerers who had been bitten by venomous snakes. They tamed two ferocious man-eating tigers. They raised from the dead thirty people who had drowned. When a woman gave birth to a child out of wedlock and accused a holy deacon of fathering her baby, Simon and Jude commanded the newborn to name his father; immediately the infant spoke and cleared the deacon.

The legends end with St. Simon's martyrdom, when a wicked pagan king sentenced him to be sawn in half. In art Simon is almost always depicted holding a large, two-man crosscut saw, the kind used to cut logs and timber and similar to the one that severed him in two. For this reason, St. Simon is venerated as the patron saint of lumberjacks.

See holy card, page 244

ST. BALTHASAR

FIRST CENTURY • FEAST DAYS: JANUARY 6 AND 11

St. Balthasar's link to playing cards is based on a belief during the Middle Ages that the Magi, the three kings who brought gold, frankincense, and myrrh to the infant Jesus, came from Persia, Africa, and Egypt. According to an ancient tradition, the name of the Egyptian king or wise man, or *magus*, was Balthasar. It was thought that gypsies came from Egypt, and gypsies were notorious for their card tricks. And so St. Balthasar the Egyptian became the patron of card manufacturers and, by extension, card players, blackjack dealers, and anyone who is having a run of bad luck at cards. (We'll have to draw the line at tarot card readers, however, since the Church looks on every type of fortune-telling and attempts to read the future as objectionable, if not out-right sinful.)

Only St. Matthew's gospel makes mention of wise men coming to worship the Christ Child, whom they called the king of the Jews. Matthew recounts: "After Jesus was born in Bethlehem, in Judea, in the time of King Herod, wise men from the East came to Jerusalem. . . . As they came into the house and saw the child with Mary, his mother, they bowed down and worshiped him. They opened their treasure boxes and gave him gifts of gold, frankincense, and myrrh."

The tradition that they were three kings is derived from Psalm 72, "May the kings of Tharsis and the isles render him tribute; may the kings of the Sheba and of Seba bring gifts! May all the kings fall down before him!" The English word *magic* comes from the Greek word *magi*, but the three wise men who traveled to Bethlehem were not magicians or sorcerers—in fact, their religious law forbade them to dabble in anything supernatural.

No one knows what became of the three magi after they returned home. A legend dating from the sixth century says that St. Thomas the Apostle met them as he was traveling to India and baptized them. Another legend says that, during her travels in the Holy Land, the empress Helen found their relics and brought them to Constantinople. Later they were transferred to the cathedral of Cologne in Germany, where they are preserved to this day in a spectacular golden shrine above the high altar.

See holy card, page 244

S. Anastasia.

S. JOANNES A CRUCE

Printed in Belgium

S. Giovanni da Capestrano

1. Martyrs • St. Anastasia   2. Meditation • St. John of the Cross
3. Mercy • St. Faustina Kowalska   4. Military Chaplains • St. John of Capistrano

261

S. Christina.

B. K.   A. Riffarth, New-York.

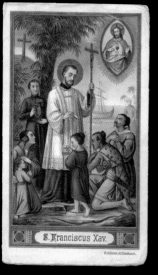

S. Franciscus Xav.

R.Kühlen, M.Gladbach.

SCTA THERESIA   A JESU INFANTE

K. BEURON 1058   MADE IN GERMANY

1. Millers • St. Christina of Bolsena   2. Miscarriages • St. Catherine of Sweden
3. Missionaries • St. Francis Xavier   4. Missionaries • St. Therese of Lisieux

1.

2.

Hl. Ulrich, Bischof † 973

Bleibt fest im Glauben, wie man euch gelehrt hat.
S. Paulus, Col. 2, 7

2891

3.

K. BEURON 1050   MADE IN GERMANY

1. Mocked for Their Religion • Blessed Kateri Tekakwitha 2. Moles • St. Ulrich of Augsburg
3. Monks • St. Benedict

263

SAINT COLUMBAN,
Pray for Us

BL. BERNARD OF MENTON
Spent his youth in penance, study and prayer.

He was made archdeacon in 966 under his Bishop, and for 42 years preached that he might banish ignorance and superstition. The famous hospital and monastery called Great St. Bernard was built by him for all travellers over the Alps, thus often saving them from death.

Spes Sancta, Newbury 23

K. SEURON 1007

1. **Motorcyclists • St. Columbanus** 2. **Mountain and Rock Climbers • St. Bernard of Menthon**
3. **Murderers • St. Vladimir** 4. **Music and Musicians • St. Cecilia**

GABRIEL POSSENTI

1838–1862 • FEAST DAY: FEBRUARY 27

Pistol-packin' saints are extremely rare. Yet, if the story about St. Gabriel Possenti is true, he was one crack shot.

Gabriel was the eleventh of thirteen children. By all accounts he grew up to be a cheerful, bright boy who was equally popular with the girls as he was with his teachers. He was devout, but not excessively so. And somewhere along the line Gabriel learned to shoot.

At age eighteen, he entered the Passionist seminary at Isola di Gran Sasso, with the intention of becoming a priest. He took the religious name Gabriel of Our Lady of Sorrows, which seems at odds with his upbeat personality. It was while he was a seminarian that he displayed his gifts as a marksman.

According to the tale, in 1860 a ragtag band of soldiers from Garibaldi's army stormed into town, pillaged and set fire to houses, and generally terrorized the residents. Gabriel confronted the raiders. In the central piazza he found a young woman fighting a soldier who was trying to drag her away. Gabriel stepped in, and during the struggle he managed to wrench the pistol from the soldier's holster. Raising the revolver he ordered the would-be rapist to back away. Meanwhile, more raiders arrived. They hooted at the sight of one of their own pinned down by a kid in a cassock. Then, just as they began to close in on Gabriel, a lizard darted across the square. Taking aim, Gabriel shot the lizard right through the head. The raiders fell silent. Gabriel ordered them to drop their weapons, and then at gunpoint he marched them out of town.

This story has become well known thanks to the St. Gabriel Possenti Society of Arlington, Virginia, whose members promote him as the patron of marksmen and handgun owners as well as self-defense and the right of private citizens to own firearms. The society has petitioned the Vatican for a formal declaration, but such official designations are rare. Much more common is a grassroots movement, in which the faithful venerate a saint as the patron of their cause. From that perspective, St. Gabriel already is the patron of marksmen and gun owners.

The run-in with Garibaldi's ruffians was the most dramatic moment of Gabriel's brief life. When he was twenty-three years old, he was ordained a priest and looked forward to joining his fellow Passionists who visited parishes throughout Italy, where, through their preaching and good example, they hoped to revive religious devotion in Catholics who had become lukewarm in the practice of their faith. Tragically, Gabriel never had the opportunity. He contracted an especially virulent strain of tuberculosis and, after a short illness, died peacefully at age twenty-four.

Of course, he was not canonized because he was a good marksman. It was his devotion to prayer, joyful outlook on life, and kindness and patience even when his time was being monopolized by someone tiresome, that made everyone who knew Gabriel come to regard him as a saint.

See holy card, page 244

ST. ANASTASIA

DIED 304 • FEAST DAY: DECEMBER 25

St. Anastasia became the patron of martyrs not simply because she died a martyr—there are thousands of other martyr-saints to choose from—but because of her heroism in risking her life to bring food, clothes, medicine, and comfort to Christians who were about to be martyred.

Anastasia was a patrician, a member of one of Rome's aristocratic families. When the emperor Diocletian began his ferocious persecution of the Church, Anastasia started visiting the prison where Christians were awaiting execution. Anastasia's husband, Publius, was a pagan. Afraid that she would be arrested and executed, he not only ordered her to stay away from the prisons, he forbade her to leave the house. Soon thereafter Publius died, and Anastasia renewed her charitable work among the martyrs. Her spiritual adviser at this time was St. Chrysogonus, a Roman official who may have secretly been a Christian priest.

When Chrysogonus traveled north to Aquileia, near present-day Venice, to serve the Christians there, Anastasia went along. There, Chrysogonus was arrested and beheaded.

Anastasia moved on to Thessalonika, in Greece, where she stayed with three sisters, Saints Agape, Chionia, and Irene. After the sisters were martyred, Anastasia moved again, this time to the Christian community in Sirmium, present-day Mitrovica, Serbia. There she was arrested and condemned to be burned alive—at last becoming a martyr herself. After the persecutions ended, Christians from Sirmium carried St. Anastasia's relics back to Rome. They rest today in the Basilica of St. Anastasia, at the bottom of the Palatine Hill.

See holy card, page 261

ST. JOHN OF THE CROSS

1542–1591 • FEAST DAY: DECEMBER 14

"The dark night of the soul" is a common phrase taken from the title of a book about the contemplative life written by St. John of the Cross. John was drawn to silence and meditation—in other words, he was best suited for cloistered life. But an encounter with the dynamic St. Teresa of Avila complicated his life considerably and prevented him from retiring to a monastery. St. John of the Cross, then, is the patron of not only all those who love meditation and the quiet life of prayer, but also those who would like to meditate more but are distracted by life's demands.

John had joined the Carmelite order and was ordained a priest just at the time that St. Teresa began her reform of the order's nuns and friars. Many convents and priories had grown lax. The old austerity had given way to opulent furnishings and expensive food and wine; gossiping with visitors took precedence over prayer. Teresa won the approval of the superior of Spain's Carmelites, as well as of King Philip II, to restore the Carmelites' original principles. But not all the friars wanted to be reformed, and they took out their frustration on Teresa's chaplain, confessor, and protégé, John of the Cross. In 1577 a band of renegade Carmelites kidnapped John and imprisoned him in their priory in Toledo. He spent nearly nine months locked inside a tiny cell, with only a three-inch-wide slit for a window. His friar-jailers gave him so little food he almost starved to death; he was refused water for washing and his habit became infested with lice; he was denied candles to dispel the gloom or a fire to warm him in winter. He was brutally flogged, bearing the terrible scars for the rest of his life.

Terrified of being locked up forever, John took refuge in meditation, mentally composing some of his finest mystical poems. He also plotted his escape. By mid-August 1578, he managed to dismantle the lock on the cell door and make a rope by tying together strips torn from his blankets. Late one night he crept out of his cell, hurried to the parapet, and used his makeshift rope to climb down the priory's outer wall. Weak and disoriented, John called upon the Blessed Virgin for help. She must have heard him because, after staggering through the city, he found himself at the door of one of Teresa's convents. Once the nuns recognized him, they brought him inside their enclosure. (Under both Church and civil law, it was forbidden for any man to enter that part of a convent.) When the friar-jailers and local police arrived looking for John, they searched everywhere except the enclosure.

Once he had regained his health and strength, John wanted to return to his quiet life, but civic and religious leaders prevented him from doing so. First he served as head of a college; next he was prior of a Carmelite house; and then he was made one of the superiors of the order in Spain. Since he had to be out among people, John took the opportunity to teach others about the joy of meditation. "Contemplation," he taught, "is nothing else but a secret, peaceful, and loving infusion of God, which,

if admitted, will set the soul on fire with the Spirit of love."

See holy card, page 261

ST. FAUSTINA KOWALSKA

1905–1938 • FEAST DAY: OCTOBER 5

It was Pope John Paul II, a contemporary of St. Faustina, who declared her "Blessed," then canonized her, and finally proclaimed her "the Apostle of Divine Mercy." All this effort was in response to seven years' worth of visions and revelations that St. Faustina received in her convent in Warsaw between 1931 and her death in 1938. "I have opened my heart as a living fountain of mercy," Christ told Sister Faustina. "Let all souls draw life from it."

St. Faustina was born Elena Kowalska, one of ten children of Stanislaus and Marianna Kowalski. Her parents farmed a few acres of rye and owned a handful of dairy cows, but they could barely support such a large family. At age fifteen, to contribute some much-needed money, Faustina went to work as a housemaid. But what she really wanted to be was a nun. As a half-literate teenager with no skills aside from housekeeping, she was hardly an attractive candidate—one religious order after another turned her away. Finally she was accepted by the Sisters of Our Lady of Mercy in Warsaw. They gave her the name Sister Maria Faustina of the Blessed Sacrament and put her to work in the kitchen.

For the first several years, Sister Faustina didn't really stand out in the convent. Then, on the night of February 22, 1931, Christ appeared before her, his right hand raised in blessing, his left hand touching the side of his chest. From his chest issued two rays of light, one red, the other colorless. Christ commanded Faustina to paint what she saw and inscribe the painting, "Jesus, I trust in you."

But that wasn't all the Lord wanted. He urged her to remind sinners to trust in his mercy, and he commanded her to petition Poland's bishops as well as the pope to establish the first Sunday after Easter as the Feast of Mercy.

Mystified and perhaps frightened by the experience, Sister Faustina reported her vision to her superior and to the priest who was her spiritual director. They both instructed her to keep a diary detailing all revelations. Her account consumes more than six hundred pages.

Like St. Bernadette of Lourdes and St. Thérèse the Little Flower, Sister Faustina contracted tuberculosis and died young. The year after her death, the Nazis invaded Poland; interest in Sister Faustina and devotion to Christ's mercy were eclipsed by the struggle to survive the nightmare of World War II. Interest was revived after the war, but it seemed likely that the Divine Mercy movement would either remain local or be crushed completely by Poland's Communist government.

Perhaps the strongest supporter was Karol Wojtyla, archbishop of Krakow who became pope in 1978. As John Paul II, he advanced the cause for Sister Faustina's canonization, encouraged Catholics to venerate Christ under the title of Divine Mercy, and fulfilled the request the Lord had made years earlier, naming the Sunday after Easter as Divine Mercy Sunday.

See holy card, page 261

ST. JOHN OF CAPISTRANO

1386–1456 • FEAST DAY: OCTOBER 23

John of Capistrano was a man who saw the world as black or white. The day he joined the Franciscans in his native Italy, he wrote down all his worst sins. He did so believing that, to begin a new life of holiness, he must first acknowledge his own wickedness.

Once ordained a priest, he held himself—and all other members of the clergy—to a high standard. This was the fifteenth century, a time when many priests were corrupt, so John published a book entitled *A Mirror for the Clergy*. In it, he held up to his brother priests all the evil they did, showing them the damage their misdeeds inflicted upon the Church and the souls of the laity. He went on to instruct them about what they must do to be worthy of their sacred office. Such a blatant attack made John unpopular with many priests and bishops, but Pope Nicholas V thought that such a holy, upright friar was just the man to convert the Hussites of Bohemia and Hungary. So that's how John

came to be in Hungary at the time of the Turkish invasion.

After conquering Constantinople on May 29, 1453, the Ottoman Turks turned toward Europe. Three years later a Turkish army of about sixty thousand marched into Hungary. Arrayed against the invaders was a force led by János Hunyadi, a Hungarian general who had been battling the Turks for at least twenty years. Joining the experienced soldiers was Father John, leading a rag-tag group of peasants armed mostly with knives, slings, and farm implements. Between Hunyadi and St. John, the Christians numbered about fifty thousand.

The Christians hunkered down behind the walls of Belgrade while the Turks encamped all around. For the first few weeks, fighting was intermittent until July 22, when several small Christian detachments skirmished with Turkish cavalry outside the city. As the Turks massed for a major attack, Father John rode out and ordered the men to take cover behind the walls. But when two thousand of Hunyadi's knights came riding out of the city, he changed strategy and led a wild charge against the Ottomans. Hunyadi, seeing Father John's maneuver, led a second charge to disable the Turkish cannons. Taken entirely by surprise, the Turks panicked, fled, and were cut down by the thousands. For his heroism in the face of the enemy, St. John of Capistrano is revered as the patron of military chaplains.

As the Ottoman conquest spread across eastern Europe, John's fortitude—his absolute unwillingness to compromise—was exactly the quality needed. In his preaching, he laid out the options as starkly as possible: The Christians of Europe could remain at home and wait for the Turks to come and kill or enslave them, or they could take up arms in defense of their families, their country, and their faith and drive out the invaders. Inspired by John's rhetoric, the outnumbered Christian forces crushed the Turks and saved all of eastern Europe from being swallowed up by the Ottoman Empire.

See holy card, page 261

ST. CHRISTINA OF BOLSENA

DIED ABOUT 250 • FEAST DAY: JULY 24

Two martyrs named Christina are commemorated on July 24, and the doubling up has caused some confusion. The histories and legends of the two women have been conflated so that it's now impossible to separate which facts and fables apply to Christina of Bolsena and which relate to Christina of Tyre. Rather than trying to sort it out, here's the story of St. Christina of Bolsena as told in most collections of lives of the saints.

Christina was a member of the wealthy Roman patrician family known as the Anicii (this part appears to be true). While in her early teens, she converted to Christianity under circumstances that remain unknown. Legend says that she celebrated her baptism by smashing every statue of pagan gods and goddesses in her parents' home; the ones made of gold or silver she broke up, distributing the fragments to the poor.

Now the story becomes a little puzzling, as the scene shifts from the Anicii villa in Rome to Lake Bolsena, in the Italian province of Tuscany, where Christina's outraged father decided to punish his daughter. He tied a millstone to her neck and threw her into the lake. But Christina didn't drown—she didn't even sink.

With Christina back safely on shore, the local magistrate stepped in, gave her a formal hearing, and then condemned her to be shot to death by arrows. This time, Christina did die.

Because of the dramatic incident with the millstone, millers have taken St. Christina as their patron.

See holy card, page 262

ST. CATHERINE OF SWEDEN

1331–1381 • FEAST DAY: MARCH 24

It's unclear why St. Catherine is invoked against miscarriages, but it may have something to do with the size of her family: She was one of eight healthy children.

Catherine's parents, Bridget and Ulf Gudmarsson, were wealthy, well connected (Bridget was related to Sweden's royal family), and deeply religious. While their children were still young, the couple decided to make a pilgrimage to the shrine of St. James at Compostela in Spain. By the time they returned, Ulf was sick with what would prove to be his final illness. Before he died, however, he arranged for thirteen-year-old Catherine to marry a man named Edgard Kryn.

Following the pattern set by her mother and father, Catherine had become very pious, and she was fortunate that Edgard was nearly as religious. Somehow this teenage girl persuaded her husband never to consummate their marriage. They lived apart within their house as austerely as any monk or nun.

Meanwhile Bridget had intensified her religious life. She founded a new religious order for men and women, the Order of the Holy Savior (popularly known as the Bridgettines), and built a double monastery-and-convent at Vadstena. It was said that every day she received visions of Christ and the Blessed Virgin Mary. Then, in 1349, Bridget said good-bye to her children and set off for Rome. Years later, Catherine confided to a friend that her mother's departure caused such distress that she forgot how to smile. In fact, after only one year, the separation had become too much, and with the blessing of the ever-patient Edgard, Catherine left for Rome. She was nineteen and, by all accounts, breathtakingly beautiful.

Rome was a mixed bag of excitement, disappointment, and frustration. Catherine was enchanted by the beauty of the churches and thrilled to be able to pray at the tombs of so many famous saints. For a woman accustomed to a healthy rural life, however, the city's squalor and oppressive heat were hard to bear. Complicating the situation was Bridget's misgivings about letting Catherine leave their house alone. Her daughter's beauty attracted attention, and Bridget had heard too many stories of lovely young women being abducted by lascivious lords, raped, or forced into marriage. "I lead a wretched life here," Catherine wrote to a friend, "caged like an animal."

Eventually mother and daughter reached an understanding. They began working as a team, visiting shrines, nursing the sick, calling on the great families of Rome to win their help and support. Until Bridget's death in Rome in 1373, the two women were practically inseparable. Then it fell to Catherine to escort her mother's body back to Sweden for burial.

The journey took eleven months, and Catherine hoped she could remain in her homeland for the rest of her life. But the country's bishops wanted Bridget to be named a saint, and they insisted that Catherine would be the best advocate for the cause. So back to Rome she went.

For the next five years, Catherine collected the testimony of those who had known her mother as well as evidence of miracles attributed to Bridget's intercession. Once the documentation was in order, she began the long trip back to Sweden. She arrived at Vadstena in July 1380, worn out and ill; she died the following March.

Catherine and Bridget were buried together. To this day, their relics are preserved in the same shrine in the Vadstena abbey church.

See holy card, page 262

Missionaries

ST. FRANCIS XAVIER & ST. THÉRÈSE OF LISIEUX

1506–1552 • FEAST DAY: DECEMBER 3
1873–1897 • FEAST DAY: OCTOBER 1

A French cloistered nun who died at age twenty-four may seem to be an odd choice as a patron saint of foreign missions. Until, that is, you understand St. Thérèse of Lisieux and the immense popularity of her cult.

As a cloistered nun, Thérèse took it upon herself to pray especially for priests—both missionaries and those who remained close to home. Next, thanks to the wide distribution of her best-selling autobiography, *Story of a Soul*, Thérèse became a religious phenomenon in the early twentieth century. Missionary priests adopted her as one of their patrons, and in 1923 Pope Pius XI made it official.

The primary patron of missionaries, however, is St. Francis Xavier, a man of tremendous zeal, energy, and optimism. As a student at the University of Paris, he met St. Ignatius of Loyola, a fellow Basque. Led by Ignatius, in 1534 Francis and five friends formed the Society of Jesus,

better known as the Jesuits. The first Jesuits hoped they all would serve as missionaries together in the Holy Land; instead, Francis was sent to southern Asia. He sailed with a convoy of Portuguese ships bound for the colony at Goa, India. The voyage took thirteen months, and Francis was seasick through most of it.

The Portuguese had been in Goa for thirty-one years, and the city was well furnished with churches, monasteries, and even a bishop. But most of the town's Portuguese population was composed of cruel, dissolute, and vicious men who abandoned the illegitimate children they had with Indian women, tortured their slaves, despised the helpless, and regarded India as their personal property to pillage as they wished.

With so much work to be done, Francis kept up an exhausting routine that included visits to the city prison and hospitals, saying Mass for the lepers, teaching the catechism to children and slaves, and writing lyrics that explained the basics of Christianity and then setting them to the tunes of popular songs. One of his toughest assignments was trying to convince the Goa Portuguese to live like Catholics instead of godless despots.

After months in Goa he sailed to the Spice Islands, in what is now Indonesia, where he met three Japanese converts to Christianity. This chance meeting piqued his interest, and once he arrived in Japan the refinement, elegance, and courtesy of the people there captivated him. But Francis could never stay long in one place. He wanted to bring the gospel to China.

With the help of a Chinese convert named Anthony, Francis struck a bargain with a Chinese merchant who, for an extravagant fee, agreed to transport him to China. Instead, the merchant abandoned Francis and Anthony on a desolate island. There, Francis fell ill and died, attended by Anthony, two slaves, and a Portuguese ship's captain who'd stumbled upon the castaways.

St. Francis Xavier set a very high standard for missionaries: It's estimated that in eleven years he converted forty thousand to Christianity. In 1904 Pope Pius X recognized his achievements by naming him as the patron saint of missionaries.

See holy cards, page 262

BLESSED KATERI TEKAKWITHA

1656–1680 • FEAST DAY: JULY 14

Life can be difficult for converts to Catholicism, particularly if their newly found faith puts them at odds with the prevailing religion or culture. Such was the case for Blessed Kateri Tekakwitha, a Mohawk Indian who became an outcast in her native community after converting to Christianity.

Kateri was born in Ossernenon, in the Mohawk Valley near Auriesville, New York. This was the same village in which three Jesuit missionaries had been martyred—St. Rene Goupil in 1642 and Saints Jean de la Lande and Isaac Jogues in 1646. In 1660 a smallpox epidemic swept through the Indian villages of New York, taking the lives of Tekakwitha's mother, father, and baby brother and leaving her face badly scarred. The orphaned Tekakwitha found a new home with two aunts and an uncle.

Once Tekakwitha became a teenager, her relatives looked for a man to marry her, but she refused. Her relatives found her reluctance to marry perplexing, but what she did next enraged them. When Jesuit missionary Father Jacques de Lamberville arrived in the village, Tekakwitha expressed interest in Christianity. She had a quick mind and absorbed the essentials of the faith so rapidly that Father de Lamberville agreed to baptize her on Easter 1676. She took the name Kateri, Mohawk for "Catherine."

News of the conversion made her an instant outcast. Her uncle and aunts looked for any excuse to beat her. She was harassed, pelted with stones, and once almost killed. As the stress of living in a hostile environment became unbearable, Kateri turned to Father de Lamberville for advice. He told her to go to the Christian Indian village of Kahnawake on the banks of the St. Lawrence River, near Montreal. To find peace and security, Kateri set out on July 14, 1677, for the village of Christian Indians, leaving her home forever. It was a two-hundred-mile journey, and Kateri made it alone, on foot.

She arrived in Kahnawake in October and immediately found a new home. By chance she met a Christian Huron, Anastasia Tegonhatsihonga, who had known Kateri's mother and invited Kateri to live with her. Safe at last among people who were Indians and Christians, Kateri felt at ease for the first time in many years. She enjoyed nearly three happy years before falling ill just as the Canadian winter was giving way to spring. On Wednesday during Holy Week, April 17, 1680, she died. At her bedside knelt the Jesuit who had been her spiritual director, Father Pierre Cholenc. Later he testified that, as he recited the prayers for the dead, Kateri's disfiguring scars disappeared. "Suddenly [her face] became in a moment so fair and beautiful that, noticing the change, I cried out in surprise." Two French settlers also saw the miracle and honored the Mohawk saint by making a wooden coffin for her (most of the dead, French and Indian, were buried wrapped in a shroud). Thanks to that gesture of respect, when the mission moved several years later, the Jesuits were able to find Kateri's relics and take them along.

See holy card, page 263

SAINT RAYMOND NONNATUS
PATRON OF CHRISTIAN MOTHERS

S. Rafael Archange

S. HIERONYME EMILIANI
ORA PRO NOBIS

1. Newborn Infants • St. Raymond Nonnatus   2. Nightmares • St. Raphael the Archangel
3. Nurses • St. Camillus de Lellis   4. Orphans • St. Jerome Emiliani

281

den 2ten · IHS · Mai.

Hl. Athanasius, Patriarch von Alexandrie.
Mein Gerechter lebt aus dem Glauben. Hebr. 10, 38.
Glaubenstreue.
Bete für jene, welche im Glauben wanken oder gleichgültig sind.

Der heilige Alexius, Bekenner.

4

SANCTUS MICHAEL ARCHANGELUS

SAINTE MATHILDE, Reine

1. Orthodoxy · St. Athanasius 2. Panhandlers · St. Alexius
Paratroopers · St. Michael the Archangel 4. Parents with Disappointing Children · St. Matilda

SAINT JEAN-BAPTISTE VIANNEY,
Curé d'Ars.

MAISON BOUASSE-LEBEL & Guérard & Cⁱᵉ — 6166 — PARIS.

SAN GIOVANNI GUALBERTO

· ST · NICOLAUS ·

H. Stubenrauch   OFCHEM

Sel. Nicolaus von der Flüe

2989   Com. appr. eccl.

Bavaria

1. **Parish Priests** · St. John Mary Vianney   2. **Park Service Workers** · St. John Gualbert
3. **Pawnbrokers** · St. Nicholas   4. **Peacemakers** · St. Nicholas of Flue

283

S Teresia — S.te Thérèse,
Hervormster der — Reformatrice de l'ordre
Carmelieten-Orde. — de N.D. du Mont-Carmel.
of Aran de Vesen-Petit-Bruges

S. BENEDETTO DA S. FRATELLO
IL CUI CORPO SI VENERA NEL
Convento di S. Maria di Gesù - Palermo

✠ Sancta-Maria-Magdalena-O.P.N.

B. JOANNA D'ARC.

1. People in Need of Grace • St. Teresa of Avila   2. People of African Descent • St. Benedict the Moor
3. Perfume Makers • St. Mary Magdalene   4. Persecuted by the Church • St. Joan of Arc

ST. ULRICH OF AUGSBURG

890–973 • FEAST DAY: JULY 4

St. Ulrich is still one of Augsburg's most beloved saints, but devotion to him was especially fervent during the Middle Ages. It was said that pregnant women who drank from his chalice would have an easy delivery; that one touch from his bishop's cross would cure anyone afflicted with rabies; and that a little earth from his grave or a little dust from his shrine would repel moles.

St. Ulrich is distinguished in another way as well: He is the first saint to have been formally canonized by the pope. In the first centuries of the Church, saints were designated by popular acclaim. Later, bishops could canonize holy men and women who had lived in their diocese. After Pope John XV canonized Ulrich in 993, Rome became the official arbiter of all saints' causes.

Ulrich served as bishop of Augsburg for fifty years, during which time he successfully juggled an active pastoral life with a private life of prayer and study. Three years after Ulrich had been installed as bishop, the Magyars swept through the region and conquered Augsburg, slaughtering many of the citizens, plundering the city, and burning the cathedral. Ulrich devoted the rest of his life to rebuilding his diocese. He had new defensive walls erected around the town, brought in merchants to revive commerce, and rebuilt or restored all the destroyed or damaged churches. When the Magyars returned thirty years later, Bishop Ulrich led the defense of the city and kept the enemy at bay until the German emperor Otto arrived with his army and drove out the invaders.

See holy card, page 263.

ST. BENEDICT

ABOUT 480–543 • FEAST DAY: JULY 11

The Father of Western Monasticism"—that is one of the titles of St. Benedict, the man responsible for transforming monastic life from a series of grueling self-tortures into a disciplined but sane routine of prayer, work, study, and recreation. Before Benedict wrote his Rule, too many men thought they could reach perfection by denying themselves food, water, adequate clothing, and sleep. To Benedict, such extremes could ruin a monk's health, drive him mad, and perhaps even lead to premature death. And so he prescribed healthy meals, clothing suitable to the climate, and sufficient hours of sleep and rest.

Benedict had withdrawn from the world when he was nineteen or twenty years old. The child of a wealthy Roman Christian family (his twin sister was St. Scholastica), Benedict became disgusted by the licentiousness of the young men and women of his class. Taking along the elderly servant woman who had raised him, Benedict left Rome for Affile, where a community of like-minded men were trying to serve God by following a kind of haphazard monastic life. After a short time, Benedict found himself drawn to a solitary life. He sent his old servant home and withdrew to a cave in a mountain ravine called Subiaco.

During the three years he lived in the cave, Benedict deepened his spiritual life while planning the basic elements of his monastic rule. When other men asked if they could live in caves near him, Benedict put his ideas into practice, forming the first Benedictine monastery at Subiaco. The way of life formulated by St. Benedict continues to this day in Benedictine monasteries throughout the world, and his Rule has served as the inspiration for virtually every religious order founded during the last fifteen hundred years.

See holy card, page 263

ST. COLUMBANUS

543–615 • FEAST DAY: NOVEMBER 23

St. Columbanus was one of those roving Irish monks who wandered up and down Europe in the sixth and seventh centuries. This love of the open road inspired the Right Reverend John Oliver, an Anglican bishop and biker, to suggest St. Columbanus as the patron of motorcyclists.

As a young man, Columbanus felt drawn to the religious life, but his good looks attracted the attention of the young women of Ireland, and he didn't entirely want to give that up. At the urging of a holy woman Columbanus decided, finally, to become a monk at the abbey of Bangor.

Columbanus was forty-two when he asked his abbot to send him as a missionary to the pagan tribes of Gaul. Accompanied by twelve monks, Columbanus set out for France, taking the long way around through Scotland and England. Once in France he preached to the pagans, founded monasteries where sometimes he agreed to serve as abbot, and other times preferred to live as a hermit. Over the next thirty years, Columbanus traveled through Germany and Switzerland and then crossed the Alps into northern Italy, where he finally settled down in Bobbio. There he rebuilt a dilapidated church dedicated to St. Peter and constructed a new monastery beside it. Even then he found it hard to stay put, so he retired to a cave near the abbey. St. Columbanus died in his cave, but he was buried in his abbey church. His relics are there still, beneath the altar in the crypt.

See holy card, page 264

ST. BERNARD OF MENTHON

ABOUT 1000–ABOUT 1081 • FEAST DAY: MAY 28

Cardinal Achille Ratti, who became Pope Pius XI in 1922, was a lifelong aficionado of mountain climbing. With his election to the papacy, he was forced to give up his favorite sport, but he was still able to do something to promote it. In 1923 Pius XI named St. Bernard of Menthon as the patron of mountaineers. By extension, St. Bernard has also become the patron of the popular contemporary sport of rock climbing.

The castle of Menthon stands on the shores of Lake Annecy in a mountainous region where the borders of France, Switzerland, and Italy meet. In all likelihood, that is where Bernard was born into a noble family about the year 1000.

As a young boy growing up in the foothills, Bernard went on rambles into the Alps. Many residents in the remote alpine valleys were either still pagans, or else they practiced an odd mixture of Christian and pagan customs. When Bernard grew up and entered the priesthood, he took these mountain regions as his parish. For the next forty-two years he traveled through the mountains, preaching the gospel in small towns and isolated farms. During these missionary expeditions, Bernard met pilgrims going to, or coming from, Rome, whose companions had died of exposure in the mountains or had been swept away by an avalanche. To help these travelers, he opened a monastery and hospice in what is known today as Great St. Bernard Pass, 8,100 feet above sea level. The saint's work continues as the monks welcome crowds of visitors, mountaineers, and hikers in the summer as well as a few hardy pilgrims, climbers, and skiers in the winter. The monastery's large dogs, known as St. Bernards, are still on the site as well.

See holy card, page 264

ST. VLADIMIR

ABOUT 956–1015 • FEAST DAY: JULY 15

f all the medieval heathen kings, Vladimir of Kiev tops the list of those least likely to convert.

Vladimir was the illegitimate son of Svyatoslav, king of Kiev. He was still in his teens when an enemy tribe killed Svyatoslav, beheaded the corpse, and turned the skull into a drinking cup. As the king's illegitimate son, Vladimir had no claim to the crown—not that he let that get in his way. He recruited an army, overthrew his half-brother, and had him assassinated. And he did not stop there. He then broke into the convent where his widowed sister-in-law had taken refuge, raped her, and added her to his harem of eight hundred concubines.

Vladimir's reckless (and successful) play for power won him the admiration of the warriors of Kiev. Now, to secure the favor of the gods, he built an enormous temple in which he enshrined images of every god in the Russian pantheon as well as every god of the Turkic tribes (just to be on the safe side). To consecrate the temple, he slaughtered a pair of his own subjects, Theodore and John, two of the very few Christians in the kingdom.

Ever eager for power, Vladimir conquered one neighboring tribe after another. He was so fearsome on the battlefield that when Basil, emperor of Byzantium, was threatened by a Bulgar invasion, he asked Vladimir for help. Vladimir defeated the Bulgars and saved Constantinople; Basil was so delighted, he offered him anything he wanted. Vladimir asked to marry Anna, the emperor's sister. The request stunned Basil. As for Anna, she refused to marry a pagan who had seven wives and hundreds of mistresses, a man who had killed his own brother and practiced human sacrifice. Desperate to honor his promise and protect his sister, the emperor agreed to the match on the condition that Vladimir become a Christian. Vladimir agreed, but no one, least of all Anna, expected him to be true to his word.

After his baptism and his Christian marriage to Anna, Vladimir returned to Kiev a changed man. He dismissed his wives and concubines and ordered his grandiose pagan temple destroyed. He urged the men of his inner circle to accept the Christian faith. He asked his brother-in-law the emperor to send him more bishops and priests, more icons, Bibles, and relics as well as trained architects to build churches throughout the realm.

His change of heart was complete. Vladimir, who had despised weakness, was now distributing alms to the helpless. Stranger still, the man who had waded hip-deep in blood now abolished the death penalty. Vladimir's dramatic change of heart made his people curious about Christianity. They listened to what the priests from Byzantium preached, and many of them asked to be baptized.

For his success spreading the Christian faith, the Eastern Church has given St. Vladimir the title "Equal to the Apostles." In the West, he is venerated as the patron saint of contrite murderers.

See holy card, page 264

ST. CECILIA

THIRD CENTURY • FEAST DAY: NOVEMBER 22

According to the story, although Cecilia's parents were Christians, they chose a pagan for her to marry. The legend goes on to say that at the wedding banquet, while the musicians played bawdy songs, Cecilia sang in her heart hymns to Christ, her heavenly bridegroom. That is how St. Cecilia came to be venerated as the patron of music, professional musicians, and students of music. In the late Middle Ages, when organs were introduced into churches, artists began to depict Cecilia as seated at one of these marvelous new instruments. It makes a lovely scene, and to this day she is almost always pictured playing the organ and singing.

During a wave of anti-Christian persecution, Cecilia was martyred in her own home. Travelers to Rome can still see the house: It is intact beneath the Basilica of St. Cecilia in the part of town called Trastevere.

Originally Cecilia was buried in the catacomb of St. Callixtus on the Appian Way. In the ninth century, the bodies of St. Cecilia; her husband, St. Valerian; his brother St. Tiburtius; and their prison guard St. Maximus were moved to a new basilica the pope had built over Cecilia's house. The relics of the four saints lie in the crypt beneath the high altar.

Inspired by St. Cecilia's legend, great composers including Handel, Purcell, and Britten have written music for her feast day. Typically on that day classical music stations play one or all of these odes to the patron of music.

See holy card, page 264

ST. RAYMOND NONNATUS

1204–1240 • FEAST DAY: AUGUST 31

St. Raymond's mother died trying to give birth to him. He was saved because, at the last moment, the midwives performed a caesarian section—hence his surname, Nonnatus, Latin for "not born." Because his life was saved just as he was trying to enter the world, Raymond is the patron saint of newborns, midwives, and obstetricians.

Raymond was born into the Spanish nobility at a time when Spain's Christians were fighting to drive out the Moors who had conquered the country five hundred years earlier. As a member of the upper class, he could have become a knight; instead Raymond entered the Mercedarians, a new religious order dedicated to ransoming Christian prisoners and slaves held by the Moors in North Africa. With a large sum of money he traveled to Algeria, where he bought the freedom of as many Christians as he could. Once the money ran out, he offered himself as a hostage if the Moors would set even more Christians free.

The Moors accepted this arrangement but locked Raymond in prison, where he was beaten, tortured, and, when it was discovered he had converted some of the prison guards, sentenced to be impaled. Raymond's life was saved by his jailers, who reminded the governor that the priest was well connected in Spain and would command a large ransom. A story, probably legendary, says that to punish Raymond for converting Muslims to Christianity, the governor of Algeria had his lips pierced, the wounds cauterized with a hot iron, and his mouth fastened shut with a padlock.

After eight months in the dungeon, the ransom arrived and the Moors set Raymond free.

In recognition of all he suffered in Algeria, Pope Gregory IX made Raymond a cardinal. Raymond accepted the honor but continued to live as an ordinary priest, dying suddenly at age thirty-six.

See holy card, page 281

ST. RAPHAEL THE ARCHANGEL

FEAST DAY: SEPTEMBER 29

The Bible says there are seven archangels, but it names only three: Saints Michael, Gabriel, and Raphael.

Raphael's one and only appearance in sacred scripture is found in the Old Testament Book of Tobit, which tells how the archangel assumed human form to serve as the protector of Tobias, a young man whose father had sent him on a dangerous mission. One of the most memorable episodes tells of Tobias's visit to his relatives Raguel, his wife, Edna, and their daughter Sarah.

Sarah was being plagued by a demon named Asmodeus. Every time she married, the demon killed the bridegroom on the wedding night. Seven times Sarah had married, and each time she was widowed by morning. So Raphael suggested that Tobias marry Sarah. Understandably, the young man balked at the idea, but the archangel promised that if the couple delayed consummating their marriage and spent their first three nights together praying, Asmodeus's hold over Sarah would be broken.

Placing their trust in Raphael, Tobias and Sarah married and for three nights prayed to God for a long and happy life together, then they went to sleep. When Sarah's family found Tobias alive the next morning, they rejoiced and invited their neighbors to a wedding banquet that lasted two weeks. Sarah's living nightmare was over, thanks to St. Raphael.

When Raphael finally revealed his true identity, Tobias and his family were terrified. "Do not be afraid," the archangel said, "You will be safe. But praise God forever."

See holy card, page 281

ST. CAMILLUS DE LELLIS

1550–1614 • FEAST DAY: JULY 14

Camillus de Lellis must have made an intimidating nurse. Six-feet-six-inches tall and powerfully built, a man who had been a soldier and a compulsive gambler, he didn't look like the nurturing type. Yet the patron of nurses revolutionized health care in sixteenth-century Italy. His hospitals were scrupulously clean, the hospital kitchen served healthy meals, and the nursing staff were trained medical professionals.

Camillus had learned about hospital mismanagement while working odd jobs in the wards of San Giacomo Hospital in Rome. San Giacomo was typical: The food was foul; hygiene was virtually nonexistent; and patients with contagious diseases were placed beside those with simple injuries—an arrangement that led to soaring mortality rates. Camillus felt he could do better. More to the point, the city desperately needed more hospitals, especially for those unable to afford medical care.

He began by renting a house in a bad part of town and turning it into a tiny hospital, where the poor were treated free of charge. In his burgeoning establishment, Camillus put into practice his novel ideas about medical care. The wards were well ventilated, patients received healthy meals, and contagious patients were quarantined. As Camillus's reputation for charity, sanctity, and common sense spread, other men volunteered to help. They formed a new religious order of priests and brothers dedicated to treating the poor. In 1930 Pope Pius XI formally named St. Camillus de Lellis the patron of nurses.

See holy card, page 281

ST. JEROME EMILIANI

1481–1537 • FEAST DAY: FEBRUARY 8

Like St. Francis of Assisi, St. Jerome decided on religious life after a stint in a dungeon. In a war against the Venetians, Jerome had been commanding one of the fortresses of Treviso. When the Venetians overran the castle, they captured him and chained him in a cell. He was thirty years old.

In his despair, Jerome turned to the Blessed Virgin Mary, who broke the chains that bound him to the prison wall and helped him escape. Back in Treviso, as a sign of the miracle wrought by Our Lady, Jerome hung his chains in the town's main church.

It took another seven years for Jerome to decide that he wanted to become a priest. He had just been ordained when a simultaneous epidemic and famine struck northern Italy. He nursed the sick, fed the hungry, and buried the dead, but he found his true vocation among the hordes of orphaned children who roamed the streets and country roads. Jerome rented large houses for the orphans, depleting his own fortune to provide them with food and clothes. As the number of orphanages increased, Jerome recruited other priests to help.

Over time, Jerome's work expanded to include a hospital and a shelter for penitent prostitutes. Yet the care of orphaned children remained his focus. In 1928 Pope Pius XI formally proclaimed St. Jerome Emiliani the patron of orphans and abandoned children.

See holy card, page 281

ST. ATHANASIUS

ABOUT 295–373 • FEAST DAY: MAY 2

In 313 the emperor Constantine signed the Edict of Milan, ending anti-Christian persecution in the Roman Empire and allowing Christians to worship freely. Yet within a dozen years, the Church was torn apart by a doctrinal crisis that would last more than a century.

Arius, an Egyptian priest, denied the Church's understanding of the Holy Trinity. In his mind, God the Son was not equal to God the Father, he was not eternal, he was not even the Son of God. Arius imagined that Christ had been fashioned out of nothing by God and was a creature on par with Adam. At a Church council in Nicea, in present-day Turkey, the bishops condemned Arius's teaching as heretical and wrote the Nicene Creed as a clear statement of what the Church believes about the Holy Trinity.

But the Arian heresy continued to spread, thanks to the encouragement of several sympathetic emperors who succeeded Constantine. Arius's greatest opponent was Athanasius, patriarch of Alexandria. Unlike other bishops who, out of fear of the emperor, waffled on the Arian subject, Athanasius boldly defended orthodoxy. For his outspokenness, the Arians and their supporters in the imperial government drove Athanasius out of Alexandria five times. He was not the only orthodox bishop who suffered persecution—the Arian emperor Constantius exiled Pope Liberius and installed an anti-pope in Rome, and the emperor Theodosius came within a heartbeat of massacring St. Ambrose and his congregation inside the cathedral of Milan. But Athanasius stood at the forefront of the fight. Both the Catholic and the Orthodox churches honor St. Athanasius, and, on his feast day, congregants sing a hymn praising the saint as the "pillar of orthodoxy [who] refuted the heretical nonsense of Arius."

See holy card, page 282

ST. ALEXIUS

DIED ABOUT 417 • FEAST DAY: JULY 17

This legend begins in ancient Rome with Alexius, a young man who was anything but a panhandler. Alexius was the son of a wealthy senator. He had a promising future, plenty of friends, and a beautiful fiancée. But on his wedding day, minutes after sitting down at the banquet table with his new bride, Alexius inexplicably yanked off his wedding ring and fled. He ran to the harbor and boarded a ship to Syria.

Upon arriving in the city of Edessa, Alexius joined the throng of beggars who huddled around the doors of the Church of Our Lady. For seventeen years, he begged outside the church, living on the scraps and castoffs of others. But, when the sacristan of the church recognized him as the missing son of a Roman senator, Alexius ran away again. This time unfavorable winds drove his ship off course, and Alexius landed, of all places, back in Rome.

His mother and father were still alive, and so was the bride he had abandoned. But seventeen years of rough living had so altered Alexius's appearance that even his own father didn't recognize him. When he begged to be allowed to live under the front steps of his parents' house, the senator gave his permission, on one condition: that every day the beggar would pray to God to bring home the family's long-lost son.

Every day for another seventeen years Alexius begged in the streets of Rome, sharing any coins or scraps of food with less fortunate panhandlers. Every night he returned to his old home and crawled under the stairs to sleep. His wife and parents never suspected his true identity.

One day Pope Innocent I was saying Mass for the emperor when he heard a voice from heaven say, "Seek the man of God. Through his prayers God will favor Rome and you." Then the voice said that the "man of God" would be found under the stairs of a senator's house. After Mass, the pope, the emperor, and their entourages went to the senator's house. The astonished family came out to meet their distinguished visitors, and then everyone peered under the staircase. There lay the beggar, dressed in his rags, dead. But in his hands he held a document that revealed his true identity and explained how he had lived for the past thirty-four years.

Pope Innocent proclaimed Alexius a saint, and the staircase from the senator's house was carried away as a relic. Part of it is still displayed in the Church of Sant'Alessio all'Aventino in Rome.

See holy card, page 282

ST. MICHAEL THE ARCHANGEL

FEAST DAYS: SEPTEMBER 29 AND MAY 8

There is, of course, the obvious visual link between paratroopers and angels, both of whom descend from the heavens to earth. But St. Michael the Archangel's patronage of paratroopers goes beyond that. First, he is a warrior angel, the captain of the good angels who drove Lucifer and the rebel angels out of heaven. Second, he is the valiant defender of the Church and of all faithful Christians.

One of the oldest shrines to St. Michael was dedicated about the year 500 on Monte Gargano in southern Italy. Legend says that on May 8, 663, the Christians of the region around the shrine were invaded by a large army of pagans. The bishop called for a three-day fast, with continuous prayers to St. Michael to come to their aid. In a vision, St. Michael promised the bishop that on the fourth day he would grant victory to the Christians.

When the three days of fasting and prayer had ended, the Christian army marched out to face the invaders. Suddenly St. Michael made his presence known in a massive earthquake that shook Monte Gargano. As both armies watched, an immense dark cloud covered the summit. Then bolts of lightning flashed from the cloud, striking down six hundred of the enemy. The survivors fled the battlefield in terror.

That is why paratroopers take as their patron St. Michael, who came down from heaven to rescue the Christians of Monte Gargano.

See holy card, page 282

Parents with Disappointing Children

ST. MATILDA

ABOUT 895–968 • FEAST DAY: MARCH 14

St. Matilda's troubles with her five children began the day her husband, Henry, died. By right, the crown would pass to their eldest son, Otto. But Otto's younger brother Henry wanted to be emperor, and what he could not have legally he tried to take by force. Henry raised an army against his brother, but Otto easily defeated the rebels, captured his little brother, and was trying to decide what to do with him when Matilda intervened, begging for clemency. Otto gave up any plans he may have had to execute Henry, and Henry swore allegiance to Otto.

With peace restored to the family, Matilda did what she loved best—endowing convents and monasteries and building new ones. She spent so lavishly that Otto insisted she stop. Then Henry the troublemaker stepped in again. For once not only did he agree with his brother, but he suggested more drastic action to prevent their mother from squandering any more on monks and nuns: The family should take charge of their mother's finances, including the property she'd inherited from their father. As her sons dispossessed her, Matilda remarked on how nice it was to see them working together at last. Then she packed her bags and went to live at her childhood home in Westphalia.

But worse was to come for Matilda. Henry made another attempt to seize the throne, this time recruiting a team of assassins. Otto survived the plot unharmed and once again treated Henry with forbearance. It was just as well—not long after his final conspiracy failed, Henry died.

As for Matilda, she spent her final years in a Benedictine convent. There, after she had given everything to the poor, including her burial shroud, she died peacefully.

See holy card, page 282

S. GEMMA ✠ GALGANI

372   VLA

S. Justinus Martyr

ST. VERONICA.

S. Germana.

Sancta Germana

S. Germaine. H. Germana.

1. Pharmacists • St. Gemma Galgani   2. Philosophers • St. Justin Martyr
3. Photographers • St. Veronica 4. Physically Unattractive • St. Germaine Cousin

Sant'Antonio Abate

Sancte Jacobe et apostole, ora pro nobis.

Hl. David.
Sieben Mal des Tages sprech ich dein Lob.
Psalm 118, 164.
The royal Psalmist.
Verlag von Carl Mayer in Nürnberg.

SEL. MARGARETHA MAR. ALACOQUE.

O möchte ich ganz Herz sein,
um Dich zu lieben, und ganz Geist,
um Dich anzubeten.

A. Müller, Innsbruck.

1. Pigs • St. Anthony of the Desert   2. Pilgrims • St. James the Greater
3. Poets • St. David the King   4. Polio • St. Margaret Mary Alacoque

Der hl. Odilo, Abt.

Gépeck. 3072.

St Pierre, priez pour nous.

St Caterina di Siena. – St Catalina de Siena.

St. Catharina Senensis.

St. Catherine of Siena. – H. Catharina von Siena.

1. Political Prisoners • St. Maximilian Kolbe   2. Poor Souls in Purgatory • St. Odilo
3. Popes • St. Peter 4. Popes • St. Catherine of Siena

St JEAN CHRYSOSTOME
A CONSTANTINOPLE.

1. Pottery Makers · St. Spiridon 2. Poverty · St. Bernadette Soubirous

Parish Priests

ST. JOHN MARY VIANNEY

1786–1859 • FEAST DAY: AUGUST 4

In France the pastor of a parish is known as the *curé*, meaning "one who cares for souls." The word is especially appropriate for St. John Mary Vianney, who spent decades tending the souls of farmers and shopkeepers in an out-of-the-way village called Ars.

In the seminary, Vianney had not been a brilliant student, but by enormous effort he passed his coursework. The bishop who ordained him, underwhelmed by Vianney's accomplishments, sent him to the backwater of the diocese, a village of fewer than three hundred inhabitants, about forty houses, and four taverns.

A priest had not been in residence in Ars since before the French Revolution. Many years had passed since Mass had been said or confessions heard or the faith taught. Furthermore, the villagers did not want a priest, and they showed their disfavor by pelting the rectory with manure. But Vianney set to work bringing the Church back to Ars—and the people of Ars back to the Church. He began by persuading the villagers to come to Sunday Mass. During the service he preached about the two most common sins in the village, drunkenness and obscene language. To ensure his parishioners knew exactly which cuss words he considered especially foul, Vianney read a list from the pulpit.

Like his parishioners, Vianney worked hard and lived poor. His diet consisted of milk and potatoes. His furniture was basic to the point of being uncomfortable. Villagers who came to early Mass found him already there, praying before the Blessed Sacrament. His constant prayer for forty-one years was, "My God, convert my parish." He developed a reputation as a perceptive and compassionate confessor, one who could touch hearts and turn lives around. Soon he was hearing confessions ten hours every day, with penitents traveling from throughout France and Europe and even a few from America. To his own surprise, he was an effective preacher. Once, when asked to preach at a neighboring parish, he arrived to find a standing-room-only crowd in the church and priests from surrounding towns seated around the altar. The sight of the crowd, all expecting to hear something astonishing, unnerved him. But he summoned his courage, climbed into the pulpit, and began to preach. After the ordeal he told a friend, "Everything went well. Everybody wept."

As word spread of his holiness, humility, and dedication to his parishioners, it appeared that Vianney would convert not only Ars but all France. Crowds came daily to confess to him, ask his advice, hear him preach. Even as he lay dying, the throngs still arrived, and, because he would soon be dead, they became even more demanding. A line of civic dignitaries formed outside his bedroom door awaiting one last confession. People in the street sent in basket after basket of holy medals for Vianney to bless. Even when it was time for the dying man to receive the Last Rites, he had to endure a crowd—twenty-two priests came in a procession to his room. On August 4, 1859, as a violent thunderstorm broke over the village, John Mary Vianney died. In 1929, in recognition of Vianney's tireless devotion to his parishioners, Pope Pius XI named him the patron saint of parish priests.

See holy card,, page 283

ST. JOHN GUALBERT

ABOUT 993–1073 • FEAST DAY: JULY 12

John was the younger son of a proud, wealthy, aristocratic family in Florence. After the murder of his elder brother Hugh, John made it his mission to hunt down and kill the murderer. By chance, on Good Friday, the two men met, face to face, in a narrow dead-end street. There was nowhere for the killer to run. As John drew his sword and stepped forward, the murderer dropped to his knees, flung out his arms, and commended his soul to God. John may not have been the best Catholic in the world, but for a man of the eleventh century it was impossible to ignore the significance of the moment. It was Good Friday, and John was about to take revenge on a man who was frightened, defenseless, and penitent. And, what's more, he had assumed the form of the crucified Christ. That proved to be too much, even for someone as worldly as John Gualbert. He sheathed his sword, forgave the murderer, and then went to the abbey church of San Miniato to thank God for stopping him before he committed such a terrible sin. As he prayed, the crucifix above the altar came to life, and Christ bowed his head in recognition of John's act of mercy.

After several years as a monk, John decided he preferred a more austere life. About twenty miles outside the city, a convent of nuns offered him a large piece of real estate called Vallombrosa. It sounded good, but in fact the gift was not terribly generous. The nuns were unloading a barren wasteland they had been unable to do anything with. But John and his monks improved the property by planting trees until their lands were covered with forest. For this reason, St. John Gualbert has become the patron of park service workers and, by extension, foresters.

See holy card, page 283

Pawnbrokers

ST. NICHOLAS

DIED ABOUT 350 • FEAST DAY: DECEMBER 6

The three gold balls that are the traditional logo of a pawnbroker's shop refer to a story from the life of the pawnbrokers' patron, St. Nicholas.

In Myra, the town in modern-day Turkey where Nicholas was bishop, there lived a widowed merchant and his three daughters. The merchant's business fell on hard times; to support his family, he sold off all their valuables, one by one. At last nothing of any value remained. With no hope of providing his daughters with a dowry and no longer able to feed them, the poor man feared that they would be forced to become prostitutes to support themselves.

About this time, the story of the impoverished family reached St. Nicholas. Late one night he took a bag of gold coins and walked to the merchant's home, where he tossed the treasure-laden sack through an open window. The merchant and his daughters were astonished by the windfall. The same thing happened the next night—another bag of gold coins came sailing through the open window. Finally, on the third night, the family was ready. As the bag flew into the house, they pulled open the front door and rushed outside, where they found Bishop Nicholas. Weeping for joy and gratitude, they kissed the saint's hands. He had given them enough to rebuild the merchant's fortunes and provide dowries for all three daughters.

Originally artists depicted St. Nicholas carrying three bags of coins. Over time, the bags became golden balls. Because the merchant had pawned all his valuables and St. Nicholas had redeemed the family, pawnbrokers took the golden balls as their emblem.

See holy card, page 283

ST. NICHOLAS OF FLUE

1417–1487 • FEAST DAY: MARCH 21

St. Nicholas learned to value peace the hard way. In the fifteenth century, his homeland, Switzerland, was not a unified nation but rather a region of rival cantons (provinces); often this rivalry erupted into open warfare. To make matters worse, France and Austria frequently attempted to seize Swiss territory and expand their borders. Beginning in his late teens and lasting until he was forty-three, Nicholas served in a series of petty wars.

At age twenty-five, he married a devout young woman named Dorothy Wissling. They had ten children—five boys and five girls. As a prosperous farmer, Nicholas provided a good life for his large family. As a religious man of unshakable integrity, he won the admiration of his neighbors. He was named a councilor of his canton and was appointed a magistrate; his reputation for fairness made him the preferred arbitrator in the most difficult local disputes.

Then, after twenty-five years of marriage and public service, Nicholas kissed his wife and children good-bye, bade farewell to his neighbors, and went into the forest to live as a hermit. He tried to live in a hut of his own making, but the local people insisted upon building him a wooden cabin and a stone chapel. The auxiliary bishop of Constance consecrated the chapel and even sent a priest to serve as Nicholas's private chaplain so that he could attend Mass every day.

In 1481 representatives from several Swiss cantons met to try to hammer out a union, but the old enmities and suspicions got in the way. When civil war seemed likely, wiser delegates suggested they call upon Nicholas of Flue to mediate. Within an hour, Nicholas had found a satisfactory solution. Then he returned to his hermitage.

See holy card, page 283

ST. TERESA OF AVILA

1515–1582 • FEAST DAY: OCTOBER 15

At age twenty-one, Teresa entered the Carmelite convent of the Incarnation in her hometown of Avila, Spain. The religious community was not a rigorous one; any visitor was admitted at any reasonable hour, and nuns from well-to-do families brought their servants with them. Teresa had a suite of rooms—a bedroom, private oratory, guest room, and even her own private kitchen. The nuns were decidedly worldly, but they did maintain the routine of daily Mass, the Divine Office, fasts, and confession at least twice a month. Still, contemplative life in the convent did not truly exist.

A few years passed and Teresa came across a book on interior prayer written by a Franciscan priest named Osuna. She dabbled a bit in contemplation but quickly gave up. Then followed a period of spiritual dryness, when all prayer seemed dull and her life lacked God's presence. She felt drawn to resume contemplative prayer, but she resisted. "On the one hand God was calling me," she later recalled, "on the other hand I was following the world." What she needed was God's grace, but she shied away from it. Eventually, however, Teresa surrendered herself to God's will and began to meditate once again. Immediately grace flooded in. She enjoyed an intense renewal of her life of prayer and even began to experience visions.

It is a common story, not only among saints but among ordinary people as well. Every day, all day long, God pours his grace upon the world. Those who accept it, who cooperate with God's will, draw closer to the Lord—as in the case of St. Teresa of Avila, the patron of souls in need of divine grace.

The easy-going life at the convent—with all its pleasures, privileges, and distractions—was not conducive to the contemplative life. So Teresa began planning a new branch of the Carmelites, one that would bring back nuns (and friars) to the order's original commitment to a life of austerity and profound prayer. By the time of her death, she had founded nine reformed Carmelite convents and two reformed priories for Carmelite friars. She met tremendous resistance from both Carmelites who did not want to be reformed and laypeople who did not want their town burdened with the obligation of supporting yet another convent of poor nuns. But Teresa persevered, supported by King Philip II of Spain as well as the superior of all Spanish Carmelites. Her resolve was further strengthened by her own life of prayer and that of her often-unwilling coworker, St. John of the Cross, a man of a genuinely contemplative character who found the quarrels and busyness of day-to-day life irksome.

St. Teresa's legacy is her collection of spiritual writings. She was the first Catholic woman to write systematically about prayer and the interior life. In 1970, upon naming St. Teresa a Doctor of the Church, Pope Paul VI praised her as "a teacher of remarkable depth." She still attracts students today: The twentieth century saw the publication of six hundred editions of her work in every major language.

See holy card, page 284

ST. BENEDICT THE MOOR

1526–1589 • FEAST DAY: APRIL 4

Benedict's parents had been captured in Africa and sold into slavery in Sicily, where a nobleman purchased them to work on his estate outside Messina; that's where Benedict was born. He served as a slave until he was freed by his master at age eighteen. Aside from the miseries of slavery, Benedict endured constant scorn and ridicule—even the poorest of the poor treated him with contempt because they believed themselves better than a formerly enslaved African. Benedict, who had been raised Catholic, tried to bear the mockery like a saint.

His patience caught the attention of the superior of a small band of Franciscan hermits living outside Palermo; he invited Benedict to join them. Perhaps Benedict had already been considering the religious life because, at the hermitage, for the first time he felt completely happy and perfectly at ease. When their superior died, the Franciscans elected Benedict to take his place.

A few years later, in a move to consolidate all of Europe's Franciscan splinter groups, the pope disbanded the Palermo hermits and ordered them to join one of the order's mainstream branches. Benedict joined the Franciscan Observants, surrendering his position as superior to work in the kitchen of his new community. His holiness and talent for administration soon became apparent, however, and he was taken from the kitchen to serve as superior, guardian of the community's property, and master of novices, surprising everyone with his comprehension of complex theological issues.

Devotion to St. Benedict is especially strong in Sicily and South America, and he is venerated as the patron of Africans and of the African missions.

See holy card, page 284

ST. MARY MAGDALENE

FIRST CENTURY • FEAST DAY: JULY 22

There are two classic depictions of Mary Magdalene: one as a penitent with her luxuriant hair cascading over her shoulders, and another in which she is looking serene while holding a beautiful alabaster ointment jar. The jar refers to a story recorded in all four gospels—that of a woman, a notorious sinner bearing such a container of perfumed oil, who arrives unannounced and enters a house where Jesus is a guest. Without saying a word to the host or the apostles or even Christ himself, she breaks open the jar and pours the scented oil over the Lord's head.

In St. Matthew's version of the episode (minor discrepancies exist among the gospel accounts), the apostles complain about the waste, saying that such precious perfume could have been sold for a large sum and the money distributed to the poor. But Christ replies that what the woman has done, she has done out of love for him. Furthermore, this anointing foreshadows his death and burial since, at that time, it was the custom to anoint the dead with expensive perfume as a final, loving tribute.

The gospels don't say that it was Mary Magdalene who performed the anointing. But a long-standing tradition in the West, one that dates back to Pope St. Gregory the Great in the sixth century, insists on the following: that the sinful woman with the jar of ointment, Mary the sister of Martha and Lazarus, and Mary Magdalene were all the same person. In recent years, biblical scholars and those studying the saints have tried to explain that Mary Magdalene and Mary of Bethany and the woman with the jar were three separate individuals. But the scholars have an uphill struggle, what with fifteen hundred years of tradition and all the visual arts working against them. Of course, if they ever do make their case, perfume makers will have to find a new patron saint.

See holy card, page 284

ST. JOAN OF ARC

1412–1431 • FEAST DAY: MAY 30

Twice St. Ignatius Loyola was imprisoned by the Inquisition. St. John of the Cross was jailed, flogged, and starved by his Carmelite brothers. St. Mary McKillop was excommunicated by her bishop. But the case of St. Joan of Arc is unique: Never before or since has a saint been put to death through the connivance of men who claimed to represent the Catholic Church.

"Claimed" is the operative word because the bishops and priests who brought about Joan's death were acting independently. Their primary loyalty was to their English overlords, not to the pope. That was especially true of the presiding judge, Bishop Pierre Cauchon, an unscrupulous man who harbored a personal grudge against Joan. Self-interest made him a willing collaborator with the English and their Burgundian allies, and his reward had been a comfortable life as bishop of Beauvais. All that came to end when the French, commanded by Joan, captured Beauvais, forcing

Cauchon to flee. The man accustomed to living like a prince now survived as a refugee, dependent on the charity of strangers. He could scarcely believe his good luck when Joan, whom he blamed for his galling situation, was sent to him for trial.

Cauchon was determined to put on a good show. He assembled 5 bishops, 3 abbots, 7 physicians, 48 doctors of theology, 42 doctors of canon and civil law, and 55 priests, lay brothers, and clerics. Joan had no lawyer, she was not permitted to call witnesses to testify on her behalf, nor could she receive counsel from churchmen on the difficult points of law and theology brought up during her trial. Those who tried to assist her were silenced or driven out of the courtroom.

When Jean Lefevre, a doctor of theology, objected to one of the questions put to Joan, Cauchon ordered him to "be silent in the Devil's name!" Jean de la Fontaine, a canon lawyer, was forced to flee Rouen after giving her legal advice. And when Father Isambart de la Pierre began explaining to her the process of filing an appeal, the Englishmen in the room closed in around him and threatened to throw the poor man into the Seine River if he didn't keep his mouth shut.

No one doubted what the court's verdict would be: The judges condemned Joan as a witch, a heretic, and an idolater. On May 30, 1431, Cauchon turned her over to the secular authorities, who burned her in the marketplace of Rouen.

But that was not the end of the story. Joan's mother, Isabelle, and her brothers Pierre and Jean appealed to Pope Callixtus III to revisit the case. Normally the trial of a peasant would not have attracted the pope's attention, but Joan's case appeared so troubling that Callixtus authorized an investigation. For nine months, a team of papal commissioners studied the transcript and heard testimony from Joan's relatives and neighbors, her comrades in arms, and even her enemies. When the commissioners reached a decision, they traveled to the site of Joan's execution. There they announced that Joan's trial had been "tainted by fraud, calumny, iniquity, contradiction, and manifest errors of fact and of law." They set aside the verdict and declared that Joan had been free from "any taint of infamy." She was completely exonerated, but a greater honor was to come. In 1920 Pope Benedict XV declared Joan to be a saint of the Catholic Church.

See holy card, page 284

ST. GEMMA GALGANI

1878–1903 • FEAST DAY: APRIL 11

St. Gemma's father was a pharmacist, but she never practiced the trade. Usually a profession's patron saint followed that line of work; in this case, Italian pharmacists likely chose her as their patron because she's such a popular saint in Italy.

There's no doubt about Gemma's sanctity or her heroic patience and courage in the face of a dreadful disease, tuberculosis of the spine. It is the supernatural side of her life that has caused the greatest debate. Some people who knew Gemma said that she bore the stigmata—that her hands and feet were wounded as Christ's had been by the nails that pinned him to the cross. Sometimes her body appeared to bear whip marks. If she heard someone curse using the name of God or Jesus Christ, she would sweat blood. It is said that she saw her guardian angel daily and that in religious ecstasies she conversed with saints.

Gemma's spiritual director be-lieved these phenomena to be real, that God had granted them to her so the world would recognize her holiness and his glory. Gemma's confessor, on the other hand, was reluctant to attribute everything to the miraculous. He wouldn't rule out the power of the imagination, and he wondered if there were other causes that perhaps medical science did not yet understand. Although the stigmata and visions have made St. Gemma an object of devotion, when the Vatican declared her Blessed in 1933, the document clearly stated that the Church was beatifying her based on the holiness of her life and that it would not rule on the strange phenomena.

See holy card, page 301

ST. JUSTIN MARTYR

ABOUT 100–165 • FEAST DAY: JUNE 1

St. Justin trained in all the major schools of pagan Greek philosophy, from the Stoics to Pythagoras to Plato, none of which satisfied his intellectual and spiritual quest for the truth. He was about thirty years old when a chance encounter with an elderly Christian man introduced him to the faith. As Justin put it, when the old man explained the Hebrew prophets and gospels, "I discovered that his was the only sure and useful philosophy." After his baptism, Justin opened in Ephesus the first Christian school of philosophy, where, in public debates, he defended the faith against Jews, Gnostics, and Roman pagans.

In ad 150, Justin moved his school to Rome, and there, drawing on the Greco-Roman philosophical tradition, he wrote a series of books—the first scholarly defenses of the Christian faith. Addressing well-educated Roman pagans, he explained that, just as the Hebrew prophets predicted the coming of the Messiah to the Jews, Socrates and Plato laid the intellectual groundwork that would make the teachings of Christ comprehensible and rational to the Greeks and Romans.

All this writing and debating made Justin a conspicuous target when the emperor Marcus Aurelius renewed the persecution of the Church. Justin was arrested with six of his students and hauled before the prefect. Incredibly, the transcript survives from their brief trial. When the prefect commanded them all to sacrifice to the gods, Justin, acting as spokesman, replied, "No one in his right mind gives up piety for impiety." For their obstinacy, Justin and his disciples were condemned to be flogged and beheaded.

See holy card, page 301

ST. VERONICA

FIRST CENTURY • FEAST DAY: JULY 12

Perhaps the most beloved, and certainly the most memorable, scene in the Catholic devotion known as the Stations of the Cross depicts St. Veronica stepping out of the crowd to wipe blood, sweat, and spittle from the face of Jesus. As a reward for her compassion, Christ left on her veil or cloth a perfect image of his face. This story is the origin of St. Veronica as the patron of photographers.

It is a wonderful story, yet none of the gospel accounts of Christ's sad journey to Calvary mention Veronica or any woman wiping the Lord's face. St. Veronica's name doesn't appear in the ancient martyrologies (the early lists of martyrs). Yet, as is the case with the best legends, her popularity endures despite the lack of evidence.

As for the relic known as Veronica's Veil, two churches claim it: St. Peter's Basilica in Rome and the Capuchin monastery of Monoppello, located in Italy's Apennine Mountains. In 2006 Pope Benedict XVI visited Monoppello and prayed before the Holy Veil, but he didn't comment on the relic's authenticity.

Medieval storytellers tried to fill in the details of St. Veronica's life. One story says that she was the unnamed woman healed of a hemorrhage after touching Christ's robe. Another relates that she brought her miraculous image of Christ to Rome, used it to cure the emperor Tiberius, and on her death bequeathed it to the popes. The most colorful story is set in France, where she was the supposed wife of Zacchaeus, the little man who climbed a sycamore tree so that he could see Jesus passing by.

See holy card, page 301

ST. GERMAINE COUSIN

ABOUT 1579–1601 • FEAST DAY: JUNE 15

Has there ever been a person completely content with his or her looks? Probably not. We know that our Stone Age ancestors applied cosmetics and styled their hair with some type of primeval goop, likely for reasons similar to our own: to look better than nature made us.

Those of us who are never satisfied with our appearance might want to invoke St. Germaine Cousin. The poor girl came into the world with a withered right arm and a disfiguring skin condition; later she developed a form of tuberculosis that caused unsightly swellings on her neck. Her father, Laurent, couldn't bear the sight of her. We don't know much about Germaine's mother, Marie Laroche, for she died soon after her daughter was born.

Laurent remarried, choosing a woman who apparently didn't know the meaning of the word *compassion*. Appalled by Germaine's looks, the new wife became the classic wicked stepmother. She would not let Germaine eat with the family and forbade

her from going near her stepbrothers and stepsisters lest they become infected. She tossed a straw pallet under the stairs and told Germaine to sleep there. If her stepmother were in an especially foul humor, Germaine would be driven out of the house to spend the night in the barn.

While Germaine was still a girl, her father put her to work tending the family's sheep. Alone in the fields, she conversed constantly with God. She began attending Mass each morning and prayed the rosary many times throughout the day. Her genuine piety, coupled with her meekness in the face of cruelty, won over her neighbors, who sympathized with the abused girl. But Germaine's family remained as coldhearted as ever.

Then the villagers began telling strange stories about Germaine. They noticed that, although she left her sheep unattended while she went to Mass, the animals never wandered off or were attacked by wolves. Once, after a heavy rain, the stream separating Germaine's field from the church flooded. Some said that Germaine arrived at Mass on time by walking across the water; others said the torrent parted for her just as the Red Sea had for Moses.

Whether prompted by these reports of miracles or the pangs of his own conscience, Laurent Cousin finally repented of neglecting his daughter. He offered her a real bed in the house and a place at the family's table. She declined. Years of abuse may have made her suspicious of these unexpected acts of kindness, or perhaps she felt self-conscious about joining a family who had never wanted her. Whatever her reasons, Germaine kept to her routine of tending sheep and sleeping under the stairs. One morning she didn't get up at her usual time, and Laurent found her dead on her pallet. She was twenty-two years old.

A fervent local cult grew around her tomb. Today Pibrac, St. Germaine's hometown, welcomes an annual pilgrimage in her honor. Visitors line up to enter the Cousin house and pray at the crawlspace where the saint lived and died.

See holy card, page 301

SAN GERARDO MAIELLA
della Congregazione del SS. Redentore

SANT'IPPOLITO MARTIRE
PREGATE PER NOI

Den Frieden
hinterlasse
ich euch,
meinen
Frieden
gebe ich
euch,
nicht wie
ihn die
Welt gibt,
gebe ich
ihn euch.

Joh. 14 27.

S. Leonhardus

1. Pregnancy • St. Gerard Majella   2. Prison Guards and Jailers • St. Hippolytus of Rome
3. Prisoners • St. Leonard of Noblac   4. Prisoners • The Holy Child of Atocha

321

268

Sancta·Christina·Mirabilis
Virgo·de·Sancto·Trudone.

3.

St. Paulus.

1. Procrastination · St. Expeditus 2. Psychiatrists and Psychologists · St. Christina the Astonishing
3. Public Relations Professionals · St. Paul the Apostle

Św. Jadwiga

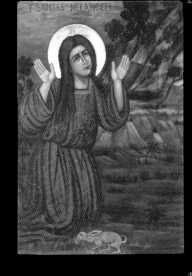

Y SANTES MELANGELL

Sanctus Dionysius

S. MARTIN DE PORRES O.P.
(1579-1639)

1. Queens • St. Hedwig   2. Rabbits • St. Melangell
3. Rabies • St. Denis   4. Racial Discrimination • St. Martin de Porres

S. SWITHIN. B.C.

Verein der christl. Familien.

(Answeiset, empfohlen und mit Ablässen versehen von Papst Leo XIII. Déposé. am 14. und 20. Juni 1892.) No. 4586.

SCÈNES DE LA VIE MONASTIQUE

St BAZILE
ET St GRÉGOIRE DE NAZIANZE
A ATHÈNES

ÉDITION DE LA TRAPPE DE N-D à AIGUEBELLE (Drôme)

1. Rain • St. Swithun 2. Ransom • St. John of Matha

ST. ANTHONY OF THE DESERT

251–356 • FEAST DAY: JANUARY 17

St. Anthony's connection with pigs is complicated. During the Middle Ages, Christians believed that prayer to him was especially effective in clearing up rashes and other skin inflammations. The precise reason is unknown, since nothing in St. Anthony's story links him with rashes. But then nothing in the story of the apostle St. Jude explains why he should be the saint of impossible cases. Some saints just develop a reputation for solving certain types of problems. Since pork fat was a common medieval folk remedy for skin rashes, the pig became St. Anthony's emblem.

Anthony was the son of a wealthy Egyptian family. When his parents died, he inherited a fortune, which he gave away to the poor, and then went into the desert west of Alexandria to live as a hermit. St. Athanasius, Anthony's contemporary and the author of his biography, says that the devil tried to break Anthony's resolve by tempting him with the pleasures of indolence, fine food and wine, and beautiful women. Through intense prayer, Anthony resisted all these temptations, at which point the devil attacked him, beating him unconscious.

Anthony returned to civilization on rare occasions—once to comfort the martyrs during a period of anti-Christian persecution and later to refute publicly the heresy of Arius. In the last decades of his life, he accepted disciples and organized them into a religious community over which he presided as abbot. He remained with his monks in the desert until one day, in 356, he laid down on the ground and died. He was 105 years old.

See holy card, page 302

ST. JAMES THE GREATER

DIED 44 • FEAST DAY: JULY 25

Jerusalem. Rome. Compostela. During the Middle Ages, these three sites were the most important pilgrimage destinations. The shrine of Compostela, which lies in northwestern Spain, is believed to be built over the tomb of St. James the Greater, one of the twelve apostles and the brother of St. John the Evangelist. According to tradition, St. James preached in Spain before returning to Judea, where King Herod had him executed (James's martyrdom is recorded in the Acts of the Apostles). The legend goes on to say that his body was miraculously transported to Spain, lost for centuries, and then rediscovered in the ninth century by a shepherd who saw a brilliant star shining over a field (*Compostela* means "field of the star"). Beneath the star was found the grave of St. James.

The authenticity of the relics at Compostela remains the subject of debate, despite the official endorsement of Pope Leo XIII in 1884. Nonetheless, during the last twelve hundred years, millions of pilgrims have ignored or suppressed such doubts and made the long journey to Santiago.

According to one of many legends, when St. James's relics returned to Spain by ship, a Christian, in his enthusiasm, rode his horse into the sea to swim out to the boat. Both horse and rider sank beneath the waves. The crowd on shore assumed they had drowned, but, by the intercession of St. James, the man and his horse reappeared and cantered onto the beach, dripping wet and covered with scallops. Ever since, the scallop shell has been the badge of pilgrims to Compostela.

In art, St. James is often depicted as a pilgrim carrying a staff and a bottle of water and dressed in heavy walking boots, a cloak, and a large hat with a scallop shell pinned to the floppy brim.

See holy card, page 302

ST. DAVID THE KING

ABOUT 1085–ABOUT 1015 BC • FEAST DAY: DECEMBER 29

At the heart of the Church's prayer life lie the Psalms. These sacred poems enrich Mass as well as the daily prayers of priests and nuns, known as the Divine Office, and they've inspired countless hymns. Tradition says that David, the shepherd boy who defeated Goliath and became king of Israel, wrote all 150 of them. Although that's probably an exaggeration, he did write some, including almost certainly Psalm 23, "The Lord is my shepherd." For that one alone he deserves to be patron of poets.

It may seem odd to honor as a saint a person from the Old Testament, since a saint is a person who tries to imitate Christ—and the holy men and women of the "old" part of the Bible lived before Jesus's lifetime. Nonetheless, devotion to a handful of Old Testament figures sprang up in the West, notably Abraham, David, Elijah the prophet, and the seven martyred Maccabee brothers. In the East, the custom is much more common and includes Adam and Eve, whose feast day is Christmas Eve.

The Bible tells us that, throughout his life, David loved music and poetry. As a teenage boy, he played his harp and sang to comfort the gloomy, erratic King Saul. Later as king himself, he moved the Ark of the Covenant to Jerusalem, where he founded twenty-four different choirs to sing at the daily sacrifices and other religious services. David was also a prophet, for some of his psalms foretell the coming of the Messiah, particularly the crucifixion: "They have pierced my hands and feet . . . they stare and gloat over me; they divide my garments among them, and for my raiment they cast lots" (Psalm 22:16–18).

See holy card, page 302

ST. MARGARET MARY ALACOQUE

1647–1690 • FEAST DAY: OCTOBER 17

At age nine, Margaret Mary Alacoque contracted polio. She spent the next six years as an invalid, confined to her bed. When she was fifteen, she had a vision of the Blessed Virgin, and, upon emerging from her ecstasy, she found that she'd been healed.

During her years alone in her room, Margaret Mary developed a deep prayer life. So when she joined the Visitation nuns, she found the form of meditation prescribed for the novices rudimentary to the point of being tedious. Yet she remained with the nuns and took her final vows.

In 1675, as she was praying before the altar in the convent chapel, Christ appeared to her. He wanted her to be his messenger, spreading throughout the world the devotion to his Sacred Heart that, he told Margaret Mary, is "burning with divine love" for all humankind. Christ asked that the Church institute a new feast day in honor of his Sacred Heart and that, for love of him, Catholics should attend Mass and receive Communion on the First Friday of each month. He promised to save all faithful Catholics who honored him by either displaying an image of his Sacred Heart in their homes or going to Mass and Communion every first Friday of the month for nine successive months.

Margaret Mary had trouble as soon as she revealed her visions. Nuns accused her of lying, and members of the clergy rejected her visions, saying the Sacred Heart devotion went too far in humanizing Christ and thus diminished his divinity. But the Jesuits, especially Father Claude de la Colombiere, the convent's chaplain, argued successfully that Margaret Mary's revelations put fresh emphasis on the perfectly orthodox principle of confidence in God's infinite love. Today veneration of the Sacred Heart of Jesus is a standard part of Catholic devotional life.

See holy card, page 302

ST. MAXIMILIAN KOLBE

1894–1941 • FEAST DAY: AUGUST 14

On the eve of the Nazi invasion of Poland, Adolf Hitler instructed the Wehrmacht, "Kill without pity or mercy all men, women, and children of Polish descent or language. . . . Be brutal. It is necessary to proceed with maximum severity. The war is to be a war of annihilation." Obedient to their Führer, between 1939 and 1945 the Nazis killed more than six million Poles—22 percent of the population—of whom approximately four million were Christians.

After Poland surrendered, new instructions came from Heinrich Himmler: "Shoot thousands of leading Poles." With ruthless efficiency, his soldiers rounded up and murdered thousands of Poland's attorneys, medical personnel, professors, and clergy. Among those arrested was Father Maximilian Kolbe, a Franciscan superior of 760 priests and brothers, the founder of an international Catholic religious movement, and the editor in chief of one of the country's largest publishing companies. As if he were not already enough of a target, Kolbe had opened his extensive religious-and-publishing complex to shelter fifteen hundred Jews. The Nazis seized Kolbe, along with the terrified Jewish men, women, and children he had been hiding, and sent them all to Auschwitz.

In the death camp, Kolbe was assigned to slave labor. At night, in violation of camp regulations, he heard the confessions of Catholic prisoners and led small groups of inmates in prayer. He worked especially hard with men who, because of the brutality of the Nazi occupation and the horrors of Auschwitz, no longer believed in God.

Late in July 1941, a man escaped from Kolbe's barracks. Karl Fritsch, the adjutant to Auschwitz's commandant, chose at random ten of Kolbe's barracks mates for special punishment: starvation in the camp's Punishment Bunker 11. One of the doomed men, a Polish army sergeant named Francis Gajowniczek, exclaimed, "My wife! My poor children! I will never see them again."

As Fritsch began to walk away, Kolbe appealed to him, "Please, I want to take the place of that man." He pointed to Gajowniczek.

"Why?" Fritsch asked. "Who are you?"

"I am a Catholic priest," Kolbe replied. "I am sick. I can barely work. This man is young and strong and he has a family. I would like to die in his place."

"Accepted," Fritsch said.

Gajowniczek returned to the line of prisoners, and Kolbe joined the condemned men. They were all stripped naked, marched across the camp, and then locked together in the bunker. As the sentence demanded, they received no food or water. On August 14, a Nazi guard entered the cell and gave Kolbe and the four surviving prisoners a lethal injection of phenol. Their bodies were burned, and the ashes dumped in an open burial pit.

Gajowniczek survived the war, as did his wife, and he later tracked down members of Kolbe's community to tell them what their founder had done for him. When the Church began investigating Father Kolbe's life, Gajowniczek's testimony was key.

In 1982 he traveled to Rome, where, from a prime location, he watched as the Polish pope, John Paul II, declared Maximilian Mary Kolbe a saint.

Francis Gajowniczek died in Poland on March 13, 1995. St. Kolbe had given him an additional fifty-four years on earth.

See holy card, page 303

ST. ODILO

ABOUT 962–1049 • FEAST DAY: JANUARY 1

Prayers for the dead are as old as the Church, and probably as old as humanity itself. In Europe's catacombs, tombstones of the earliest Christians beg passersby to pray for the souls of those buried there. But the custom of a feast day devoted to prayers for the dead was late in coming. It began in 998 when St. Odilo, the abbot of Cluny in France, was inspired to dedicate a day in honor of departed souls. For this commemoration, he chose November 2, the day after the feast of All Saints. Odilo's logic was faultless: After honoring all the souls in heaven, it makes perfect sense to pray for all the souls still detained in purgatory.

Originally Odilo introduced the custom as a day when the monks of Cluny would pray for the deceased members of their order. Within a few years, the idea caught on in other parts of Europe. It was expanded to become a day commemorating all the faithful departed, in both public and private prayers.

Odilo was also responsible for conceiving the "Peace of God." The eleventh century was an especially violent era, when bloody-minded barons thought nothing of assembling a private army to avenge some slight or advance their own interests. To allow hot tempers to cool (and give innocent civilians a break from almost perpetual war), Odilo argued that no wars should be waged during the seasons of Advent and Christmas and Lent and Easter. He also requested that churches be a sanctuary for anyone seeking protection. Odilo's peace plan was not observed universally, but enough barons adopted it to make it modestly effective.

St. Odilo was revered in Cluny until the French Revolution, when revolutionaries scattered the monks, looted the abbey, and burned the saint's relics.

See holy card, page 303

331

ST. PETER &
ST. CATHERINE OF SIENA

DIED ABOUT 67 • FEAST DAYS: JUNE 29, FEBRUARY 22
1347–1380 • FEAST DAY: APRIL 29

Rome is the city of the popes because it was there that the apostle St. Peter—the first pope—taught the gospel and was martyred during Nero's persecution of the Christians. In St. Matthew's gospel Christ says, "You are Peter, and upon this rock I will build my church, and the gates of Hell shall not prevail against it. I will give to you the keys of the kingdom of heaven. And whatever you bind on earth shall be bound in heaven and whatever you loose on earth shall be loosed in heaven" (Matthew 16:18–19).

Aside from the gospels, the oldest document suggesting that St. Peter's successors exercised authority over the churches is St. Clement I's *Letter to the Corinthians*, written about the year 95. Clement wrote to heal dissensions that had divided the Christians of Corinth into rancorous camps. The fact that it is Clement who steps in suggests that his author-

ity was recognized by Christians outside Rome. Furthermore, we know that the letter was revered by subsequent generations of Christians—seventy years later, St. Dionysius, Bishop of Corinth, reports that the Christians of Corinth read it at Mass.

St. Clement's letter is just one example of the preeminence the Church of Rome enjoyed among the other churches. As St. Gregory of Nazianzen, the great Greek bishop, theologian, and preacher, observed in the fourth century: "Regarding the faith . . . Rome has kept a straight course from of old, and still does so, uniting the whole West by sound teaching, as is just, since she presides over all and guards the universal divine harmony."

The second patron of the popes is St. Catherine of Siena, the twenty-fourth of twenty-five children of a prosperous wool-dyer's family. A mystic who lived as a nun without ever formally entering a convent, Catherine was a fearless champion of all that was right, good, and true. She felt no qualms about correcting nobles, kings, and even the pope himself. Her life's goal was to see the pope return to Rome.

That may seem like an odd ambition, but by Catherine's day it had been decades since a pope had lived in Rome. In 1309 Pope Clement V, at the invitation of the king of France, took up residence in Avignon, in the south of France. Given the political upheavals in Italy at the time, the temporary relocation of the papacy seemed judicious. But sixty-three years and six popes later, the papacy was still in Avignon, and it was firmly under the influence of the French king.

Meanwhile Rome had become dilapidated and depopulated, and the independency of the papacy was compromised by its intimate relationship with the kings of France. The way St. Catherine saw it, the only solution was for the pope to return to Rome, where he could revitalize the city that was the heart of the Church and act free from the interference of the meddling French. In the summer of 1376, twenty-nine-year-old Catherine traveled to Avignon to convince Pope Gregory XI it was time to come home. Gregory wanted to go, but he was hesitant—his advisers frightened him with tales of cutthroats and poisoners who would lie in wait for him along his way to Rome. Catherine had to put tact aside and address the Holy Father in forceful terms.

"Courage, Father," she said, "be a man! I say to you that you have nothing to fear. But if you neglect to do your duty, then indeed you have cause to fear. It is your duty to come to Rome; therefore, come."

See holy cards, page 303

ST. SPIRIDON

270–344 • FEAST DAY: DECEMBER 12

A debate between St. Spiridon and a pagan Greek philosopher led to the former becoming the patron of pottery makers. The philosopher was willing to concede that some aspects of Christianity were rational, but the doctrine of the Trinity struck him as lunacy. Seeing a fragment of broken pottery at his feet, St. Spiridon picked it up and used it as an illustration. When the three elements of clay, water, and fire come together, Spiridon said, the pottery maker creates a pot in the same way that the unity of the Father, Son, and Holy Spirit make up the Trinity.

Spiridon supported his wife and daughter by working as a shepherd on the island of Cyprus. Legend says that one night robbers entered the pen to steal some of the family's sheep, but the power of God immobilized them. When Spiridon came out the next morning, the robbers were still there, motionless as statues. Spiridon prayed for God to be merciful, and the men were released.

Before they slunk off, the shepherd gave them a ram—payment, he said, for having stood watch over his flock all night.

During Diocletian's persecution, Spiridon was arrested and sentenced to slavery in the mines in Spain. Before he left, the torturers put out his right eye and then hamstrung him. After the emperor Constantine legalized Christianity throughout the Roman Empire, Spiridon was released. Back home in Cyprus, Spiridon decided to become a monk, and his wife and daughter took vows as nuns. Yet even after becoming bishop, he still tended a small flock of sheep.

St. Spiridon's mummified body is enshrined in a small church on Corfu, where devotion to him is so strong that the overwhelming number of male children born on the island are baptized with the name Spiridon.

See holy card, page 304

ST. BERNADETTE SOUBIROUS

1844–1879 • FEAST DAY: APRIL 16

At her birth, Bernadette joined a family of comfortable means. Her mother, Louise Casterot, and father, François Soubirous, had taken over her grandfather's mill, a business that had always generated a tidy income for the Casterots. But Bernadette's parents had no head for business. They extended credit to the most unreliable characters, wasted time and money sitting around drinking wine with customers, and were slipshod about keeping the mill clean and operating efficiently. As the paying customers stayed away, the family's income dried up. They lost the mill. Then followed a depressing downward spiral: François could not find steady work, and they could not afford to rent even the most miserable house.

The year Bernadette turned thirteen, the family hit rock bottom. They had no money. Their furniture had been confiscated by a landlord to whom they owed back rent. They were reduced to begging for shelter from one of Louise's cousins, who had an empty room on the ground floor of his house. The space had been the *cachot*, or town jail, but since it was perpetually damp and overlooked a cesspool, the prisoners had been moved to healthier quarters. The cousin offered the dank room to his down-and-out relatives. It was there that Bernadette, her sister, and her two brothers experienced all the miseries of the destitute—cold, hunger, sickness, and the humiliation of being infested with lice.

About a year later, on February 11, 1858, while gathering firewood at a grotto known as Massabielle, Bernadette saw a young woman dressed all in white, with a blue sash around her waist and a golden rosary in her hands. This vision was the first in a series of the Blessed Virgin Mary that Bernadette experienced over the next five months. Our Lady's message was simple—pray for all sinners, she said, and then she asked that a chapel be built on the spot. At Mary's direction, Bernadette uncovered the grotto's spring that has made Lourdes a pilgrimage destination. Although the Virgin had never said that the sick who visited her chapel would be healed, the sudden, inexplicable healing of several townspeople made Lourdes internationally famous.

Bernadette was the model visionary. She would not touch or bless the sick; she denied having any special powers; she accepted no money or gifts; and she never even mentioned her experiences in the grotto. To escape the throngs who besieged her, she enrolled in a convent boarding school and then joined the Sisters of Notre Dame at Nevers, a full day's coach ride from Lourdes. As a nun she was modest, conscientious, quietly devout, and never attracted attention. In other words, aside from the five months of visions, Bernadette's life was unremarkable.

The last four years, though, were one long Calvary, as she suffered from chronic asthma as well as tuberculosis of the bone, a horribly painful disease that proved fatal. For her patience in suffering, her humility, her uncomplicated piety, and her refusal to exploit her visions, Bernadette Soubirous was canonized in 1933.

See holy card, page 304

ST. JOHN CHRYSOSTOM

ABOUT 347–407 • FEAST DAY: SEPTEMBER 13

On the printed page, St. John's sermons are masterpieces; they must have sounded even better live. As a tribute to his genius as an orator, the Greeks gave John the title Chrysostom, which means "the golden mouthed."

Like all great public speakers, John knew how to grab and hold an audience's attention. First and foremost, he always emphasized a single overriding point. But around this central theme he wove illustrative examples from the events of the day as well as episodes from the Bible and the lives of the saints. The result was a sermon that was compelling, entertaining, and often poetic, yet full of advice on how to be a better Christian.

As bishop of Constantinople, John was the foremost prelate in the Eastern world. He used his pulpit not only to encourage the ordinary layman and laywoman in the pews, but also to confront the great controversies and crises of his day. He castigated the avaricious who would not take pity on the poor. He attacked immoral clergy who scandalized the faithful and brought the Church into disrepute. He censured husbands and wives who made light of their marriage vows. And he reminded worldly bishops and haughty nobles who exploited the weak and defenseless that God sees all and forgets nothing. On one occasion, when preaching against the sins of certain high churchmen, John assured his congregation, "The floor of Hell is paved with the skulls of bishops."

For his fearlessness, John's enemies had him exiled twice from Constantinople. During his second banishment he died from exhaustion and mistreatment. Although he is recognized in the West as a brilliant orator and a Doctor of the Church, the Christians of the East especially venerate St. John Chrysostom as a champion of the faith.

See holy card, page 304

ST. GERARD MAJELLA

1726–1755 • FEAST DAY: OCTOBER 16

As a child, Gerard Majella was so good and prayed so intensely that his mother told the neighbors her boy "was born for heaven." He took up the trade of tailor but longed to enter the religious life. So at age twenty-six he closed his shop and joined the new order of the Redemptorists. The priests and brothers came to look upon Gerard as their prize recruit. He never broke any rules and apparently never committed any sins, yet he was personable and popular with everyone, whether fishermen or nobility.

Soon reports arose of Gerard working miracles. No fewer than twenty individuals made known to St. Alphonsus Liguori, the founder of the Redemptorists, that Gerard had revealed to them sins they had been unwilling to confess. A poor family said that, through Gerard's prayers, their meager supply of wheat was miraculously replenished for months on end. And a mother and father swore that after their son had fallen off the edge of a cliff, Gerard had brought the child back to life.

One day Brother Gerard was leaving the home of his close friends the Pirofalo family when one of the daughters ran after him—he had dropped his handkerchief. "Keep it," Gerard told her. "Someday you'll find it useful." Within a few years Gerard had died, and the woman had married and became pregnant. The labor went badly; in her fear and agony the woman remembered what Gerard had said, and she asked for the handkerchief. Pressing it against her belly, she prayed to him for help. Immediately her labor pains diminished, and she delivered a strong, healthy child.

As the Redemptorists spread across Europe and then to the Americas, they told the story of the young mother. Ever since, countless expectant mothers and women who are having trouble becoming pregnant have turned to St. Gerard for help.

See holy card, page 321

ST. HIPPOLYTUS OF ROME

DIED ABOUT 258 • FEAST DAY: AUGUST 13

About one hundred years after St. Hippolytus's death, St. Ambrose wrote that the martyr was a Roman soldier assigned to guard Christian prisoners arrested during the emperor Valerian's persecution of the Church. One of his prisoners was St. Lawrence, the deacon who Ambrose says converted Hippolytus. As for Hippolytus, he passed on his new faith to his elderly nurse Concordia and nineteen slaves in his household.

Shortly after St. Lawrence was roasted alive, Hippolytus's conversion was revealed to the Roman authorities. He, Concordia, and his Christian slaves were all arrested and arraigned together before the magistrate. To strike terror in the slaves' hearts, the judge ordered Hippolytus to be beaten and tortured. But that didn't shake the constancy of the new Christians. Even seeing poor Concordia flogged to death didn't induce Hippolytus and his surviving servants to sacrifice to the Roman gods. They were condemned to death and led to execution outside the walls of Rome. How the slaves died is unknown, but tradition says that Hippolytus's arms and legs were tied to four horses that were then driven in four different directions, tearing him apart.

The story of Hippolytus, Concordia, and their companions appears to be a blend of fact and legend. Nonetheless, with the endorsement of the great St. Ambrose, it seems probable that this martyr once worked as a prison guard.

See holy card, page 321

ST. LEONARD OF NOBLAC &
THE HOLY CHILD OF ATOCHA

DIED ABOUT 559 • FEAST DAY: NOVEMBER 6
FEAST DAY: DECEMBER 15

Devotion to St. Leonard as the patron of prisoners dates back to the First Crusade. In 1100 Bohemund, a Norman knight and one of the crusade's leaders, was captured by a Turkish tribe who kept him chained in their dungeon. On the verge of despair, the knight prayed for deliverance to St. Leonard, a holy hermit who had lived in the forest near Limoges during the sixth century. After three years of captivity, the Turks released Bohemund. When he returned home to France, the crusader made a pilgrimage of thanksgiving to St. Leonard's tomb at Noblac, where he left a gift—a heavy chain made of silver, like the one that had shackled him.

We know little about St. Leonard aside from a few facts: He lived during the reign of Clovis, the first Christian king of the Franks, and his queen, Clothilde; he was a hermit; and, after his death, people in and around Limoges venerated him as a saint. To fill in the gaps, legends later arose, such as the one describing how Clothilde, while nine months pregnant, went hunting with Clovis in the forest, near Leonard's hut. In the middle of the hunt the queen went into labor. She had brought none of her attendants, no village or midwife was handy, and the nearest shelter was Leonard's hut. Leonard had no experience delivering a baby, but prayer got them through the ordeal—the queen delivered a healthy baby boy.

In gratitude Clovis gave Leonard an enormous tract of land, which later became the monastery of Noblac, and made the hermit part of his inner circle of advisers.

Another legend says that after a battle, when Leonard pleaded with Clovis to be merciful to his captives, the king promised to free every prisoner Leonard thought worthy. This

Am 22ten   IHS   Juni.

Der hl. Alban.

Martirer.

Daran werden Alle erkennen, daß ihr meine Jünger seid, wenn ihr einander liebt. Joh. 13, 35.

Erweise gerne Liebesdienst.

Bete für die von der Selbstsucht Befangenen.

S. IGNATIUS A LOYOLA

3.

Sanctus Alphonsus Maria de Liguorio.
Episcopus, Ecclesiæ Doctor et Congregationis
SS. Redemptoris Fundator.

B. Kühlen, Typogr. Apost. M. Gladbach.

1. Refugees • St. Alban   2. Religious Retreats • St. Ignatius of Loyola
3. Religious Vocations • St. Alphonsus Liguori

Our Lady of Guadalupe
DOHENY HACIENDA ❧ THOMAS AQUINAS COLLEGE

St André Corsini.

S^{tus} Andreas Corsinus

ST EULALIA.
Verlag v. Carl Mayer in Nürnberg

1. Rights of Native Peoples • St. Turibius of Mogrovejo 2. Right-to-Life Movement • Our Lady of Guadalupe
3. Riots • St. Andrew Corsini 4. Runaways • St. Eulalia of Merida

S. Guido, patroon van Anderlecht.

S. GUIDO, O.P.N.

· ST · NICOLAUS ·

S. URSULA.

1. Sacristans · St. Guy of Anderlecht   2. Sailors · St. Nicholas
3. Salmon · St. Kentigern   4. Schoolgirls · St. Ursula

He that shall do and teach; he shall be called great in the kingdom of heaven. Math. V. 19.

B. Albertus Magnus.

B. K.   A. Hiffarth, New-York.

Sainte Adelaïde.

St. Angela de Fulgineo

1. Scientists • St. Albert the Great   2. Sculptors • Four Crowned Martyrs
3. Second Marriage • St. Adelaide   4. Sexual Temptation • Blessed Angela of Foligno

legend may be the reason why Bohemund, as he languished in prison, invoked St. Leonard's help.

Devotion to the Holy Child of Atocha dates back to the thirteenth century, when the Moors conquered Atocha (now a neighborhood of Madrid) and imprisoned all the town's men. The Moors refused to give food or water to the captives. They did permit provisions to be brought in but insisted that they must be delivered by children under the age of twelve who could feed only their own family members. Prisoners who had no children, or whose children were age twelve or older, were left to starve.

The women of Atocha turned to the Blessed Virgin for help, begging her to intercede with her son for their own sons, brothers, and husbands. That night a little boy, dressed like a pilgrim from Compostela (Spain's national shrine), appeared in the prison with a basket of food and a jug of water—hardly enough for all the captives. Yet as the child went from man to man, each one ate and drank his fill, and the basket and the jug were constantly replenished. As the little boy returned to the prison night after night, the captives and the women of Atocha realized that he was the Christ Child.

Devotion to the Holy Child of Atocha spread throughout Spain and is especially strong among Spanish-speaking Catholics in the Americas. The Holy Child's original shrine stands near the Atocha train station in Madrid.

See holy cards, page 321

ST. EXPEDITUS

FOURTH CENTURY • FEAST DAY: APRIL 19

Puns on saints' names are common, but that a saint named Expeditus should be invoked against procrastination seems just too good.

St. Expeditus was a real person: He was one of six Armenian Christians, possibly Roman soldiers, martyred in Melitene. His fellow martyrs are Saints Hermogenes, Gaius, Aristonicus, Rufus, and Galata. Documentary evidence suggests that St. Expeditus was venerated in Germany as early as the seventeenth century, but how he became the saint of procrastinators is harder to determine.

The version of the story with the widest circulation claims that in the nineteenth century the relics of a martyr, along with a statue, were shipped from Rome to a Paris convent. Neither the statue nor the relics were labeled, but the shipping crate was marked *Spedito*, which the nuns assumed was the name of the saint. The sisters Latinized the word into St. Expeditus. It's a good story, but it sure sounds like a holy urban legend.

Nonetheless, devotion to St. Expeditus spread, especially in France, South America, and New Orleans, where he has become a favorite voodoo *loa*, or spirit.

In art, St. Expeditus is usually dressed as a Roman soldier, holding in one hand the palm frond that is the symbol of martyrdom and raising above his head a cross on which is inscribed the Latin word *Hodie*, meaning "today." Sometimes he is shown trampling on a raven that is labeled *Cras*, Latin for "tomorrow."

See holy card, page 322

ST. CHRISTINA
THE ASTONISHING

1150–1224 • FEAST DAY: JULY 24

In the long list of saints, St. Christina is hard to classify. Reading her story today, it seems likely that she suffered from schizophrenia (which explains her role as the patron of psychiatrists and psychologists). The question is, can a schizophrenic be a saint? During Christina's life, her neighbors wondered that, too. The Church has never clearly stated its position, and Christina has never been canonized formally. But by popular acclaim she has been venerated as a saint since the thirteenth century.

Christina grew up with her two older sisters in the town of Saint Trond in Belgium. At age twenty-two she suffered some type of severe fit, possibly catalepsy, which led her family and friends to believe she had died. During Christina's funeral, as the priest chanted the prayer "Agnus Dei" in preparation for Communion, Christina suddenly sat up in her coffin, jumped out, and climbed (some sources say levitated) to the church

rafters. Panicked mourners ran out of the church, all except Christina's eldest sister and the priest, who commanded her to come down.

Once her friends were calm enough to listen, Christina explained how she had visited hell and purgatory and then traveled to heaven, where Christ asked if she would return to earth to bring sinners to repentance. Christina agreed to go back to save souls, with the understanding that she would act in ways "never seen before among mortals." That was an understatement.

She climbed into treetops or to the summit of church steeples and castle towers, saying she couldn't bear the smell of humans. She wandered through graveyards weeping hysterically for those who had died impenitent. She threw herself into fires, icy rivers, and thorn bushes. Her sisters tried to lock her up, but she was cunning and always escaped.

One day Christina wandered into the parish church, climbed into the baptismal font, and poured holy water over her head until she was completely drenched. After her "bath," she was much less agitated and her behavior much less eccentric. Instead of avoiding people, she confronted the region's most hardened sinners—not to reproach them but to beg charity for the poor and the sick. Christina said that if she could move such people to be merciful now and again, God would be merciful to them later.

At the end of her life, the nuns at the local convent of St. Catherine took her in. For once Christina was at peace and appeared pleased to slip quietly toward death. But one nun, Sister Beatrice, kept pestering her with metaphysical and mystical questions. Reluctantly, Christina answered. When she'd had enough, she made the sign of the cross over the nuns, leaned back against her pillow, and gave up her troubled spirit.

See holy card, page 322

ST. PAUL THE APOSTLE

DIED ABOUT 65 • FEAST DAYS: JANUARY 25 AND JUNE 29

Public relations professionals have got to love St. Paul, who made himself "all things to all men" to reach the widest possible audience for his "product"—the Christian faith. Each of the leading apostles offered something important to the fledgling Church: St. John the Evangelist was its first mystic and theologian; as bishop of Jerusalem, St. James the Lesser kept the loyalty of Jewish Christians by emphasizing the Jewish roots of Christianity; St. Peter, as the first pope, sorted out the Church's first personality conflicts and theological quarrels; and St. Paul was the first apostle to use classical Greek philosophy to explain the Christian message, thereby making it more appealing to Gentiles throughout the Roman Empire.

St. Paul is fascinating. He was a Jew, born in Tarsus in what is now Turkey; his parents named him Saul and sent him to Jerusalem to be educated by a rabbi, but they also apprenticed him to a tentmaker so that he'd be able to support himself.

As a devout Jew, Saul opposed Christianity and hated Christians. Having been commissioned by the high priest in Jerusalem to imprison Jews who had converted to Christianity, he was on his way to Damascus to round up more Christians when a flash of light threw him from his horse. A voice from heaven asked, "Saul! Saul! Why do you persecute me?" Terrified, Saul replied, "Who are you, Lord?" The voice answered, "I am Jesus, whom you are persecuting." Then Christ instructed Saul to continue to Damascus and await the next message.

Saul's men were nearly as frightened as he was since they, too, could hear the voice but couldn't see anyone. Their terror only increased when Saul got to his feet and found he was blind. Led by his men, he staggered into Damascus, where he found shelter among the city's Christians. There, he was baptized, upon which his sight was restored. He later changed his name to Paul, probably for the sake of the Greek-speaking pagans he chose as his "target audience": the classical Greek word *saulos* means "effete" and "conceited," but *paulos* means "rest" or "calm."

Paul's conversion complicated his life. Faithful Jews denounced him as a traitor and some wanted to kill him: Christians, including the apostles, were suspicious that he might be trying to trick them. St. Barnabas, a disciple the apostles trusted completely, assured the Christians of Jerusalem that Paul's conversion was sincere, and he introduced Paul to St. Peter and St. James. But Paul didn't remain long in Jerusalem. He had chosen the wider Roman world as his mission, and for the next twenty years he traveled throughout the Middle East, Turkey, Greece, the Aegean islands, and eventually to Rome itself, preaching the gospel, establishing churches, and gathering disciples like Saints Titus, Timothy, and Luke.

Along with St. Peter and countless other Christians, St. Paul was martyred during Nero's ferocious Christian persecution. His Roman citizenship proved to be an advantage. Condemned criminals who were not citizens of Rome could be executed in the grisliest fashion, which is why St. Peter was crucified upside down. But St. Paul invoked his privilege of citizenship, and so he died a swift death, beheaded by a sword.

See holy card, page 322

ST. HEDWIG

1371–1399 • FEAST DAY: SEPTEMBER 28

S t. Hedwig, or Jadwiga (her Polish name), was one of those remarkable women rulers who appeared throughout Europe in the Middle Ages. At age thirteen, she was crowned queen of Poland and almost immediately demonstrated her abilities as a shrewd negotiator.

Poland was threatened by invasion from the Russians, Mongols, and Tartars. On its eastern border lay the kingdom of Lithuania, an outpost of paganism in Christian Europe and an aggressive military power led by the warrior-king Jagiello. Yet the more pressing problem was posed by the Teutonic Knights, a German operation that was part religious order, part freelance army. The Knights conquered bits of Poland's border, claiming the territory for Germany.

Hedwig was betrothed to William, an Austrian prince. Although it was an arranged match, after several meetings the teenagers fell deeply in love. Given all the raids they had endured from the Teutonic Knights, the Polish aristocracy refused to accept a German-speaking prince as their next king. They insisted that Hedwig break off the engagement to William so that she could instead accept a marriage proposal from Jagiello.

Although it broke her heart, the young queen did as the nobles demanded. One saving grace was that she saw a way to turn the marriage to her country's advantage. She told Jagiello she would marry him on three conditions: they would unite their two countries into a single nation; Jagiello would become a Catholic; and he would do everything possible to convert his people. The maneuver was canny. By marrying Jagiello she made a husband out of a potential enemy, expanded her kingdom, and reinforced her own army, which could now defend the country against invaders.

With her country's borders secure, Hedwig devoted herself to revitalizing intellectual life in Poland and establishing the Church in Lithuania.

She became the main patron of the first bishop of Vilnius in Lithuania. She refounded the rundown university in Krakow and sponsored a new college for Lithuanians in Prague, the intellectual and artistic capital of Eastern Europe.

Hedwig was twenty-eight when she and Jagiello expected their first child. Tragically, the baby died in childbirth, and Hedwig died soon after. The grateful people of Poland and Lithuania began to venerate her as a saint immediately after her death. The popular devotion received papal approval in 1997, when John Paul II formally declared Hedwig to be a saint.

See holy card, page 323

Rabbits

ST. MELANGELL

DIED ABOUT 590 • FEAST DAY: MAY 27

During the Middle Ages, Welsh Christians referred to rabbits and hares as "Melangell's lambs" and considered it a sacrilege to kill any of the furry little animals within the parish boundaries.

St. Melangell was an Irish princess. She planned to become a nun, but her father, the king, had already chosen her husband. Rather than submit to the marriage, Melangell fled to Wales, where she built a little hut in the woods near present-day Pennant. One day while reading outside her hut, a frightened hare ran into the clearing, leapt into her lap, and hid up her sleeve. A moment later a pack of snarling dogs and a hunter burst onto the scene. At the sight of Melangell, the dogs whimpered and slunk back into the woods. The astonished hunter, a Welsh prince named Brochwel, asked the woman who she was and what she was doing in his forest. When he heard Melangell's story, he declared that she was "a true handmaiden of the true God." On the spot, the prince do-nated to Melangell a large expanse of his favorite hunting ground and declared it a sanctuary for rabbits and all other animals forever.

Melangell lived for another thirty-seven years and her land became a sanctuary for all animals, just as the prince had promised. She also expanded the privilege to include human fugitives.

The rabbit has become St. Melangell's emblem, and artists tend to portray her at the dramatic moment of the hunting dogs running out of the woods and the terrified hare peaking out from the saint's sleeve.

See holy card, page 323

ST. DENIS

DIED ABOUT 250 • FEAST DAY: OCTOBER 9

Finding the connection between St. Denis and rabies takes a little work. One story says that the barbarian king Clovis (about 466–511), after he had become a Christian, commanded the monks of the Abbey of St. Denis to open up the martyr's tomb so he could view the relics. After gazing at them for a while, the king reached into the sarcophagus, snapped off a piece of bone, and then strolled out of the church. Soon thereafter, as punishment for his sacrilege, Clovis went insane.

King Clovis went mad after desecrating the relics of St. Denis. Madness is a symptom of rabies. And so St. Denis is invoked against rabies. Logical, no?

St. Denis was a missionary who became the first bishop of Paris. Together with St. Rusticus, a priest, and St. Eleutherius, a deacon, he brought large numbers of pagan Parisians into the Church. Jealous of the bishop's success, the pagan priests stirred up the people and the magistrates against Denis and his companions. They were all arrested and beheaded on the Parisian hill known ever since as Montmartre, "martyr's mountain."

The Abbey of St. Denis lies about twenty miles from Montmartre, and how the body of St. Denis got there is one of the more colorful stories in the legends of the saints. After the executioner had struck off the saint's head, Denis stood up, picked it up, and walked to the site of the abbey church, where he laid down at his final resting place.

For many centuries, the Abbey of St. Denis was the favorite burial place of France's royal family, a custom that made the church a target during the French Revolution. A revolutionary mob smashed the tombs, desecrated the bones of kings and queens, and destroyed the relic said to be the skull of St. Denis.

See holy card, page 323

Racial Discrimination

ST. MARTIN DE PORRES

1575–1639 • FEAST DAY: NOVEMBER 3

Martin's difficulties began the moment he was born. His mother, Ana, an African who had once been a slave, was the mistress of Don Juan de Porres, a Spanish nobleman. Because Martin inherited his mother's African features, Don Juan refused to acknowledge him as his son or to support the family.

About the time Martin turned seven, Don Juan had a change of heart. He recognized Martin as his own, gave him his surname, and provided for Ana so that she and the children (Martin had a sister by this time) wouldn't live in poverty.

Martin wanted to join the Dominicans, but his mixed-race background got in the way. Peruvian law barred anyone with Indian or African blood from joining any religious order. His only option was to enter as a *donado*, a layman who was essentially a servant at the monastery but was permitted to live among the Dominicans and wear the habit. In recognition of Martin's distinguished father, the Dominicans' superior stretched the law and let Martin take the vows of a lay brother. Not all the friars were so broad-minded, however. Almost daily a priest or a brother mocked or insulted Martin because he had been born black and illegitimate.

To many others, Martin was a saint. It was said he healed a priest whose gangrenous legs were about to be amputated and that he brought back to perfect health another priest on the brink of death. Martin's patience, humility, and unquestionable holiness made him one of the most beloved and respected men in Lima. When he died, two bishops, the king's viceroy, and a judge of the royal court claimed the honor of serving as his pallbearers—a public rebuke to those who still looked down on Martin as an illegitimate descendant of slaves.

See holy card, page 323

ST. SWITHUN

DIED 862 • FEAST DAY: JULY 2

St. Swithun was born and raised in Winchester and eventually became the town's bishop. He loved his home and, as bishop, used his influence and wealth to introduce improvements. He restored old neglected churches and built new ones in those parts of the diocese that needed a priest. To boost the economy, he built a bridge over the Itchen River, making it easier for farmers and tradespeople to bring produce and other goods to market.

Swithun never lost his affection for his old neighbors. One day while he was sitting on the bridge and watching the workmen put on the finishing touches, a countrywoman walked by, balancing a basket of eggs on her head. As a malicious joke, one of the workmen jostled her, and down fell the eggs. Using strong language, Swithun scolded the workman. Then he knelt beside the weeping woman and made the sign of the cross over the shattered eggs. At once they were whole again.

As bishop of Winchester, Swithun was guaranteed burial in a prime location inside his cathedral. Yet on his deathbed he instructed the monks to bury him in the churchyard, with the common folk. They obeyed the bishop's wishes, but in 971 Winchester's new bishop and monks revisited their predecessors' decision. Leaving a saint lying in the dirt was irreverent. So they built a splendid shrine inside the cathedral and set July 15, 971, as moving day for the relics. At the exhumation a torrential downpour soaked the procession, which the townsfolk took as a clear sign of the saint's displeasure. Ever since, St. Swithun has been invoked to bring rain during a drought or to stop rain when a flood threatens.

See holy card, page 324

ST. JOHN OF MATHA

1160–1223 • FEAST DAY: FEBRUARY 8

The day after he was ordained a priest, as he was saying his first Mass, St. John of Matha had a vision of an angel accompanied by two Christian captives. The apparition was puzzling. Sometime afterward John was discussing it with Felix of Valois, a hermit and also later a saint, when it struck them that the vision might be a sign that John should dedicate his life to ransoming Christians held prisoner or enslaved by the Moors.

In the late twelfth century, the Moors still occupied more than half of Spain. Spanish Christians living under Moorish rule who fell afoul of their overlords were often sold into slavery. Spanish Christian soldiers captured in battle against the Moors were locked away in dungeons or sent off to the slave markets of Morocco, Tunisia, and Algeria. The number of captive Christians in St. John's day ran to the tens of thousands; since no one was trying to win their release, John of Matha made it his cause.

In Paris he gathered a group of courageous men who were willing to travel into hostile territory to negotiate the captives' release. They called themselves the Order of the Most Holy Trinity and of Captives—Trinitarians for short. They fanned out across France and Italy, calling upon nobles and bishops and pleading for the funds needed to buy the freedom of their fellow Christians.

John and his Trinitarians were somewhat successful—they did ransom hundreds of captives. But there were thousands more that the Moors refused to liberate. As for the details of John's adventures in Moorish lands, we know almost nothing. Incredibly, it didn't occur to the early Trinitarians to keep any records of their rescue missions.

The Trinitarians have survived to this day, and they are still involved with prisoners, working as prison chaplains.

See holy card, page 324

Real-Estate Transactions

ST. JOSEPH

FIRST CENTURY • FEAST DAYS: MARCH 19 AND MAY 1

Small plastic statues of St. Joseph have become one of the hottest items in religious gift shops. Prospective homebuyers bury the statuette in the lawn of the property they want, pointing the saint's head toward the house. Those wanting to sell their houses buy the statuette, too, but they point the head toward the street. It is one of the odder saint-related phenomena of our time, and no one can say for sure how the trend began.

The link between St. Joseph and houses is not far-fetched. As the husband of the Blessed Virgin Mary and the foster father of Jesus, he has always been associated with a happy home. One likely source for the statue-burying custom comes from the life of another saint who was intensely devoted to St. Joseph. Blessed André Bessett (1845–1937), a French Canadian Brother of the Holy Cross, dreamed of honoring his favorite saint by building a shrine on Mount Royal, overlooking Montreal.

He had a plot in mind, but the landowners refused to sell. After years of fruitless negotiations, Brother André took a pocketful of St. Joseph medals and buried them all over the piece of land he wanted for the shrine. The next time he approached the owners with an offer, they accepted.

The link to Brother André seems more plausible when one notices that Pope John Paul II declared him "Blessed" in 1982, and the custom of burying St. Joseph statues began to mushroom about 1984.

See holy card, page 324

ST. BASIL THE GREAT

329–379 • FEAST DAY: JANUARY 2

St. Basil came from a remarkably virtuous family: His grandmother, parents, and four of his nine brothers and sisters are recognized as saints. They were wealthy and generous to the needy, but Basil took his family's bounty a step further. When famine struck their province of Cappadocia, he worked with the servants in a soup kitchen that fed hundreds every day. This personal involvement in the needs of the world became his guiding principle and the cornerstone of his reform of monastic life in the East.

In Basil's day most monks and nuns were hermits living in isolated corners of the deserts of North Africa and the Middle East. Arguing that men are "sociable beings, and not solitary or savage," he urged the hermits to form communities near towns and cities where ordinary Christians could profit from their prayers and, inspired by their example, deepen their own religious life. The monks and nuns could take in orphans and open schools, recruiting a new generation for the religious life. To this day in the Eastern Church, St. Basil's guidelines for monks and nuns remain the standard.

Basil himself became a priest and eventually bishop of Caesarea, his hometown. To keep his people faithful to orthodox doctrine, he preached every morning and evening, and always to enormous crowds. (As was the case with so many bishops of the fourth century, Basil had trained as an orator.) With his family fortune, he built a huge hospital at the city gates.

The great trial of his life was the rise of the Arian heresy, which taught that Christ was not the Son of God but a lesser being. When the emperor Valens became an Arian, he sent a delegate to order all the bishops of the Church to accept Arianism, too. Basil refused and derided those Christians who had allowed themselves to be seduced by the Arian heresy. Stunned, the emperor's delegate remarked that no one had ever dared to speak to him in such a way. "Perhaps," Basil replied, "you have never yet had to deal with a bishop."

The strain of running a diocese, combating the Arians, and reforming monasticism all took their toll on Basil. He died shortly before his fiftieth birthday. The Church joined his feast day with that of his close friend St. Gregory of Nazianzen, who preached the sermon at Basil's funeral. In it, Gregory said he looked forward to their reunion in heaven, where they would "receive the reward of the battles we have fought and the attacks we have resisted."

See holy card, page 324

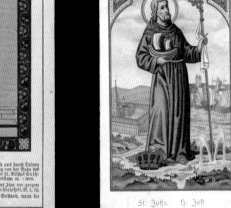

St. Joffe.   H. Joft.

S. MARGARITA DE CORTONA.

1. **Shepherds** • **St. Cuthbert**   2. **Shipwrecks** • **St. Jodocus**
3. **Shoemakers** • **SS. Crispin and Crispinian**   4. **Single Mothers** • **St. Margaret of Cortona**

ST. LIDVINA.

St MARCULPHE
ET LE LIÈVRE.

ÉDITION DE LA TRAPPE DE N-D. D'AIGUEBELLE (Drôme)

3.

Sanctus Petrus Claver Confessor S.J.

1. Skaters • St. Lydwina   2. Skin Rashes • St. Marculf
3. Slavery • St. Peter Claver

362

MARIA SS. DELLA NEVE

BIENHEUREUSE LOUISE DE MARILLAC

1. Snakebites • St. Patrick 2. Snow • Our Lady of the Snow
3. Social Workers • St. Louise de Marillac 4. Soldiers • St. George

S. Blasius

S. Benedictus

2085   CASM

St. Notker

Ll. M. K. Beverwijk - Holland   16.

1. Sore Throats • St. Blaise   2. Spelunkers • St. Benedict
Stammering and Other Speech Impediments • St. Notkar Balbulus   4. Statesmen and Politicians • St. Thomas

ST. ALBAN

DIED EARLY THIRD CENTURY • FEAST DAY: JUNE 20

The case of St. Alban is the earliest known of a Christian being executed in England. He lived in the Roman town of Verulamium (present-day St. Albans). It was a time of anti-Christian persecution, but, as a pagan, Alban was not troubled by the authorities. That is, until one day someone came pounding on his door. A stranger, a Christian priest, begged Alban to hide him from soldiers in pursuit. Alban pulled the frightened man inside and bolted the door.

Over the next few weeks, Alban became impressed by his guest, named Amphibalus, who spent long hours in prayer and contemplation. He asked the priest to instruct him in the Christian faith and baptize him. Soon after Alban's conversion, the soldiers arrived on a house-to-house search for Christians. Alban urged Amphibalus to save himself and then pulled on the priest's robe. A moment later the soldiers burst into the room, demanding to know who and what Alban was. "My name is Alban," he said, "and I worship the only living God." The soldiers tied Alban's hands behind his back and led him to the magistrate.

In court Alban admitted again that he was a Christian and that he would not sacrifice to pagan gods. He confessed that he was not a priest, but he would not say where the priest he had sheltered could be found. At the magistrate's command, soldiers marched Alban to Holmhurst Hill, where they flogged him and then cut off his head. A few days later, Amphibalus was captured and beheaded, too.

A Benedictine abbey was built on the site of St. Alban's martyrdom, and the relics of both saints were enshrined there until the Reformation, when King Henry VIII ordered the shrines to be destroyed.

See holy card, page 341

Religious Retreats

ST. IGNATIUS OF LOYOLA

1491–1556 • FEAST DAY: JULY 31

For the last four hundred years, Catholics who make a religious retreat under the direction of a priest have most likely followed the system set down by St. Ignatius of Loyola in his book *Spiritual Exercises*. Before his conversion, Ignatius had been arrogant, vain about his appearance, defensive in matters of honor, and much more interested in attaining glory than in growing in virtue.

His change of heart came during his long convalescence from a crippling battle wound. The ideas he presents in *Spiritual Exercises* emerged from his own conversion experience. The book is basically a step-by-step program designed to help Christians detach from those things the world considers essential—physical comfort, respect, success, even good health. It further instructs them to dedicate themselves to discovering God's will and doing it, no matter how difficult, unpleasant, or dangerous it may be. To emphasize this

point, Ignatius composed this prayer to be said by the retreatant: "Take O Lord and receive my entire liberty, my memory, my understanding, and my whole will. All that I am and all that I possess you have given me: I surrender it all to you to be disposed of according to your will. Give me only your love and your grace; with these I will be rich enough and will desire nothing more."

It takes thirty days to complete Ignatius's regimen. Since most people cannot leave work and family for a full month, the method has been adapted for a three-day retreat. Even in the abridged version, the goals are the same: the examination of one's actions, motivations, and desires and the resolution to give up anything that keeps one from doing the will of God.

See holy card, page 341

ST. ALPHONSUS LIGUORI

1696–1787 • FEAST DAY: AUGUST 1

In St. Alphonsus Liguori's day, there were seventy-five thousand priests in his homeland, the Kingdom of Naples. But that doesn't mean that religious life was flourishing. Thanks in large part to the custom of parents passing all their property to the eldest son, younger male family members had to find some other way to support themselves. Many chose careers in the Church, especially as administrators, which spared them the hard work of running a parish and brought them a comfortable income. Furthermore, under the laws of Naples, the clergy paid no taxes. While not every priest in Naples was a self-interested money-grubber, enough were, dragging the priesthood into disrepute.

To convert wayward clerics, encourage hardworking parish priests, and revive religious life among ordinary Catholics, Alphonsus started a new religious order, the Congregation of the Most Holy Redeemer, commonly known as the Redemptorists. The men who joined him were spe-

cially trained to be effective preachers and gentle but persuasive confessors. The Redemptorists spent most of their time on the road, traveling from parish to parish, or town to town, where they held a mission. Typically the mission lasted several days, during which time the visiting Redemptorist—through reverent Masses and inspiring sermons, long periods in the confessional and special devotions to the Blessed Sacrament and the Blessed Virgin—set new standards of parish life for the local clergy to follow. They increased parishioners' fervor as well.

Almost from the start, Alphonsus's order thrived. The Redemptorists flourished in southern Italy, where bishops competed to have the zealous priests come to work in their dioceses. Within Alphonsus's own lifetime he saw his priests and brothers spread first to Austria, then to Poland and Germany. In 1832 the first Redemptorists arrived in America.

See holy card, page 341

ST. TURIBIUS OF MOGROVEJO

1538–1606 • FEAST DAY: MARCH 23

It must have come as a shock to St. Turibius when both King Philip II of Spain and Pope St. Pius V named him bishop of Lima, Peru. He was a devout, intelligent man, but he had never thought of becoming a missionary. In the first place, Turibius was not a priest, he was a lawyer. True, he was an expert in both civil and ecclesiastical law, and he had served as an advisor on legal matters to the Inquisition in Granada. But aside from his work for the Church, Turibius was still a layman who had not given any thought to entering the priesthood.

King Philip refused to take no for an answer. The Spanish colony of Peru needed an archbishop, and Philip was determined to send a man who possessed a reputation for piety, energy, humility, and who had good organizational skills as well. Turibius was the ideal choice. All that remained was to ordain him a priest and then consecrate him a bishop. Pope Pius V, pleased with the king's choice, dispensed with the customary waiting period and permitted Turibius to go through the ceremonies in record time.

Whatever his misgivings may have been, Turibius accepted the appointment. But, travel conditions being what they were in the sixteenth century, it took him a year to reach Lima.

By 1581, the year Turibius arrived in his diocese, the Inca had been subdued and most of them were at least nominally Christian. Three items stood at the top of the new bishop's very long list of priorities: recruit priests who spoke the native languages; try to keep the Spanish colonial government from meddling in Church affairs; and protect the native peoples from being abused and exploited by the colonists. In addition to these concerns, Turibius had to contend with the size of his diocese—it covered eighteen thousand square miles.

First he had a new catechism translated into Quechua and Aymara, the two major Inca languages; then he insisted that priests assigned to Indian parishes be fluent in both languages. He encouraged mission priests to get the Inca involved in parish life by asking them to direct the choir, care for the church, and serve as religious teachers. Then, to understand his people and see what they needed, Turibius made a long, hard tour through his diocese. To reach all his parishes and missions, he scaled the Andes, crossed dangerous rivers, and followed trails through the jungles—almost always on foot. During the twenty-five years he was bishop, Turibius made the journey three times.

The effort paid off. Bishop Turibius became loved and revered among the Inca, who were awestruck that such a man would go to such lengths to visit them, stay as a guest in their huts, eat their food, and teach them the faith in their own language. He could have remained in Lima, living like a colonial prince, but Turibius never lost his humility. Even as he was dying, he dragged himself to his cathedral to receive Communion one last time, saying it was not proper for God to come to him.

See holy card, page 342

OUR LADY OF GUADALUPE

APPEARED 1531 • FEAST DAY: DECEMBER 12

Our Lady of Guadalupe is especially beloved in Mexico. Her image is everywhere—in churches and homes, on buildings and T-shirts, and mounted on the dashboards of trucks and taxis. Millions visit her shrine outside Mexico City every year. Recently the right-to-life movement in the United States has adopted her as their patroness because, it is said, the miraculous image of the Virgin Mary shows her pregnant with the Infant Jesus. The proof, they say, is the position of the sash the Virgin wears. It is high up, under her breasts, which is said to be how the Aztec women of Mexico wore it when they were pregnant.

On December 9, 1531, Juan Diego, a Nahua Indian who had recently converted to Christianity, was on his way to Mass when he heard singing on the summit of Tepeyac Hill. Curious to discover the music's source, he followed a trail up the hill and at the summit met a young woman, dark-skinned, beautifully dressed, and standing amid dazzling light. Speaking to Juan in Nahuatl, his own language, she introduced herself. "I am the ever Virgin Holy Mary, Mother of the true God," she said. "I am your merciful mother, to you and to all the inhabitants of this land." Then Mary instructed him to go to Juan de Zumárraga, the bishop of Mexico City, and tell him to build a church in her honor on the spot.

Twice Juan tried to persuade the bishop to do as Mary had asked, and twice the bishop turned him away. He wasn't surprised that the bishop didn't take such a poor peasant seriously. "I am a small rope," he told Mary, "a tiny ladder, the tail end, a leaf." He urged her to ask someone with more status to deliver her message. Instead, Mary promised to give the bishop a sign that would prove to everyone for all time that what Juan Diego had reported was true. She commanded him to return to Tepeyac and gather flowers there. At the top of the hill, he discovered gorgeous Castillian roses, growing six months out of season. He picked flowers until his *tilma*, or cloak, was full. Then he carried them back to Mary, who took each rose in her hand before replacing it in Juan Diego's cloak.

Tucking up the edges of his cloak so that not a single rose would fall out, Juan hurried to the bishop's palace. De Zumárraga was with some of his chaplains and several servants when he entered the room. "You asked for a sign," Juan said. "Now look." He opened his *tilma* and the magnificent roses cascaded onto the floor. But more astonishing than the roses was the image on his cloak—a perfect portrait of the Virgin Mary as Juan had seen her, beautifully dressed and with the dark complexion of an Indian.

Convinced that Juan's message had truly come from the Mother of God, Bishop de Zumárraga built a church on Tepeyac Hill and enshrined the miraculous image over the high altar. The Franciscan and Jesuit fathers made copies of the image to carry with them on missionary journeys among Mexico's tribes. The story of the Virgin Mary appearing as an Aztec princess to a Nahua Indian and speaking in the Nahua language captivated the Indians of Mexico. Within a decade of the apparition, nine million had converted to the Catholic faith.

See holy card, page 342

ST. ANDREW CORSINI

1302–1373 • FEAST DAY: FEBRUARY 4

From the twelfth through the fifteenth century, the cities of Italy were tumultuous places where rival families, political parties, and even neighborhoods struggled for dominance. Many famous names fell victim to the unrest. Dante was exiled by his political enemies, and the Pazzi family tried to settle their feud with the Medici by murdering Lorenzo the Magnificent as he attended Mass. Even Shakespeare heard of the troubles; the love story of Romeo and Juliet is set against the backdrop of bloody-minded Italian families rioting in the streets of Verona. During this difficult period, the pope named St. Andrew Corsini as bishop of Fiesole, a town near Florence. Making peace among his diocese's warring factions was Andrew's priority. Incredibly, he succeeded, which inspired the pope to send him to Bologna to put an end to that city's civil strife. Because St. Andrew was renowned as a peacemaker, he is invoked against riots and civil disturbances of all kinds.

As a teenager and young man, Andrew had shown no signs of sanctity. He filled his days and nights with booze, sex, brawling, and the occasional petty theft. Once he returned home to find his mother weeping. At first she wouldn't say what troubled her, but Andrew persisted until she revealed that, when she was pregnant with him, she'd dreamed of giving birth to a wolf. She'd dismissed it at the time, but now the dream struck her as prophetic. His mother's complaint pierced Andrew's heart. Not only did he give up his wild life, he joined the Carmelite order, was ordained a priest, and spent the rest of his life trying to atone for the sins of his former life. Even after he was named a bishop, he continued to sleep on the floor, a penance he'd adopted as an ordinary Carmelite friar.

See holy card, page 342

ST. EULALIA OF MERIDA

ABOUT 290–ABOUT 304 • FEAST DAY: DECEMBER 10

According to Prudentius, the fourth-century Spanish Christian poet, St. Eulalia was the daughter of a Christian family in Merida. She was about twelve years old when the emperor Diocletian ordered an empire-wide persecution of Christians. Despite her youth, her zeal to join the martyrs was so intense that her mother dragged her off to the family's estate in the country. It didn't matter. Eulalia escaped from the villa and ran back to Merida, arriving just as the morning session of the city court began. Marching up to the tribunal, she denounced the presiding magistrate for trying to terrify innocent people into denying the true God.

Out of consideration for Eulalia's youth, and recognizing her as a member of a noble family, the judge tried to calm her. But by this point Eulalia was beyond the reach of soothing words. She knocked over the statue of a god on the courtroom's little altar, trampled the offerings, and then, for good measure, spat at the magistrate. Now the magistrate treated Eulalia as a criminal rather than as an excitable girl. She was given one more chance to sacrifice to the Roman gods. Still she refused. There in court the torturers stripped her to the waist, lacerated her sides with sharp hooks, and scorched her breasts with flaming torches. Yet even in her agony, Eulalia still mocked the judge. Finally he ordered her taken outside and burned at the stake.

Secretly the Christians of Merida collected St. Eulalia's bones and ashes and buried them. The tomb of the girl who ran away to become a martyr instantly became a goal of pilgrims. Today St. Eulalia's relics are enshrined within a silver casket in a magnificent basilica in Merida.

See holy card, page 342

ST. GUY OF ANDERLECHT

ABOUT 950–1012 • FEAST DAY: SEPTEMBER 12

St. Guy was born into poverty and remained poor all his life. By the time he was in his teens, he was already working as a field hand for a local lord. On Sundays and holy days, when no work was done, Guy spent long hours in and around Anderlecht's village church. The parish priest noticed and offered to hire Guy as sacristan. It was his dream job—he accepted at once. Now he spent all day in the church, cleaning the interior, caring for the sacred vessels, preparing the altar every morning for Mass. He even lived there, in a small room in the back.

He was still dirt poor, but working in the church was better than walking behind a plow horse. One day a merchant from Brussels passed through the village and met Guy after Mass. He liked the young man (Guy was not yet twenty years old at the time) and thought he would help him advance in the world. The merchant offered Guy a share, gratis, in a new trading venture. If it succeeded, Guy would be rich. This was his first opportunity to make a lot of money, and Guy leapt at it. He even made the trek to Brussels to see the merchant ship set sail, but it sank in the harbor and all the goods on board were lost.

Feeling that he had succumbed to the deadly sin of avarice, Guy made a penitential pilgrimage to Rome, walking the entire way. Then he went on to Jerusalem. A few years later he returned to Anderlecht and again took up the job of sacristan. He died in his beloved church.

St. Guy's devotion to his work—the joy he felt being in the presence of the Blessed Sacrament all day—has made him the patron and model for church sacristans.

See holy card, page 343

ST. NICHOLAS

DIED ABOUT 350 • FEAST DAY: DECEMBER 6

For the last seventeen hundred years, St. Nicholas has been one of the most popular saints of both the East and West. Although devotion to him is negligible in the United States (thanks to the confusion that he's Santa Claus—but that's another story), St. Nicholas is enormously popular in Europe and especially in the East.

A sure sign of St. Nicholas's popularity in the Middle Ages is the number of legends that have been told about him and the variety of people, professions, and causes that have taken him as their patron saint. Two stories explain why St. Nicholas is venerated as the protector of sailors.

During Nicholas's lifetime, a ship was caught in a violent storm at sea. Fearing for their lives, some of the sailors cried out, "Bishop Nicholas! If it is true what we have heard, that you are a saint who works miracles, help us now!" Immediately Nicholas appeared on the deck. "You called me," he said, "and I am here." Then the bishop rallied the astonished sailors, helped them secure the rigging and canvas, and commanded the storm to cease. The howling wind stopped, the sea became calm, and Nicholas vanished.

Years later, after St. Nicholas had died, a storm overtook a ship full of pilgrims bound for the Holy Land. Suddenly the terrified passengers and crew heard a loud cracking sound and saw the mainmast begin to break. As they called upon St. Nicholas for help, he appeared above the ship, grasped the broken mast and restored it, and then calmed the storm.

See holy card, page 343

ST. KENTIGERN

ABOUT 520–603 • FEAST DAY: JANUARY 13

The most extravagant legends have grown up around the Celtic saints, which makes their stories especially good reading.

Kentigern's mother was a married woman when she became pregnant by a man who was not her husband. Her outraged family dumped the poor woman into a cart and ran it off the edge of a cliff above Scotland's Firth of Forth. Incredibly she survived the fall into the sea, made it to shore, and gave birth safely to a baby boy she named Kentigern. Mother and child were warming themselves beside a shepherd's fire when along came an abbot, St. Serf. He offered Kentigern's mother a home and volunteered to adopt her son and raise him in the monastery. Serf became very fond of the child, calling him "Mungo," which means "dear boy." Some churches in Scotland are dedicated to the saint under that nickname.

Kentigern grew up to be a monk and eventually was consecrated as the first bishop of what is now Glasgow. Like all Celtic saints, he had a reputation as a wonderworker who specialized in solving seemingly impossible situations. When St. Serf's pet robin died, Kentigern restored it to life. Once in midwinter, when he had dozed off and let the monastery's fire go out, he kindled a new one with nothing but the frozen branches of a hazel tree.

After Kentigern became bishop, the queen came to him with an especially difficult problem. She had begun an affair with one of her husband's knights and had given the knight a love token. The problem was that the token, a ring, was one the king had given to her. One evening as the knight lay sleeping, the king saw his ring on the faithless man's finger. Carefully, without waking the knight, the king slipped it off and hurled it into the Clyde River. The next morning the king asked his wife to show him the ring. If the king did not execute his queen and her lover, he would at the very least banish them, and they would be disgraced for life. What, she implored Kentigern, should she do?

The bishop told her not to worry and sent her home. Then he summoned one of his monks and commanded him to go fishing. The monk caught a fine salmon that he carried back to the bishop. Kentigern slit open the salmon's belly, and out tumbled the missing ring.

Legend says that during a period of political upheaval in Scotland St. Kentigern was driven out of Glasgow. He traveled south to Wales, where he stayed with St. David, the monk and bishop who would become the patron saint of Wales. Kentigern spent many years with the Welsh. Then a new Scottish king invited him to return home to Glasgow and govern his diocese once again. Kentigern died in Glasgow at age eighty-five; tradition says that he was taking a bath at the time. St. Kentigern's tomb lies in the Lower Church of Glasgow Cathedral.

See holy card, page 343

ST. URSULA

LIFE DATES UNKNOWN • FEAST DAY: OCTOBER 21

The legend of St. Ursula is pretty hard to believe. Even during the Middle Ages, Christians had their doubts about it. The story is complicated, but here's the basic outline. Ursula was a British princess engaged to a pagan prince. Hoping to dissuade the prince from marrying her, or at least to convert him to Christianity, Ursula insisted upon a three-year waiting period, during which time she and eleven thousand of her virgin companions would make a pilgrimage to Rome. The prince did not object.

In Rome, the arrival of so many pious virgins led by a British princess caused a sensation. The pope received them in a private audience and then decided, along with many of his cardinals, to join the ladies on a pilgrimage to Cologne to venerate the relics of the Magi, the three kings who had brought gifts to the Christ Child. Tragically Urusla, her companions, the pope, and the cardinals all arrived in Cologne on the day the Huns had overwhelmed the city. The barbarians turned on the pilgrims, slaughtering them all. Ursula died in a rain of arrows, and so arrows have become her emblem.

Because Ursula traveled with an immense multitude of young ladies, schoolgirls have taken her as their patron saint. That practice was reinforced in 1535, when Angela Merici, an Italian nun and also later a saint, founded a new teaching order dedicated to the education of girls. She called her community the Order of St. Ursula. The Ursulines were the first teaching sisters to come to North America, opening schools for girls in Quebec and Montreal in the seventeenth century and in New Orleans in the early eighteenth.

See holy card, page 343

ST. ALBERT THE GREAT

ABOUT 1206–1280 • FEAST DAY: NOVEMBER 15

St. Albert the Great is best known as the man who taught theology to St. Thomas Aquinas. It was he who said that if Thomas was a dumb ox, as Thomas's fellow theology students called him, then he was one ox whose bellowing would be heard around the world.

But Albert was not only a theologian, he was also a scientist in the modern sense of the word. He wrote forty books on the natural sciences; in all of them he argued that, when it comes to scientific investigation, "experiment is the only safe guide." Eight hundred years ago, St. Albert was following a method of inquiry that today we take for granted—he went outside to see and study first-hand the workings of nature. "The aim of natural science is not simply to accept the statements of others," he wrote, "but to investigate the causes that are at work in nature." Albert's warning about accepting the statements of others was a gentle rebuke to his contemporaries, who still believed in some of the wilder ideas about the animal kingdom, for example, that barnacle geese were hatched out of trees. To deflate these medieval urban legends, Albert published a book on zoology—again, based on direct observation. He was the first man ever to accurately describe a Greenland whale, and to do so he hiked up his Dominican habit, climbed into a boat, and joined a whale hunt.

Scientists in their labs, students agonizing over the next biology exam, people wishing to correct the misguided notion that believers in God cannot have a scientific outlook—all could do no better than to invoke St. Albert the Great.

See holy card, page 344

FOUR CROWNED MARTYRS

ABOUT 305 • FEAST DAY: NOVEMBER 8

Technically five martyrs, rather than four, form this group: Claudius, Nicostratus, Symphorian, Castorius, and Simplicius. The first four had been Christians, friends, and coworkers for many years. Simplicius was a pagan who, inspired by the other four, converted to Christianity. The November 8 feast day is dedicated to the four, with St. Simplicius as an add-on.

The Four Crowned Martyrs were master sculptors in a quarry in Pannonia, a region that included parts of present-day Hungary and Serbia. Simplicius, their fellow sculptor, thought it must be their religion that made the men so skillful. As he took instruction in the faith, however, Simplicius realized that there was more to Christianity than improving one's job skills.

On a visit to the quarries, the emperor Diocletian admired the work of Claudius and his four friends. He commissioned them to carve a statue of Asclepius, the god of medicine, but the Christian sculptors refused to make an image of a pagan god. Diocletian wanted to leave the five men in peace, but a crowd of local people demanded that the blasphemers of the gods be punished. To keep the peace, Diocletian ordered the arrest of all five. They were flogged, sealed up in lead chests, and then drowned in the Danube River.

Christians recovered the chests and gave the martyrs a proper burial. A few years later the relics were transferred to Rome, where they are enshrined today in the ancient Basilica of the Four Crowned Martyrs.

See holy card, page 344

F. Fuchs.

Hl. Cassian.
Deine Wege, Herr, zeige mir und weise
mir deine Pfade. (Ps. 24, 4.)
Cum appr. eccl.

Déposé «St. Norbertus, Wien. — Mit kirchl. Genehmigung.

St. Leopold.

R. Margreiter.   GL 1038

ST. MARTHA

SANT'ANDREA AVELLINO

1. Stenographers and Secretaries · St. Cassian of Imola   2. Stepchildren and Stepparents · St. Leopold the G
3. Stressed by Guests · St. Martha   4. Stroke · St. Andrew Avellino

1.

ST. BRIGID

Was born in Ireland in the sixth century. She received the veil from St. Mel, the nephew of St. Patrick

S T. BRIGID built herself a cell under an oak tree. She was joined by many others and they formed a religious community which branched out into other communities, all acknowledging her as their Mother. She worked many miracles. She is also known as St. Bride.

Spes Sancta, Newbury 18

2.

3.

1. Students • St. Brigid   2. Swans • St. Hugh of Lincoln
3. Swimmers • St. Adjutor

Hl. Philomena.

Stark im Schwachen groß im Kleinen,
Ist der Glaube, gottgegeben,
Selig sind die Herzensreinen,
Gott sie schaun im ewgen Leben.

Commissariat of the Holy Land Washington D.C.

S. CLARA ASSISIENSIS

San Antonio M.ᵃ Claret

1. Teachers • St. John Baptist de la Salle 2. Teenagers • St. Philomena
3. Television • St. Clare of Assisi 4. Textile Workers • St. Anthony Mary Claret

1.

S. Augustinus

2086   CASM

2.

LE CHRIST ET LE BON LARRON

3.

CON
JVN
GO
R

T
IBI
CHRI
ST
E

SANCT·CYRIACVS·MART

VLA 411   Made in Austria

S. Cyriacus Martyr

1. Theologians • St. Augustine of Hippo   2. Thieves • St. Dismas
3. To Drive Away the Devil • St. Cyriacus

Second Marriage

ST. ADELAIDE

ABOUT 931–999 • FEAST DAY: DECEMBER 16

Medieval history is full of stories of daughters from royal or noble families whose fathers married them off to form a political alliance or extend the family's power. One of these unhappy women was St. Adelaide. At age two, she was engaged to a Provençal aristocrat. That marriage never took place; instead, at age sixteen she was married to Lothair, the king of Italy. Three years later she was a widow, her husband poisoned by a powerbroker named Berengar who wanted the crown for himself. Now Berengar tried to force Adelaide to marry his son. When she refused, he locked her in a prison. Somehow Adelaide managed to escape and made her way to German territory, where she begged the king, Otto the Great, for protection. Not only did Otto drive off Berengar, he married Adelaide himself.

We don't know if the union was a happy one, but it was certainly eventful. Adelaide and Otto had five children, and the pope crowned the couple Holy Roman Emperor and Empress. After twenty-two years of marriage, Otto the Great died and Adelaide was widowed once again. The joy of seeing her eldest son, Otto II, become king was diminished thanks to Adelaide's daughter-in-law, a thoroughly unpleasant Byzantine princess named Theophano, who delighted in instigating trouble between mother and son.

More deaths followed. Both Otto II and Theophano died in quick succession, leaving a little boy, Otto III. The German nobles and bishops asked Adelaide to act as regent until her grandson was old enough to rule. At age sixty, for the first time in her life, Adelaide was in complete control. As regent she demonstrated what a queen should be—wise, generous, and forgiving. Once her grandson was an adult, Adelaide retired to a convent she had built near Cologne, where she spent her final years among women who, like herself, preferred a quiet life.

See holy card, page 344

BLESSED ANGELA OF FOLIGNO

ABOUT 1248–1309 • FEAST DAY: JANUARY 4

One must read between the lines of Blessed Angela's memoirs to learn the nature of the terrible sin that haunted her all her life. She admits that, after her marriage to a wealthy merchant, she developed a taste for luxury—fine clothes, splendid jewels, rich food, rare wines. She was proud; she was a gossip; and she dressed and carried herself in a way to attract men's attention—and that leads one to believe that Angela cheated on her husband. She says that in 1285 she did something so bad, she feared she would go to hell. She says that she went to confession but was too ashamed to tell the priest what she had done. From the standpoint of Catholic theology, she then made matters worse by going to Communion. According to Church doctrine, a Catholic who consciously receives Communion with an unconfessed mortal sin on the soul commits sacrilege. Now Angela was certain that hell was waiting for her.

At long last, however, Angela did something right. She prayed to one of her favorite saints, Francis of Assisi, to help her find a confessor she could trust. The saint appeared to her, saying, "Sister, if you would have asked me sooner, I would have complied with your request sooner. Nonetheless, your request is granted." Excited and relieved, Angela hurried to church, where she found not just any priest, but a relation whom she loved and admired. To him she revealed all her sins, received absolution, and felt peace at last.

See holy card, page 344

ST. CUTHBERT

634–687 • FEAST DAY: MARCH 20

s a boy, St. Cuthbert watched his family's sheep on the hillsides above Melrose, in northern England. Nearby at Bamberg was a monastery where the elderly and much-loved St. Aidan had retired after a busy life establishing the faith in the borderlands between England and Scotland. Aidan died on the night of August 31, 651. Cuthbert was out on the hillsides, guarding his sheep as usual, when a brilliant light split open the night sky and he saw angels carrying St. Aidan's soul to heaven. At that moment Cuthbert decided to become a monk.

He entered the monastery at Melrose, where he struck everyone as an ideal candidate. Still in his late teens and very strong, Cuthbert enjoyed any kind of outdoor work. He learned Latin quickly and loved the hours spent chanting in the choir with his fellow monks. When the monks founded another monastery nearby, Cuthbert was sent there to serve as guest-master. His friendly,

outgoing personality made him a favorite with all visitors to the new establishment.

For more than a century, monks and nuns in Britain and Ireland had developed ways of living, praying, and keeping the liturgical calendar that differed from the traditions of the rest of the Catholic Church. Repeatedly the pope and his emissaries urged the British and Irish monks and nuns to adopt the Roman customs, but many were reluctant to give up their traditions. Finally in 664, St. Hilda, the most respected abbess in Britain, hosted a synod at her abbey at Whitby to decide the question. The delegates voted to adopt the Roman model, but the monks of Lindisfarne Abbey resisted. Fearful of a schism, the bishops of Britain agreed that Cuthbert should be appointed abbot of Lindisfarne. He had been trained in the old British rite, so perhaps through his tact and kind nature he could bring the monks into unity with the rest of the Church. It was a wise gamble, for Cuthbert succeeded in persuading the Lindisfarne monks to adopt the Roman usage.

St. Cuthbert became a beloved saint in England. So much so that even during the Reformation, the men whom Henry VIII appointed to dismantle shrines and scatter the bones of the saints could not bring themselves to harm St. Cuthbert's relics. They did strip the shrine of its valuables, but they left the saint's remains intact, buried beneath the church floor, at the very spot where his shrine had stood. St. Cuthbert's bones lie there in Durham Cathedral to this day.

See holy card, page 361

ST. JODOCUS

DIED 668 • FEAST DAY: DECEMBER 13

Briefly St. Jodocus had been king of Brittany, but after a pilgrimage to Rome he abdicated and became a hermit. Bretons at the time were a seafaring nation, with plenty of first-hand experience of all the perils of the sea. Once he retired to his rough chapel in the forest, Judocus prayed daily for the safety of all mariners. And so he became their patron, invoked especially against shipwreck.

As a hermit, Judocus did not have much, but whatever he had he shared with anyone who asked. One story tells how he had nothing in his hut but a piece of bread. A poor traveler asked for something to eat, so Jodocus cut the bread in half and gave it to the hungry stranger. In quick succession, three more travelers came to the door looking for something to eat, and to each one Joducus gave a share of his bread. By the time the fourth man arrived, the remaining bread was too small to divide, so Judocus gave it all away. People who heard the story said that the four travelers were in fact four apparitions of Christ who had come to experience for himself Joducus's generosity.

The place where Joducus was buried became known as Saint-Josse-sur-Mer, or St. Joducus by the Sea, which made it convenient for sailors to pray at his shrine. In 902 monks from Brittany brought a few of the saint's relics to Winchester Cathedral. Visitors to the church reported a sudden flurry of miracles, which established St. Joducus's cult in England. The English had a hard time pronouncing the Breton saint's name, so they modified it to St. Joce, or Joyce.

See holy card, page 361

Shoemakers

SS. CRISPIN & CRISPINIAN

DIED 285/86 • FEAST DAY: OCTOBER 25

We know that Crispin and Crispinian, two brothers, were beheaded for the faith in Soissons, France, on October 25 of either 285 or 286. The rest of their story is probably pure legend.

The brothers were Romans who had moved to Soissons to preach the gospel. As master shoemakers, they earned enough to support themselves and give something to the poor. They spoke of Christ to everyone who came to the workshop, which made them an easy target during a time of anti-Christian persecution.

The magistrate alternated between bribes and threats to make the brothers abandon Christianity, but Crispin and Crispinian were unmoved. The torturers stretched them on a rack, cut long strips of flesh from their bodies, and drove awls under their fingernails before at last beheading them both.

Shoemakers took the two brothers as their patrons. In England devotion to them spiked after King Henry V won his famous victory over the French at Agincourt on their feast day. In his play *Henry V*, Shakespeare gives the king a rousing speech in which he makes a prediction about the feast day of the shoemaker saints:

And Crispin Crispian shall ne'er go by,
From this day to the ending of the world,
But we in it shall be remembered—
We few, we happy few, we band of brothers.

See holy card, page 361

ST. MARGARET OF CORTONA

1247–1297 • FEAST DAY: FEBRUARY 22

By the time she was thirteen years old, Margaret had grown into a beautiful, flirtatious, overconfident girl, eager to get away from an unhappy life with her father and stepmother. When Arsenio, the fifteen-year-old son of the local baron, paid attention to her, Margaret was flattered. When he invited her to move into the castle as his mistress, she didn't hesitate. The historical record doesn't tell us much about Arsenio, but what has survived suggests that he was a direct, candid young man. He told Margaret at the outset that he would never marry her. A peasant could be his mistress, but never his wife. She heard him but didn't believe him. She was confident that, given time, she could change his mind—that one day she would be a baroness.

The couple lived together for nine years and had one son. Yet still Arsenio didn't ask Margaret to marry him. Ever the optimist, she remained with her lover, waiting for the moment when a wedding would lead them both out of mortal sin and legitimize their son.

Then one day Arsenio went off to tend to some business on one of his family's outlying estates. The date of his return came and went without any word that he was delayed or sick or injured. As the days passed, Margaret became increasingly anxious. Then Arsenio's dog returned alone to the castle. He found Margaret, grabbed her dress in his teeth, and, backing up, pulled her toward the door. As the dog headed for the woods, Margaret followed. When they were out of sight of the castle, the dog stopped beside a shallow pit covered with dry brush and began to whine. With trembling hands Margaret cleared away the debris until she saw Arsenio's body. The sight of her handsome lover, now dead and decomposing, shocked her. Weeping and lamenting, she wondered who murdered Arsenio and why. Then, to her surprise, her mind took a different turn: She wondered if Arsenio had had time before he died to beg for God's mercy. In that moment, Margaret was overwhelmed by the recognition that for nine years she and Arsenio had lived entirely for their own pleasure, without any thought for the state of their souls. That was the beginning of her conversion.

Unwilling to remain at the castle, and certain to receive a cold welcome at her father's house, Margaret took her son and headed for Cortona, where the Franciscan fathers had a reputation for helping repentant sinners. As it happened, the Franciscans exceeded their reputation. They found a home for Margaret and her son, found work for her in a hospital, arranged for the boy to study at an academy in a nearby town, and helped Margaret overcome her past and become a saint.

Originally St. Margaret was recognized as the patron of penitent women. Recently she has come to be venerated as the patron of single mothers.

See holy card, page 361

ST. LYDWINA

1380–1433 • FEAST DAY: APRIL 14

Fifteen-year-old Lydwina was ice-skating with some friends on the Schie River when one of the girls lost her balance and collided with her. Lydwina hit the ice hard, striking her head and breaking a rib. Her friends carried her home and the family sent for a doctor, but in the days that followed her condition worsened; she suffered from bouts of violent vomiting and was in constant pain. Weeks later, still unable to get out of bed, Lydwina could add profound depression to her growing list of ailments.

Since the accident Lydwina's parish priest, Father John Pot, had stopped by often. He knew Lydwina had hoped to enter a convent. Now he suggested that she accept her current pain-wracked condition as a substitute for the life of self-sacrifice she would have lived as a nun.

Father Pot's suggestion appealed to Lydwina. As she began a routine of concentrated prayer and meditation, her depression lifted and her pain diminished. Neighbors stopped by to ask her counsel on spiritual matters; her advice was so down-to-earth and helpful that townspeople began to regard her as their saint. When a new pastor dismissed her as a faker, neighbors caused such an uproar that the bishop sent theologians to examine her. After lengthy conversations with her and with witnesses, the commissioners concluded that Lydwina was a devout and faithful Catholic. The bishop was so impressed by what he had heard of the young woman that he instructed the parish priests to bring her Holy Communion twice each week—a rare privilege at a time when most Catholics received Communion only once a year, at Easter.

In spite of her injuries, St. Lydwina is the patron of all amateur and professional ice-skaters, hockey players, and by extension everyone who uses roller blades, roller skates, and skate boards.

See holy card, page 362

ST. MARCULF

DIED 558 • FEAST DAY: MAY 1

After coronation, one of the first things a king of France did was travel to Corbigny to pray at the tomb of St. Marculf, and then touch the relics. It was believed that the saint was able to transfer to him the power to heal a skin rash known as scrofula, or the king's evil. All the monarch had to do was touch the afflicted person, and, through St. Marculf's prayers, the rash would clear up.

How Marculf acquired a reputation for healing inflammations and irritations of the skin is unknown. He was born in Bayeux, the son of a wealthy Christian family. After his parents died, he gave away his entire fortune and went off to live as a monk. He moved around a great deal in northern France, and everywhere he went he founded a monastery. At one point he moved to the Island of Jersey, one of the Channel Islands between England and France. The islanders liked Marculf, especially after he saved them from an invasion of Saxon pirates. As the pagans had drawn near, Marculf stood praying on the shore. Suddenly a violent storm crashed down on the fleet, destroying all the ships and drowning all the raiders.

The tradition of the king touching the bones of St. Marculf survived into the eighteenth century. Unfortunately, Marculf's link to the royal family made his shrine a target during the French Revolution. In 1793 a mob rampaged through the church where his relics were enshrined, broke open the tomb, and destroyed the remains of the saint.

See holy card, page 362

ST. PETER CLAVER

1580–1654 • FEAST DAY: SEPTEMBER 9

As a young man, Peter Claver found it difficult to make up his mind about his future. Should he enter the religious life or live as a layman? Should he be a Jesuit, active in the world, or retire to a cloistered life in a monastery? Should he remain in Spain, his homeland, or accept an assignment in the New World? Finally, after years of dithering, Claver joined the Jesuits, agreed to go to the mission in Cartagena, Colombia, and there asked to be ordained a priest.

In Cartagena, Claver found his purpose in life. He was assigned to assist Father Alphonsus de Sandoval, a fellow Jesuit who worked in the slave pens at the harbor. Cartagena was one of the main ports for the African slave trade, and every month ships brought a thousand or more terrified captives into the city. After their long voyage sequestered in the dark holds of the ships, many of the enslaved Africans were sick, injured, undernourished, and dehydrated. Father de Sandoval brought them medicine, food, water, and what comfort he could offer. From the moment Father Claver joined him, he worked with true fervor. Around the docks he found African slaves and freedmen to act as interpreters so that he could learn what the newcomers needed while beginning to teach them the rudiments of Christianity. Generally he had a couple weeks with each new shipload, for the traders waited until the Africans had recovered from the voyage before putting them up for sale. It is said that in the forty-four years he worked in the slave pens, Claver baptized three hundred thousand Africans.

More certain is Father Claver's dedication to his African parishioners. Many were sold beyond his reach, to far-off farms and cities, but he never abandoned those who were purchased by masters in and around Cartagena. He visited them regularly, continuing their religious instruction, saying Mass and bringing them the sacraments, and intervening on the behalf of those with their harsh masters.

Most of the white colonists of Cartagena tolerated Father Claver, but some despised him. They complained that he kept slaves from their work and that he was committing sacrilege by giving the sacraments to the Africans. Certain well-to-do ladies let it be known that they would not set foot into any church or chapel where he had said Mass for a congregation of slaves.

In 1654 Father Claver, now seventy-four years old, was working in the slave pens as usual when he collapsed. As word spread that he was dying, a large crowd of enslaved Africans gathered in front of the Jesuit residence. Shortly after midnight, when his death was announced, the Africans broke down the gates and surged into the residence to see, for the last time, one of the few men in the New World who had treated them as human beings.

See holy card, page 362

ST. PATRICK

ABOUT 390–ABOUT 461 • FEAST DAY: MARCH 17

Even people who can't tell the difference between an archangel and an abbess know that St. Patrick drove the snakes out of Ireland. The legend is one of the oldest and most enduring. And it's true that, to this day, no serpents live in Ireland. Of course, it's also true that Romans who visited the island centuries before Patrick noticed the country was snakefree. In modern times it has been common to view the story metaphorically, with the snakes representing the false gods and heathenish practices of the pre-Christian Irish, which St. Patrick banished from the island.

St. Patrick was not an Irishman; he was British, born in a town called Bannaventa, close to the border of England and Scotland. About the year 406, raiders from Ireland attacked the town and carried off some of the inhabitants as slaves: among the captives was sixteen-year-old Patrick. In Ireland he was put to work as a shepherd. For six years he lived almost entirely outdoors, ill-clothed, underfed, and close to despair. Although raised in a Christian home, young Patrick had never taken Christianity seriously, but now, with no one else to turn to, he began to pray to the God he had always scorned. And his prayers were answered—Patrick escaped, returned to his family in Britain, and then went to France to study for the priesthood.

After his ordination he had a dream in which he heard the voices of millions of Irish crying, "Come back, young man, and walk among us once again!" Patrick interpreted the dream as a call to convert the Irish to Christianity. His interpretation was reinforced when Pope St. Celestine sent him as a missionary bishop to Ireland.

It is said that St. Patrick converted all the Irish. Well, not exactly. But he did convert so many, and changed their worldview so thoroughly, that it was light work for his disciples to complete the conversion of the entire country.

See holy card, page 363

OUR LADY OF THE SNOW

FEAST DAY: AUGUST 5

Every winter for generations, Catholic schoolchildren have prayed to Our Lady of the Snow to grant them a snow day.

According to an old legend, on the night of August 4, 352, at the height of a steamy Roman summer, Our Lady appeared to a senator named John and his wife, commanding them to build a church in her honor on the Esquiline Hill. That same night, she also appeared to Pope Liberius and gave him the same instructions.

The next morning, John, his wife, and the pope met on the Esquiline Hill, where they found something extraordinary: Outlined in snow was the plan for the basilica the Blessed Virgin wanted them to build. The church built on the spot is the Basilica of St. Mary Major. To commemorate the miracle of the snow, every August 5, during Mass in the basilica, a shower of white roses petals are released from above to fall onto the congregation.

The basilica is called "Major" be-cause it's the most important church in the West that is dedicated to the Blessed Virgin. As such, it's filled with extraordinary works of art, including a series of fifth-century mosaics that extend along the length of the main aisle. The ceiling was gilded with the first shipment of gold to arrive in Europe from the New World—the gift of Ferdinand and Isabella.

The church is rich in relics as well. Beneath the high altar, in a crystal and gilt bronze casket, are pieces of wood said to be from the Bethlehem manger in which Mary placed the Christ Child.

See holy card, page 363

ST. LOUISE DE MARILLAC

1591–1660 • FEAST DAY: MARCH 15

More than three hundred years ago, Louise de Marillac, a widow, moved into Paris, taking a house near the church where a priest named Vincent de Paul operated an ambitious mission to the poor, the desperate, and the abandoned. From their meeting emerged a remarkable partnership. Vincent, always overextended, never had time to oversee his charitable organizations; Louise, a woman with a great love for God and superior management skills, was eager to do good.

In various towns around France, Father Vincent had gathered women who had time and money to spare and instructed them to see to the needs of the poorest in their parishes. It was an inspired idea, but in many cases once Father Vincent moved on, the Ladies of Charity (as they called themselves) lost their initial fervor. Louise de Marillac proved to be the solution. Her first assignment was to visit all parishes that had a Ladies of Charity organization and revitalize them. Her tour convinced Louise of two things—the Ladies were willing to give money, but they recoiled from the hands-on work of nursing the sick, feeding the hungry, and tending abandoned or orphaned children. The organization needed hardy young women from the working classes who were accustomed to long days of toil, and so Louise founded a new order of nuns, the Daughters of Charity.

Devout young women from the country flocked to the new order, and soon Louise and her sisters were staffing orphanages, shelters for the mentally ill, homes for the elderly, hostels for the homeless, free schools for poor children, a ministry to convicts, and even battlefield hospitals during wartime. Her religious order was the first to tend the poor and needy at every stage of life, from cradle to grave. In recognition of her achievements, in 1960 Blessed Pope John XXIII named St. Louise de Marillac the patron of social workers.

See holy card, page 363

ST. GEORGE

DIED ABOUT 303 • FEAST DAY: APRIL 23

There have been lots of soldier-saints, but none has ever achieved the fame of St. George. Blame it on the dragon. The story of the fearless knight slaying a fearsome monster to save an innocent princess is simply irresistible. Of course, just about every mythology in the world has a story of a hero who rescues a maiden by killing a maiden-eating beast. But what sets St. George's story apart from all the others is this: Instead of ending with the wedding of the hero and the maiden, George's legend ends with a mass baptism of the princess, the king, and all the people of the realm.

The fragments of information about St. George don't say that he was a soldier. But as is often the case with the oldest and most popular saints, that's hardly the point. George's courageous death as a martyr inspired countless legends (including grisly tales of how he endured dozens of gruesome tortures before death released him).

Two things elevated George to military status—first, the Byzantine army's decision to adopt him as their patron; and second, the dragon legend. When the Crusaders from western Europe passed through the Byzantine Empire in the late eleventh century, they heard the stories of the warrior-martyr St. George; considering their mission, he seemed the ideal patron saint. And after it was said that St. George, along with St. Demetrius and St. Theodore, rode down from heaven to aid the Crusaders in a battle outside Antioch in 1098, his place in the hearts of soldiers was secure.

Crusaders took his story back home, and scores of countries, provinces, cities, and towns adopted St. George as their guardian, especially of their armies in times of war.

See holy card, page 363

S. MAGNUS.

Sumptibus Fr. Pustet, Ratisbonæ.

S. BAMBINO GESÙ DI PRAGA

Sancte Andrea, Apostole, ora pro nobis.

HIN DVRCH FROHES GEFILDE GELEITET SIE
HL. KINDER FARBIG AVS BLVMENGEFLECHT
TRÄGT SIE DIE KRONE DES SIEGES ✠ ✠ ✠

VLA 367

S. Felicitas M.

1. To Drive Away Vermin • St. Magnus of Fuessen   2. To Ensure Prosperity • Holy Infant of Prague
3. To Find a Husband • St. Andrew   4. To Have Male Babies • St. Felicitas of Rome

1.

2.

S. APOLLONIA.

3.

4.

SANCTUS CHRISTOPHORUS

1. To Make a Good Confession • St. Pio of Pietrelcina 2. Toothache • St. Apollonia
3. Tour Guides • St. Bona of Pisa 4. Travelers • St. Christopher

SCS MENAS MART

K. BEURON 1019

LE SAINT HOMME JOB

Abbaye Ste Gertrude, Louvain. G. 81. Th. Galle sc.

Sanctus Gommarus

Steendr. Kn. Lambrechts-Van de Velde, Deurne-Antwerpen.

1. Traveling Salesmen • St. Menas   2. Tuberculosis • St. Thérèse of Lisieux
3. Ulcers • St. Job   4. Unhappy Marriage • St. Gummarus

O. Rosenbaum   S círk. schv.   B B 1006

SV. CYRIL A METODĚJ

S. GUDULA.

Unity of the Western and Eastern Churches · St. Cyril and St. Methodius   2. Unmarried Women · St. Gud

3. Vampire Hunters · St. Marcellus of Paris

ST. BLAISE

DIED ABOUT 316 • FEAST DAY: FEBRUARY 3

Every February 3, crowds of Catholics line up to have their throats blessed. The custom is ancient, and it's a popular way to honor the saint of sore throats, St. Blaise.

Blaise was bishop of Sebaste, the town known today as Siras, in Turkey. During a wave of anti-Christian persecution, he was arrested. As the soldiers escorted him to prison, they encountered a pathetic scene: a wolf was running off with a small pig its mouth, and trying to catch the beast was a poor widow. In a loud voice Blaise commanded the wolf to stop. To everyone's astonishment, the animal did as he was told. "Release the pig," Blaise said. Once again the wolf obeyed. As the pig scurried back to its mistress, the wolf slunk away into the forest, and the guard led Blaise to prison.

That night, as Blaise sat alone in his dark cell, he had a visitor. The widow whose pig he saved had brought him a basket of food and two tall wax candles to dispel the gloom.

Blaise was scheduled for execution the next day. Before he left his cell, another visitor came to see him: it was a mother carrying her young son who was choking to death on a fish bone. The woman begged the saint to save her son's life. Taking the two candles, Blaise made a cross, placed it against the child's throat, and blessed the dying boy. Immediately the bone was dislodged and the boy climbed out of his mother's arms, completely well.

To this day, on Blaise's feast day, Catholic priests make a cross from two wax candles, and, while holding it against each congregant's throat, they pray, "Through the intercession of St. Blaise, bishop and martyr, may God deliver you from all evils of the throat and from every other evil. In the name of the Father, and of the Son, and of the Holy Spirit. Amen."

See holy card, page 364

ST. BENEDICT

ABOUT 480–543 • FEAST DAY: JULY 11

As wealthy patricians, St. Benedict's parents could afford to send their son to study at one of the best academies in Rome. The teachers may have been excellent, but the students were of a distinctly lower caliber. Benedict was disgusted to discover that his fellow students were ignorant, intellectually lazy, and shamelessly immoral. Some boys might have transferred to another school; instead, Benedict chose to give up the secular world altogether and live for God alone.

About forty miles from Rome, high in the mountains, was a place called Subiaco—Benedict walked there, imagining he could lose himself in the wilderness. He wasn't far from the town when he met a monk named Romanus, who lived in a neighboring monastery. Romanus pointed Benedict toward a spacious cave, gave him the religious garb of a monk, and promised to bring food.

The cave where St. Benedict made his home is still extant, overlooking a dramatic ravine on a peak above the town's monastery. It is a large cave that, over the centuries, the Benedictine monks have converted into a church. But the look and feel of the place hasn't been spoiled. Once inside, no pilgrim can doubt having entered a cavern beneath the mountain.

Benedict spent several years living in anonymity before word began to circulate about the holy man living at Subiaco. Others seeking a holy life made the trek up to his cave and built huts for themselves nearby.

See holy card, page 364

Stammering & Other Speech Impediments

ST. NOTKAR BALBULUS

ABOUT 840–912 • FEAST DAY: APRIL 6

Balbulus is the Latin word for "stammerer," and it's the nickname St. Notkar acquired when he was a schoolboy at the abbey of Saint Gall in Switzerland. The epithet stuck, even after he became a monk and a saint. As a student, Notkar was especially interested in music, and, although he stammered when he spoke, he sang with perfect clarity.

Notkar spent the rest of his life at St. Gall, where his jobs included abbey librarian, guest-master, and master of the school. He was a wise and sympathetic man whom visitors consulted on a host of matters, spiritual and secular—even the Holy Roman Emperor, Charles the Fat, came to Notkar for advice. But music remained his lifelong love. He acquired manuscripts from Rome to improve the quality of Gregorian chant at St. Gall while also expanding the monks' musical repertoire.

His life's work was *The Book of Hymns*, an extensive collection of Gregorian songs. Thanks to Notkar, these lovely compositions from the basilicas of Italy spread throughout Germany and France. It is said that he wrote two especially beautiful hymns, "Veni, sancte Spiritus," in honor of the Holy Spirit, and "Dies Irae," sung in Masses for the dead. It's possible that Notkar did indeed compose them, but it's more likely that he introduced and popularized them in the lands north of the Alps.

St. Notkar died at St. Gall, where one of his brother monks eulogized him as "stammering of tongue but not of intellect . . . assiduous in prayer, reading, and copying, versed in knowledge [and] a master of the chant."

See holy card, page 364

ST. THOMAS MORE

1478–1535 • FEAST DAY: JUNE 22

Public service was a key part of the More family tradition: Thomas's father had been a respected judge, and his maternal grandfather had been sheriff of London. But Thomas would climb higher than anyone could have predicted.

Thomas More is one of the most likable of the saints. A devoted family man, he and his wife, Alice, raised four children and took in orphans as well. He had a charming personality and, as a lawyer, his quick mind and eloquence made him a formidable opponent in the courtroom. His writings, especially *Utopia*, brought him international fame. And his wisdom and integrity won him the trust of Thomas Cardinal Wolsey and Henry VIII.

That was the Thomas More the world knew and loved. The other Thomas More spent part of each day at Mass and in prayer and meditation. His Catholic faith was the core of his life, and ultimately it was his faith that would get him into trouble.

At Cardinal Wolsey's death in 1529, the king appointed Thomas to be Lord Chancellor of England. It was the realm's second-highest office, after the king himself, and Thomas was the first layman to hold it. Henry had a problem that he expected the Lord Chancellor to fix: He wanted a son. Henry's queen, Catherine of Aragon, was forty-four years old and unlikely to have any more children. She had given birth to several baby boys, but they'd all died within a few days; only the princess Mary survived to adulthood. Yet her father did not consider Mary a suitable heir to the throne. First of all, Henry didn't believe a woman could rule, and so he wanted a male heir. But perhaps more to the point, he had become infatuated with twenty-three-year-old Anne Boleyn, whom he wanted as his wife, something he could do only if the pope annulled his marriage to Catherine.

At first, Thomas was able to keep his distance from the king's suit. But in 1531 Henry got tired of waiting for the pope's decision. He ordered the archbishop of Canterbury to declare his marriage to Catherine dissolved; then he married Anne Boleyn and made an even bolder move by proclaiming himself "Protector and Supreme Head of the Church in England." Henceforth the king, not the pope, had ultimate spiritual authority in England, and the people wouldn't be members of the Roman Catholic Church but of the Church of England.

Unable to support Henry's whims, Thomas resigned his office as Lord Chancellor, taking care not to comment on the king's divorce or his claim to supreme spiritual authority in England. It didn't matter. He was still arrested and imprisoned in the Tower of London. After fourteen months of confinement, Thomas was brought to trial on a charge of treason. The trial was rigged from the beginning, yet Thomas's skillful defense won the sympathy of the jurors and spectators. Then a false witness stepped forward, claiming that Thomas had admitted he rejected the king's title as supreme head of the church in England. The perjured testimony reminded the ju-

rors what they were supposed to do: find Thomas guilty and sentence him to death.

The sentence was carried out on Tower Hill, on July 7, 1535. On the scaffold, Thomas asked the large crowd to bear witness that he was giving his life "for the faith of the Holy Catholic Church" and to remember that he died "the king's good servant, but God's first." Then he knelt down and recited Psalm 51, the "Miserere." He forgave, blessed, and kissed the headsman, then laid his neck on the block. The executioner beheaded Thomas More with a single blow of the ax.

In 2000, Pope John Paul II—in recognition of St. Thomas More's integrity, sense of justice, and unswerving commitment to the truth—named him the patron of statesmen and politicians.

See holy card, page 364

ST. CASSIAN OF IMOLA

DIED ABOUT 250 • FEAST DAY: AUGUST 13

The oldest surviving source for the story of St. Cassian is the Christian poet Prudentius (348–about 405), who wrote many longish poems on the lives of martyrs.

Cassian was a schoolteacher in Imola, about twenty-seven miles from Ravenna, in northern Italy. During a period of anti-Christian persecution, he was arrested and arraigned before the province's governor. The governor offered to spare Cassian's life if he sacrificed to the gods; Cassian refused. All that remained was for the governor to pronounce the death sentence. In a moment of macabre inspiration, the governor decreed that Cassian's current and former pupils should be the ones to put him to death.

While the guards rounded up the schoolboys, Cassian was stripped and tied to a stake. The boys who showed up for the execution were armed with clubs, knives, and the sharp-pointed iron styluses they used to write their assignments on wax tablets (the Roman world's version of notebooks). The little monsters hurled their tablets at their teacher's face, slashed him with knives, and battered him with clubs. But the boys with the styluses were the worst, carving letters and numbers and excerpts from their lessons into Cassian's flesh.

The Christians of Imola gave Cassian's body a decent burial, and his tomb became a place of pilgrimage (Prudentius visited it while en route to Rome). Because pens were used in St. Cassian's martyrdom, he became the patron of stenographers and secretaries. Strange to say, there's no evidence of St. Cassian being invoked by schoolteachers, especially those saddled with rotten students.

See holy card, page 381

ST. LEOPOLD THE GOOD

1073–1136 • FEAST DAY: NOVEMBER 15

St. Leopold loved children. He married a widowed noblewoman named Agnes, and into the palace she brought two young children from her first husband. Leopold raised them as his own. Over the years, Agnes and Leopold had eighteen children, eleven of whom survived to adulthood. By all accounts Leopold was a gentle, loving father who made no distinction between his stepchildren and the children he fathered with Agnes.

The couple ruled over Austria, a land that in the early twelfth century was still largely wild and uninhabited. As an expression of his religious devotion, Leopold founded several important monasteries that still survive, including Heilegenkreuz in Lower Austria, which possesses a relic of the True Cross, and Klosterneuberg on the Danube, right outside Vienna. The latter was his favorite place, and he asked to be buried there.

Leopold had a practical reason for founding these monasteries, too. Although the sites he chose were in the wilderness, he knew that once the monks arrived they would make the land productive and attract people to settle in the region.

As ruler of Austria, Leopold's priorities were the peace and prosperity of his people. As a player on the European political stage, he sided with the pope against kings who were trying to assume the right to appoint bishops in their own lands.

When Leopold died, all his children and the people of Austria mourned him as an honest and holy prince. In addition to being venerated as the patron of stepchildren and stepparents, St. Leopold the Good is also one of the patrons of Austria.

See holy card, page 381

ST. MARTHA

FIRST CENTURY • FEAST DAY: JULY 29

If any saint understands the stress of preparing the house for guests, it's St. Martha. After all, she served dinner to the Son of God.

The gospels of St. Luke and St. John tell us that Martha, her sister Mary, and their brother Lazarus were close friends of Jesus. St. Luke describes one of the Lord's visits to the family's home in Bethany. Martha was rushing about preparing a meal and trying to make everything perfect for Jesus. Meanwhile, Mary was not helping at all. Instead, she sat on the floor, at the Lord's feet, so as not to miss a word that he said. Martha found the situation galling; two thousand years after the event we can still hear the irritation in her voice as she appeals to Jesus, "Lord, do you not care that my sister has left me to serve alone? Tell her then to help me." Christ answers, "Martha, Martha, you are anxious and troubled about many things; one thing is needful. Mary has chosen the good portion, which shall not be taken away from her" (Luke 10:40-42).

Legend says that after Christ's ascension into heaven, Martha carried the gospel to southern France. Once while she was preaching, a teenage boy tried to swim across the Rhone River, the better to hear her. The current, however, was stronger than the young swimmer, and he drowned. When his grief-stricken family and friends brought the boy's body to Martha, she prayed earnestly to Christ. Addressing the Lord as "my dear guest," she begged him to restore life to the young man. Her prayer done, Martha stood up and took the boy's hand. Immediately he came back to life.

See holy card, page 381

ST. ANDREW AVELLINO

1521–1608 • FEAST DAY: NOVEMBER 10

Andrew Avellino is probably the only saint whose original name was Lancelot. He lived with the moniker until he was thirty-five years old, when he entered a religious order that permitted members to take a new name—in his case, Andrew.

Born in Naples, by the time young Lancelot was twenty-six, he had become a lawyer who practiced both civil and church law and was ordained a priest. A calm, level-headed man, he won the admiration of his archbishop, who gave him a challenging assignment. The Convent of the Archangel in Naples had become notorious for the immorality of the nuns. The archbishop wanted Lancelot to persuade the sisters to keep their vows. From the day they met, the nuns hated him and resisted every reform he tried to implement. When he insisted that they return to the cloistered way of life, he was attacked and beaten by the nuns' lovers.

He was carried, half-dead, to the house of the Theatine priests, where he was protected and cared for. By the time he recovered from the attack, Lancelot had decided to join the Theatines, giving up his baptismal name and adopting the name Andrew. He became a tremendous asset to the order, not only as an eloquent preacher and skillful spiritual director who brought many sinners back to the Church but also as the priest who trained new recruits. He eventually was elected the superior of the Theatines.

Years later, on the morning of November 10, 1608, eighty-seven-year-old Andrew suffered a massive stroke and died as he approached the altar to say Mass. He is the saint invoked against stroke, and against sudden death as well.

See holy card, page 381

ST. BRIGID

ABOUT 452–525 • FEAST DAY: FEBRUARY 1

St. Brigid was born when Ireland was making the momentous shift from a pagan nation to one of the most devoutly Christian countries in Europe. The tension was played out in her own family: Brigid's father was a pagan, her mother was a Christian. One story claims that St. Patrick himself baptized the infant Brigid. That may seem unlikely, but it is possible—Patrick was still alive at the time.

More certain is the later part of the story. When Brigid decided to become a nun, she and eight companions received the veil from St. Mel, one of St. Patrick's nephews. They set up their convent at Kildare, where the druids had venerated a sacred oak tree and kept a perpetual fire burning in honor of the Celtic gods. Brigid and her nuns tended the fire, too, but they "baptized" it, consecrating the eternal flame to Christ, the eternal Light of the World.

This marriage of the Celtic and the Christian became the hallmark of Brigid's mission. At Kildare she opened Ireland's first Christian school, where she taught her pupils Christian doctrine and classical learning as well as the poetry, mythology, music, and customs of pre-Christian Ireland. The Irish trace their commitment to Christ and their reverence for their Celtic heritage to St. Brigid.

At her convent, Brigid established a scriptorium, where books from the Continent could be copied and disseminated throughout the country. The finest work her scriptorium ever produced was the magnificently illustrated *Book of Kildare*. In the twelfth century Giraldus Cambrensis, a Welsh priest, examined the book during a visit and declared that it must have been made by an angel. Giraldus's enthusiasm gave birth to a new legend about St. Brigid, that the *Book of Kildare* was a collaboration between the saint and an angel.

See holy card, page 382

ST. HUGH OF LINCOLN

1140–1200 • FEAST DAY: NOVEMBER 17

In the nearly one thousand years since they were first founded in a remote valley in the French Alps, the Carthusian monks and nuns have never required a reformation. Every other religious order, of both men and women, has grown lax or worldly at one time or another, but the Carthusians have always remained true to their original vision. Pope Innocent XI (reigned 1676–89) once quipped, "The Carthusian order need not be reformed, for it has never been deformed."

The Carthusian life is very strict. Each monk lives alone in complete silence in his own tiny house. Three times a day, the monks gather in the church for Mass and prayers, but for the rest of the day, including mealtimes, each one is solitary. The goals of Carthusian life are to grow in love of God, increase in personal holiness, and offer prayer and penances to God for the salvation of the outside world.

The Carthusians have produced countless saints, although very few are known outside the order. St. Hugh of Lincoln, however, was the first Carthusian canonized by the Church. In his early twenties, he visited the Grande Chartreuse, the first Carthusian monastery, and met St. Bruno, the man who founded the order. The Carthusian commitment to sanctity appealed strongly to Hugh, and he entered the order when he was twenty-five. He would've been happy to spend the rest of his life at the Grande Chartreuse, but in 1181 Henry II of England founded a charterhouse (the term for a Carthusian monastery) as part of his penance for the murder of St. Thomas Becket, and he invited Father Hugh to come to England and serve as prior. With the approval of his brother monks, Hugh set out across the Channel.

Once he arrived in Somerset, everyone from the king to the peasants was completely taken with him. He was saintly—that was unmistakable—but he also possessed great personal charm that made everyone feel at ease. It is said that even babies felt drawn to him. Insisting that it would be a sin to let such a man vanish into a cloister, both the king and the bishops pressured Hugh to accept the office of bishop of Lincoln. Never again would Hugh know the peace of the cloister, but as bishop he was able to do a great deal of good in the world. For example, as Richard the Lionheart prepared to join the Third Crusade, anti-Semitic violence erupted across England. Alone and unarmed, Bishop Hugh confronted angry mobs, kept them from attacking Jews, and persuaded them to release those they had already taken captive.

St. Hugh's emblem is a swan, a reference to a bird that lived at his estate at Stowe. The swan became attached to Hugh, following him around the grounds, eating from his hand, and even sleeping in his room at night. It is said that when Hugh was dying, no one could lure or drive the swan away from the saint's bedside.

See holy card, page 382

ST. ADJUTOR

DIED 1131 • FEAST DAY: APRIL 30

When Pope Urban II launched the First Crusade in 1095, Adjutor, a Norman knight, answered the call. He fought in the battle for Jerusalem and, after the Holy City was in Christian hands, stayed on as part of the garrison. He was on patrol outside Jerusalem when he was ambushed by Saracens. They dragged him to one of their strongholds, a fortress on a rocky islet off the Palestinian coast, where they loaded his wrists and ankles with heavy chains and locked him alone in a cell. From time to time, his jailers amused themselves by torturing their prisoner.

The knight tried to keep up his courage, but with no hope of escape or rescue, he was close to despair. In his desolation he turned for help to his favorite saint, St. Mary Magdalen. Legend says the saint appeared in Adjutor's cell, shattered his chains, and then transported him outside the fortress. Adjutor dove into the sea and swam to shore. When he arrived safely in Crusader territory, he was still wearing lengths of his broken chains. After a blacksmith struck them off his wrists and ankles, Adjutor kept the shackles as a reminder of his miraculous deliverance from prison.

Back in France, Adjutor became a Benedictine monk in an abbey near the Seine River. A stretch of river near the abbey was troubled by a dangerous whirlpool that had taken the lives of many boatmen. One day, Adjutor took a link from his old chains and, in the company of the local bishop, rowed out to the edge of the whirlpool. As the bishop sprinkled holy water and prayed for God's mercy, Adjutor tossed the link into the whirlpool. At once the water became calm, safe at last for boatmen and swimmers alike.

See holy card, page 382

ST. JOHN BAPTIST DE LA SALLE

1651–1719 • FEAST DAY: APRIL 7

John Baptist de la Salle was a wealthy priest assigned to the cathedral of Rheims when a layman named Adrian Nyel asked for his help in opening a school for the city's poor children. John liked the idea so much that with his own money he rented a house for the school's teachers and paid their salaries. As he became more involved with the school, John concluded that most of his teachers had no idea about the most effective way to instruct children.

The teachers who felt John was meddling in their profession quit, but those who stayed on worked with him to develop a revolutionary teaching method that is followed today in virtually every public, private, and parochial school.

In the seventeenth century, children were taught to read and write in Latin first, and in their own language later. John and his teachers reversed the process, beginning with the vernacular and bringing Latin into the curriculum later. Generally a teacher read aloud to the class from the textbook. John introduced a question-and-answer method that encouraged children to think and participate. At the time, individual attention was unheard of, but John argued that not everyone learns or understands at a uniform pace. He instructed his teachers to be patient and creative. John even included good manners in his program, saying that as children of God everyone, regardless of rank, must be treated with courtesy and respect.

The men who adopted John's method organized themselves into a new teaching order, the Brothers of the Christian Schools, better know as the Christian Brothers.

See holy card, page 383

ST. PHILOMENA

ABOUT 150(?) • FEAST DAY: AUGUST 11

St. Philomena exists in a kind of liturgical limbo. Since 1805 she has been a favorite saint enjoying a reputation as a wonderworker. Five popes encouraged devotion to her, and many saints, including St. John Vianney, St. Frances Xavier Cabrini, St. John Neumann, and St. Anthony Mary Claret, reported that, through her intercession, miracles had been wrought on their behalf. Then, in spite of the enthusiastic support of so many holy men and women, not to mention her popularity throughout the Catholic world, in 1961 Pope John XXIII suppressed the cult of St. Philomena, citing a lack of historical information. The next step was to dismantle her shrine in Mugnano, near Naples, Italy, but the pope died before he could take that step, and his successor, Pope Paul VI, declined to do so. And so St. Philomena is in the odd position of having her cult officially suppressed, but her relics still available for public veneration.

The story begins in 1802, during an archaeological examination of Rome's Catacomb of Santa Priscilla. The investigators found an intact tomb bearing the inscription PAX TECUM FILUMENA (Peace be with you, Philomena). Inscribed on the tombstone were three arrows, a palm, and two anchors. The anchor is a Christian symbol of hope; the palm symbolizes martyrdom; and the three arrows were thought to indicate the type of death the martyr had suffered. Inside the tomb were the complete bones of a young girl about fourteen years old. Some of the archaeologists examining the grave assumed, based on the inscription and other decorations, that they had found a virgin martyr named Philomena. Since the style of the inscription could be dated to about the middle of the second century, it's likely she died around the year 150. The one thing missing was any mention of a martyr named Philomena in any of the martyrologies, the ancient lists of Christians martyred during the first centuries of the Church.

During the nineteenth century a Neapolitan nun, Sister Maria Luisa, reported a series of visions of the saint that purported to tell the complete story of Philomena's life. The "visions" were obviously false, and the Church authorities ignored them.

What no one has been able to dispute, however, is the extraordinary number of miracles brought about by the intercession of St. Philomena. Clearly some saint in heaven is answering the prayers addressed to her.

Because of her enormous popularity, St. Philomena was adopted as the patron of everything from sterility to money problems, but as a teen martyr she was especially recommended to teenagers.

See holy card, page 383

S. NICOLA DA TOLENTINO AGOSTINIANO

MODENA, SOC. LIT. S. GIUSEPPE   N. 4085   DEPOS.

Die hl. Godeleva, Martyrin.

SAINTE FLORE.

Fab

COPR. 1931 ST. ANTHONY'S GUILD, PATERSON, N. J.   0236

ST. MARIA GORETTI

1. Vegetarians • St. Nicholas of Tolentino   2. Victims of Battery • St. Godelieve
3. Victims of Betrayal • St. Flora of Cordoba   4. Victims of Rape and Sexual Assaults • St. Maria Goretti

421

Pietra offerta per il compietamento
della Basilica di S. Gennaro ad Antignano

S. ONUPHRIUS, Anachoreta.
Die Bezähmung der Zunge und die unablässige Erhebung der Liebesneigung zu Gott erwärmt den Geist gar bald mit göttlicher Gluth.
St. Joa. sent. 69.

Carl Paellath Schrobenhausen.

Saint Brendan of the Sea

Sainte Paule.

Sancta Paula Vidva Ora Pro Nobis

1. Volcanic Eruptions • St. Januarius   2. Weavers • St. Onuphrius
3. Whales • St. Brendan   4. Widows • St. Paula

H. Vincentius Diaken en Martelaar

B. Columba de Reate. V.

sancta Margarita virgo et martir

1. **Wine · St. Vincent**   2. **Witchcraft · St. Columba of Rieti**
3. **Wolves · St. Edmund the King**   4. **Women in Labor · St. Margaret of Antioch**

1.

SAINT TERESA BENEDICTA OF THE CROSS
EDITH STEIN
1891 - 1942

2.

St. Francis de Sales.

3.

S. Clemens P.

1. 𝔚orld 𝔜outh 𝔇ay • 𝔖t. 𝔈dith 𝔖tein 2. 𝔚riters • 𝔖t. 𝔉rancis de 𝔖ales
3. 𝔜achtsmen • 𝔖t. 𝔠lement of 𝔯ome

ST. CLARE OF ASSISI

1193–1253 • FEAST DAY: AUGUST 11

St. Clare of Assisi was the first woman to join the religious movement that would become known as the Franciscans. On the night of Palm Sunday 1212, eighteen-year-old Clare slipped out of her parents' house and hurried to a chapel outside town where St. Francis of Assisi and his disciples were waiting for her. There, amid the flickering light of candles and torches, Clare took the traditional vows of poverty, chastity, and obedience. Then Francis cut off her hair and gave her a nun's habit to wear. Since there was no Franciscan convent yet, Clare went to live nearby with a hospitable community of Benedictine sisters.

In the thirteenth century, all nuns and monks took a vow of poverty, meaning that they would own no personal property. The religious order to which they belonged, however, did own farmland, forests, mills, flocks and herds, and even real estate in cities and towns, all of which generated income to support their communities.

St. Francis adopted a more radical notion of poverty. Like Christ and the twelve apostles, he and his disciples had no source of income whatsoever. From day to day they never knew if they would sleep in someone's home, in a barn, or in a field. From hour to hour they didn't know where their next meal was coming from. For all their basic needs, they trusted completely in divine providence and the charity of the people around them. Clare, the daughter of Italian aristocrats, had decided to make Francis's ideal her own.

Soon other women had joined her—including her mother and sister—and by 1226 they had a convent of their own called San Damiano, outside Assisi. The convent was not a concession but a necessity; it was too dangerous for women to wander the roads as did Franciscan men. But in every other respect the nuns were faithful to St. Francis's principles. They owned nothing, surviving entirely on charity.

But the rule of a new religious order requires papal approval, and for many years this support eluded Clare and her sisters. A succession of popes urged them to modify St. Francis's ideal so that the nuns would have some degree of financial security. On this point, however, Clare refused to compromise. The disagreement between her and the popes dragged on for forty-two years. Finally, as she lay on her deathbed, Pope Innocent IV gave his blessing to the Franciscan rule in all its rigor. As a tribute to Clare's holiness, to say nothing of her determination, Innocent traveled to Assisi to personally present her with the document.

Clare died soon thereafter, and Innocent began her canonization process immediately. During the proceedings, a nun from the San Damiano convent testified that one Christmas Eve, St. Clare was so ill she couldn't leave her bed to attend Midnight Mass. After all the sisters had gone to the chapel, Clare sighed and said, "Good Lord, look, I have been left here all alone with you." At that moment, God granted Clare a vision in which she saw and heard the Mass as clearly as if she had been present in the convent chapel. In 1958, when television was new cutting-edge technology, Pope Pius XII recalled this story. Interpreting the vision as a kind of miraculous simulcast, he named St. Clare of Assisi the patron of television.

See holy card, page 383

ST. ANTHONY MARY CLARET

1807–1870 • FEAST DAY: OCTOBER 24

Antonio Juan Claret y Clara was twelve years old when he began working in his father's thread and textile factory in the village of Sallent, in Catalonia. For the next nine years he toiled as a common laborer, but he felt his true calling was the priesthood. At age twenty-one Anthony entered the seminary, was ordained a secular priest seven years later, and received his home parish as his first assignment.

Spain at this time was still recovering from the devastation of Napoleon's invasion and the civil war that followed. Religious life had suffered, too; many Spanish Catholics had only the barest understanding of their religion. To remedy this situation, Anthony began holding group retreats and parish missions throughout Catalonia. He was so effective that, in 1842, his religious superiors relieved him of all parish work and appointed him a full-time missionary for the entire province of Catalonia, with thirteen cities and four hundred towns under his jurisdiction.

Word of Anthony's work had reached Rome, where Blessed Pope Pius IX named Anthony archbishop of Santiago, Cuba. The archdiocese of Santiago covered half the island of Cuba, yet it had not had a bishop in fourteen years. Immediately Anthony devoted himself to the missionary work he loved. He traveled to every town and cluster of villages in his archdiocese, and he gave a mission in each one. He heard confessions for five or six hours a day, preached retreats to parish priests, and worked heroically to bring Catholics who had drifted away from the faith back to the Church. It took Anthony eighteen months to make one complete tour of his archdiocese, but the results of his labors were astonishing. The record books show that, in his first two years as archbishop of Santiago, Anthony confirmed one hundred thousand people, brought three hundred thousand to the confessional, married nine thousand couples who had never been wed by a priest, and reconciled three hundred married couples who had separated.

Because large segments of the archdiocese were not served by a priest, Anthony opened fifty-three new parishes. The archdiocesan seminary was barely functioning (it hadn't ordained a priest in thirty years). Anthony revitalized it. Many of the parish clergy were living in poverty, so Anthony raised the salary of all diocesan priests. Furthermore he opened hospitals and schools and invited back religious orders that had left the archdiocese years before.

Anthony's success enraged the Church's enemies in the government and in society at large. Fifteen attempts were made on his life, the most serious at the city of Holguin, where a knife-wielding assassin attacked him in church, slitting open his cheek from ear to jaw. When the court sentenced the would-be killer to death, Anthony interceded until the sentence was commuted to life in prison.

Sadly, this man who was so active and so successful as a bishop was compelled to leave Cuba and return to Spain to be the personal confessor to the queen, Isabella II. Anthony loathed the pettiness and superficiality of the royal court; to escape it and feel useful again, he helped prepare seminarians for ordination and gave missions in the parishes of Madrid.

Anthony was liberated from court life by the revolution of 1868. Unfortunately the revolutionaries were violently anticlerical, and they expelled Anthony and all other members of religious orders from Spain. He found refuge in a Cistercian monastery in Narbonne, France, where for the first time in his life he lived quietly with nothing to do. He died unexpectedly on October 24, 1870.

See holy card, page 383

ST. AUGUSTINE OF HIPPO

354–430 • FEAST DAY: AUGUST 28

St. Augustine was a man of tremendous intellectual gifts, and his ideas have had an enduring impact on Western thought. Martin Luther and John Calvin wrestled with his theory about predestination. His writings on the human will inspired Arthur Schopenhauer and Frederick Nietzsche. Recently the debate among Catholic thinkers, Catholic politicians, and the Vatican concerning the rightness of the invasion of Iraq was framed by St. Augustine's theory of the just war.

Although his mother, St. Monica, raised him as a Christian, at age fifteen Augustine cast aside the faith, took a mistress, and joined the Manicheans, a sect that believed two gods—one good, the other evil—battled for control of the world, a battle that evil invariably won. Monica was outraged by her son's defection from the Catholic Church. The first time he came home after becoming a Manichee, she barred the door and refused to let him in. Nonethe-

less, she always prayed for her son's conversion, keeping an eye out for a bishop who would have the intellectual depth to take him on.

In 386 Monica found such a man in St. Ambrose. The entire family—Monica, Augustine, his mistress, and their son—was living in Milan, where Augustine taught philosophy. One Sunday Monica convinced Augustine to accompany her to Mass to hear Bishop Ambrose preach. Augustine was impressed by what he heard; over the next year, he and his son met often with Ambrose privately to discuss the Catholic faith. These discussions came to fruition on the night before Easter 387, when Ambrose baptized Augustine and his son. Not since St. Paul had the Church received such an important convert.

Augustine went on to become a priest and, later, a bishop who was known for both his saintliness and his expansive knowledge. He wrote the first autobiography, which he called *Confessions*, because people are "curious to know the lives of others but careless to amend their own." He dedicated much of the wisdom within to his mother, whose devotion to Christian ideals inspired him. Candidly revealing his foibles and follies, he shared with readers the sins he had committed and the weaknesses that plagued him. In his time as well as our own, people find comfort and encouragement in his examination of the soul and the conflict between good and evil.

Augustine had a genius for making the profundities of theology understandable to ordinary people. He wrote: "This is the business of life: by labor and prayer to advance in the grace of God till we come to that height of perfection in which, with clean hearts, we may behold God."

See holy card, page 384

ST. DISMAS

DIED ABOUT 30 • FEAST DAY: MARCH 25

All four gospels tell us that Christ was crucified between two thieves. St. Luke's gospel gives us a more complete story. As the three men were dying on their crosses, the "bad thief" mocks Jesus, saying, "Are you not the Christ? Save yourself and us!" At which point, the "good thief" speaks up. "Do you not fear God?" he asks his companion. "We are receiving the due reward for our deeds; but this man has done nothing wrong." Then, addressing Christ, he says, "Jesus, remember me when you come into your kingly power." "Truly I say to you," Jesus replies, "today you will be with me in Paradise."

By the year 400, Christians were venerating the man who repented at the last moment and received as his reward a place in Paradise. By 600, tradition had given both thieves a name: The bad thief was Gestas, the good thief was Dismas. Exactly when the good thief became the patron of thieves specifically, and of all criminals in general, is unknown, but several prison ministries operating today are dedicated to St. Dismas. A burst of renewed interest in him occurred in 1961, when the film *Hoodlum Priest* was released. It tells the story of Father Charles Dismas Clark (played by Don Murray), who served as a prison chaplain and helped convicts turn their lives around.

St. Dismas plays a significant part in another story as well. In November 1950, during the Korean War, North Koreans captured twelve hundred American troops. Among the prisoners was Father Emil Kapuan, a chaplain from Pilsen, Kansas. In the POW camp, the North Koreans kept their American prisoners on starvation rations, so Father Kapuan took to stealing food from the guards' storeroom. Each night, before he crept out of the barracks on a pilfering expedition, Father Kapuan always invoked St. Dismas, the good thief.

See holy card, page 384

ST. CYRIACUS

DIED 303 • FEAST DAY: AUGUST 8

Fact and legend are intermingled in the story of St. Cyriacus, a deacon martyred outside Rome, along with perhaps as many as twenty fellow Christians. By the end of the fourth century, Roman Christians were commemorating the anniversary of his martyrdom on August 8. It's the legendary parts of St. Cyriacus's story that have made him the saint invoked against the devil.

According to this tale, Cyriacus was a wealthy Roman patrician and close friends with the emperor Diocletian. About the time Diocletian began his persecution of the Church, Cyriacus became a Christian and was ordained a deacon. He used his tremendous wealth to help the poor, especially enslaved Christians condemned to build the immense structure known as the Baths of Diocletian. In the meantime, Diocletian's daughter Artemesia became possessed by the devil. When the physicians and priests of Rome failed to free the girl, Diocletian sent for Cyriacus, who succeeded in exorcizing the demon. In gratitude, Artemesia and her mother, Serena, converted to Christianity. Then Diocletian sent Cyriacus to the king of Persia, whose daughter Jobias happened to be possessed, too. Cyriacus triumphed again, and the king of Persia and everyone in his palace became Christians.

Cyriacus returned to Rome, where Maximian, Diocletian's coemperor, arrested the holy deacon along with Christians named Largus, Smaragdus, and Crescentianus, among others. They were tortured, dragged outside the city, and then beheaded.

During the Middle Ages, St. Cyriacus was one of the Fourteen Holy Helpers, a group of saints believed to be especially effective against common troubles—in his case, driving away the devil.

See holy card, page 384

ST. MAGNUS OF FUESSEN

DIED ABOUT 666 • FEAST DAY: SEPTEMBER 6

It's possible that St. Magnus was one of the small crowd of Irish monks who, in the seventh and eighth centuries, traveled as missionaries to France, Germany, Switzerland, and the Low Countries. It is said that he came to the Continent with two of the most famous Irish missionaries, St. Columbanus and St. Gall. More certain is that, for twenty-six years, he was a missionary among the pagan tribes in and around Fuessen in Bavaria, where he built a little chapel and house for himself. As more and more disciples joined him, Magnus then built a monastery.

St. Magnus's association with vermin comes from a wonderful medieval legend. The land he chose for his monastery was the home of a fierce dragon. Armed with holy water, he made the sign of the cross and drove out the monster. But when he discovered a baby dragon, he spared it. He kept the little creature as a pet, teaching it to kill rats and mice as well as insects that damaged the peasants' crops.

Another legend tells how Magnus pondered how to improve the lives of the region's impoverished peasants. While walking in the woods, he encountered a bear that showed him a vein of iron ore so large it would support the people of Fuessen for generations. As a reward, St. Magnus gave the bear a cake, which so delighted the bear that he showed Magnus and his monks several more veins of ore.

St. Magnus died at Fuessen, where he was buried. His relics are still preserved in the town's baroque basilica of St. Magnus.

In some parts of Bavaria and Switzerland, during the Middle Ages St. Magnus was numbered among the Fourteen Holy Helpers because he kept mice, rats, and insects away from the crops.

See holy card, page 401

HOLY INFANT OF PRAGUE

IMAGE CARVED ABOUT 1500 • FEAST DAY: 3RD SUNDAY IN MAY

This statue of the Holy Child Jesus, always dressed in elaborate garments, came from Spain to the Czech Republic in 1587 as a wedding present to Polyxena Manrique de Lara, a Spanish noblewoman who married William of Rozumberk, a Czech nobleman. In her will, Polyxena left the statue to the Carmelites at the Church of Our Lady of Victory in Prague.

In 1631, during the Thirty Years War, General Gustavus Adolphus and his army of Swedish Lutherans captured Prague. The Protestants looted every Catholic church and religious building in the city, including that of the Carmelites. After the Swedes had moved on, a priest found the discarded statue, its hands broken off, in a pile of rubbish behind the church's high altar. While cleaning it, he heard a child's voice say, "Give me my hands, and I will give you peace. The more you honor me, the more I will bless you." The priest had a craftsman fashion new hands for the statue, the right raised in blessing, the left extended and holding an orb. After the statue was placed in the church, visitors reported miracles worked by the Holy Infant of Prague.

In response to the miracles, the Carmelites erected a magnificent altar for the sculpture. The archbishop of Prague presented it with a little crown of gold and jewels and, as was customary at the time, the statue was always dressed in ornate robes.

The original statue is still in Our Lady of Victory in Prague, where today it has a wardrobe of more than seventy garments, the oldest dating to 1700. Devotion to the Infant of Prague has spread around the world, and it is a custom to place a coin beneath the statue to bring prosperity to the house.

See holy card, page 401

To Find a Husband

ST. ANDREW

FIRST CENTURY • FEAST DAY: NOVEMBER 30

People in every society practice divination, special methods by which they try to tell the future. As Christianity spread across Europe, such fortune-telling practices were often the toughest to root out. In desperation, some parish priests "baptized" the old superstitions by replacing the folk magic with prayers to the saints. In Scotland, women waiting for husbands were encouraged to pray to St. Andrew, no doubt because he is Scotland's national saint. They certainly prayed—in fact, that's how St. Andrew came to be regarded as the patron of women looking for a spouse. But they hedged their bets by incorporating some of the ancient arts of divination.

On St. Andrew's Eve, November 29, a single Scotswoman would throw her shoe at the door. If it landed with the toe pointing out, it meant that within a year she would marry and leave her parents' house. If it landed with the toe pointing into the room, it meant she would not wed that year.

Another superstition involved sitting up on St. Andrew's Eve, listening for barking dogs. The sound would foretell the direction from which the woman's future husband would come.

German women picked up the custom of invoking St. Andrew to help them find a spouse, too. In German-speaking lands, an unmarried woman was told to pray to St. Andrew the night before his feast day, then go to bed naked. In her dreams, St. Andrew would send a vision of her future husband.

See holy card, page 401

435

ST. FELICITAS OF ROME

DIED 165 • FEAST DAY: JULY 10

There's no doubt a Roman widow named Felicitas was martyred in 165. That same year, seven Christian men were also martyred in Rome; their names were Felix, Philip, Martial, Vitalis, Alexander, Silanus, and Januarius. In the mid-fourth century, Pope St. Damasus wrote an epitaph for St. Felicitas's tomb in which he mentions that she was martyred with her sons, but he doesn't say how many or give their names. Also at that time, the list of Christians martyred in Rome records the execution of Saints. Januarius, Felix, Philip, Silanus, Martial, Vitalis, and Alexander, but it doesn't mention if they were brothers or if their mother was St. Felicitas. An ancient tradition in Rome affirms that these eight martyrs were a family; that may be true, but from a documentary standpoint, this type of case gives historians headaches.

It is said that Felicitas and her sons were denounced to the authorities by pagan priests who resented the family's success in bringing new converts into the Church. The case caught the attention of the emperor Marcus Aurelius, who ordered the family to be split up and executed separately. Januarius was scourged to death. Felix and Philip were beaten to death with clubs. Silanus was thrown off a cliff. The three youngest brothers, Martial, Vitalis, and Alexander, were beheaded. Felicitas was imprisoned for four months after the martyrdom of her children, and then she was be-he-aed, too.

Details aside, the story of a heroic Christian woman who produced seven sons, all of whom became saints, has for centuries served as an inspiration for mothers, especially those who yearn for a baby boy.

See holy card, page 401

To Make a Good Confession

ST. PIO OF PIETRELCINA

1887–1968 • FEAST DAY: SEPTEMBER 23

In spite of his canonization, the affectionate name for this saint is still Padre Pio. He is revered around the world as one of the great wonderworking saints of the twentieth century. It's said that he displayed the stigmata, wounds in his hands and feet like those that Christ suffered when he was nailed to the cross. Hundreds, perhaps thousands, of people say they were healed of serious, even life-threatening, illnesses by the prayers of Padre Pio. But the most popular legend about him—and this story is impossible to prove—claims that in 1947 a young Polish priest studying in Rome traveled to Padre Pio's monastery in southern Italy. Padre Pio heard the priest's confession and then made a prediction—some day the young man would be pope. The priest was Father Karol Wojtyla, later known as Pope John Paul II.

The story springs out of two things that are indeed true. Before he became pope, Father Wojtyla and Padre Pio did meet several times, and Padre Pio was an extraordinary confessor. It is said that he could "see" sins that a penitent had kept secret for years—those that he or she had always been afraid to confess to any priest. Once he exposed these secrets in the confessional, Padre Pio assured the sinners that God forgives everything, as long as we are willing to repent and make a fresh start at living a virtuous life. Padre Pio's apparently supernatural gift of perception, combined with his deep compassion and down-to-earth advice, made him an extremely popular confessor. People came from all over the world to confess to him. The lines of people standing outside his confessional were so long that the superiors at his monastery took a drastic step: No one could confess to Padre Pio unless they had made a reservation.

See holy card, page 402

ST. APOLLONIA

DIED 249 • FEAST DAY: FEBRUARY 9

Original firsthand accounts of the martyrs of the early Church are very rare, but they do exist. One example is the letter written by Bishop Dionysius of Alexandria in 249 to a colleague, Bishop Fabius of Antioch, describing the persecution of Christians in Egypt. The emperor Decius had just commanded all citizens of the empire to appear before a special commission and worship the gods of Rome. Those who refused were to be arrested, tried, and executed.

Soon the prisons were full of Christians. In Alexandria, pagan mobs refused to wait for the orderly process of Roman law. A riot began when a seer denounced the Christians as inhuman monsters bearing no loyalty to the emperor and no reverence for the gods. Citizens who heard the seer's rant rampaged through the streets, hunting for Christians. The riot spread into every district of Alexandria, with mobs attacking Christians in the streets or breaking into homes and dragging the inhabitants outside the city walls, where the pagans had built an enormous bonfire. Any Christian who refused to sacrifice to the gods was thrown into the flames. No one was spared.

Bishop Dionysius wrote that, during the riot, the mob seized a "wonderful old lady [named] Apollonia." As they drove her out of the city, they beat her so savagely that they broke or knocked out all of her teeth. At the bonfire, they threatened to burn her alive if she didn't pray to the Roman gods. Apollonia asked for time to consider. The mob fell quiet as it waited for her decision, and in that moment Apollonia threw herself into the flames.

Because of the abuse she suffered on her way to death, St. Apollonia is invoked against toothache. She is also the patron saint of dentists.

See holy card, page 402

Tour Guides

ST. BONA OF PISA

1156–1207 • FEAST DAY: MAY 29

Throughout the Middle Ages, journeying to shrines was a popular activity that combined religious devotion with the commonplace desire for a change of scenery, and maybe a bit of adventure, too. Many pilgrims set out on their own. But given the dangers—from being swept away by an avalanche to being attacked by bandits—those who were wise traveled in a large group led by an experienced guide who knew the safest roads, most comfortable inns, and best time of year for travel.

St. Bona set out on her first pilgrimage when she was only fourteen years old. Her destination was the Holy Land, where she could pray at Christendom's holiest shrines and visit her father, who had enlisted as a crusader. Her journey to Palestine was uneventful, but on the way home to Pisa her ship was captured by pirates. The bandits seized Bona, intending to sell her into slavery. By chance, some pilgrims from Pisa heard of Bona's plight and ransomed her.

In spite of her encounter with the pirates, Bona never lost her enthusiasm for pilgrimages, but she did become more cautious. Her next destination was the tomb of St. James at Compostela in Spain. This time she took the precaution of traveling with a large group. That first trip to Compostela inspired her to become a pilgrimage leader. She made eight more expeditions to the shrine of St. James, each time leading a large band of pilgrims. St. Bona was everything a traveler hopes for in a tour guide— she was knowledgeable, helpful, friendly, vivacious, and sympathetic. In recognition of her exceptional qualities, in 1962 Pope John XXIII extended her patronage by formally naming her the patron saint of flight attendants.

See holy card, page 402

ST. CHRISTOPHER

DIED ABOUT 250 • FEAST DAY: JULY 25

St. Christopher is one of the most popular and most recognized saints on the calendar. At one time, it was common for automobiles to display his image on the dashboard, and his medal dangled from countless keychains. So in 1969, when word spread that Pope Paul VI had removed St. Christopher from the calendar, Catholics and non-Catholics alike were stunned, even a bit worried. Who would protect them on their travels?

In fact, it was all a terrible misunderstanding. In that year, the pope revised the Church's calendar of saints. To place greater emphasis on holy seasons such as Advent and Lent, some feast days were shifted and some saints' days were removed altogether. In the ensuing confusion, people began to say that St. Christopher had been demoted or that he had never existed. (We know in fact that he did exist and was martyred in Lycia, in what is now Turkey, sometime in the mid-third century.) To make matters worse, bishops and parish priests who should have cleared up the mess failed to do so. And so it became "common knowledge" that St. Christopher was no longer a saint.

Rest assured, St. Christopher is still a saint in good standing. He even kept the feast day he's always had, July 25. But since he shares that date with an apostle, St. James the Greater, the Vatican instructed priests to say Mass on that day in honor of St. James—because any one of the twelve apostles always outranks any other saint.

But there are exceptions to this rule. If the parish is dedicated to St. Christopher, or if the region has an especially strong devotion to St. Christopher, or even if the priest's name is Christopher, then Mass on July 25 may be celebrated in his honor.

The story of how St. Christopher became the patron of travelers is well known. He was a tall, powerful man. When he became a Christian, he went to live beside a dangerous river, where he put his strength to use carrying travelers safely to the other side. One day a little boy asked to be carried across. Christopher grabbed his staff, put the child on his shoulder, and stepped into the water. But with each step the waves rose higher, the current grew stronger, and the little boy's weight increased. Christopher was afraid he would lose his step, that both he and the boy would drown. At last, exhausted and gasping for breath, he crawled onto the bank on the opposite shore.

"Boy," Christopher said, "who are you?"

The little boy answered, "Today, on your shoulder, you carried the Creator of the world. I am Christ your king." Then the Christ Child vanished.

See holy card, page 402

ST. MENAS

DIED ABOUT 300 • FEAST DAY: NOVEMBER 11

Christianity arrived early in Egypt. Tradition says that St. Mark the Evangelist began preaching in Alexandria in the year 43. It's impossible to prove whether that's accurate, but it is true that, by the year 300, Egypt possessed one of the largest Christian communities in the Mediterranean world.

St. Menas was born into an Egyptian Christian family about 280. When he was fourteen, he took a job as a camel driver in merchant caravans. At fifteen, he joined the Roman army. Three years later, when the emperor Diocletian began persecuting Christians, Menas fled into the desert. What began as the life of a fugitive developed into that of a hermit. A year or two of solitude and prayer gave Menas fresh courage, so much so that he walked into an amphitheater where Christians were being martyred and announced that he was a Christian, too.

The dignitary presiding over the games ordered Menas's immediate execution. The torturers chopped off his hands, gouged out his eyes, and then cut off his head. Christians managed to recover his body, and they buried it at a place known today as Karm Abu-Mina, south of Alexandria. Almost immediately Menas became one of the popular saints in Egypt, and his burial place was famous for the miracles that occurred there. Traveling merchants—who adopted Menas as their patron saint—told his story to their clients and business colleagues, and soon pilgrims from every corner of Europe, North Africa, and Asia Minor were visiting the martyred saint's tomb.

The Church in Egypt still cherishes St. Menas. In 1943, after the Allied victory at the Battle of El Alamein, the Orthodox patriarch of Alexandria published an open letter praising "the holy and glorious great martyr Menas, the wonder-worker of Egypt," who by his prayers had saved the country from Nazi occupation.

See holy card, page 403

ST. THÉRÈSE OF LISIEUX

1873–1897 • FEAST DAY: OCTOBER 1

There's no reason why the world should have ever heard of Thérèse Martin. She grew up in Lisieux, an obscure town in Normandy, and rarely ventured beyond the tightly knit circle of her immediate family and relatives. At age sixteen, she entered the Carmelite cloister, which completely shut out the world, and she died there when she was only twenty-four. In spite of her rather isolated life, St. Thérèse has a following among believers that is on par with St. Joseph, St. Anthony, and St. Jude. She even has a nickname, "the Little Flower." And in 1997 Pope John Paul II declared her a Doctor of the Church, which sets her among the Church's intellectual and mystical heavyweights.

How did it happen, this evolution from obscurity to worldwide fame?

It all began the year after Thérèse's death, when the Carmelites published her spiritual autobiography, *The Story of a Soul*. The crucial point in the book is the idea that even the humblest, most mundane task, if done for love of God, can draw one closer to him and make one grow in holiness. At first many readers dismissed Thérèse's "Little Way," as she called it, as late nineteenth-century French sentimental piety. But even the fiercest skeptics have been surprised to find that her approach to sanctity is really quite mainstream—Saints John of the Cross and Teresa of Avila advocated the same idea, as did Thomas á Kempis in his book, *Imitation of Christ*.

Miracles account for the other facet of St. Thérèse's popularity. She has a reputation for answering prayers. On her deathbed she promised that, upon reaching heaven, she would rain down miracles on the world "like a shower of roses."

Dying was hard for Thérèse. It began in the early-morning hours of Good Friday 1896, when she awoke to find her mouth filled with blood. It was the first symptom of tuberculosis. In obedience to the Carmelite rule that a nun must not keep an illness a secret, Thérèse reported the incident to her superior, Mother Marie de Gonzague. She insisted she was in no pain and didn't need to see a doctor.

In the months that followed, Thérèse's condition deteriorated, yet she never asked to be excused from some of the more rigorous aspects of life as a Carmelite nun. Nor did Mother Marie make such an offer. For years biographers have speculated about why Mother Marie was not more maternal with Thérèse. Three of Thérèse's four sisters were with her in the convent; some of the nuns gossiped that the Martin girls had formed a family clique within the religious community, the prime goal of which was to pamper their baby sister. Mother Marie may have been among those who resented the Martin sisters. It's also possible that, given the severity of the Carmelite rule, the mother superior felt that nuns should not be coddled. Certainly she could not be accused of indulging Thérèse; even when the young nun was in agony, Mother Marie would not permit the doctor to administer morphine to ease the pain.

Without painkillers, Thérèse's death from tuberculosis was sheer torture. She would gasp, "Holy Virgin, I can get no earthly air!" Yet the nuns came to her bedside repeatedly, pestering her to say something memorable and uplifting. She resented being cast in the role of "the sweet, dying saint" and rarely gave her visitors what they were hoping for. After months of suffering she died saying, "My God, I love you!"

Everyone from foreign missionaries to florists to airline pilots have taken St. Thérèse as their patron, but she is especially dear to those who, like her, suffer from tuberculosis.

See holy card, page 403

ST. JOB

LIFE DATES UNKNOWN • FEAST DAY: MAY 10

Nicholas II, the last czar of Russia who, with his wife and their five children, was murdered by Bolsheviks in 1918, was born on the feast of St. Job. He always took the coincidence as a bad omen, attributing to it all the unhappiness of his life—his father's early death, his son and heir's hemophilia, Japan's humiliating defeat of Russia in the war of 1905, the disastrous First World War, and of course the revolution that drove him from power.

St. Job is the subject of the Old Testament Book of Job, a man the Bible describes as "blameless and upright, one who feared God, and turned away from evil." With God's permission, Satan tested Job by taking away all the good things God had given him—his wealth, his servants, even the lives of Job's ten children. Finally, Satan afflicted Job with a loathsome disease that covered his body with ulcers.

Job's story is the most troubling, yet most fascinating, in the Bible because it examines suffering and asks why God doesn't intervene to shield the good from misery and pain. In despair, Job's wife urges him to put an end to his trouble. "Curse God," she says, "and die." Job, of course, will do nothing of the sort. "The Lord gave," he says, "and the Lord has taken away; blessed be the name of the Lord." Three friends who come to comfort him tell Job that he must have deserved this punishment for some secret sin, but Job rejects that argument—he has been faithful, loved God, and repented all his sins. Finally, God himself enters the story, chiding Job and all the characters for even attempting to fathom the workings of the Lord. But although God doesn't give Job a straight answer about why there is suffering in the world, he does at least restore everything that Job lost, and he heals him of his ulcers.

See holy card, page 403

ST. GUMMARUS

717–774 • FEAST DAY: OCTOBER 11

Even saints aren't immune from a miserable marriage, but few put up with as much as St. Gummarus. A nobleman's son, he was born near the town of Lier in what is now northern Belgium. His father, hoping to see his son become wealthy and influential, sent him to serve the French king Pepin the Short (the father of Charlemagne). While at Pepin's court, Gummarus's family arranged for him to marry a noblewoman named Guinmarie. The match was disastrous.

Gummarus was mild, gentle, and devout. He was generous to his servants and tenants and charitable to the poor, the sick, and the helpless. Guinmarie, on the other hand, was a shrill, shrieking harpy who regarded every penny Gummarus gave to unfortunates as money wasted. The couple quarreled constantly, and nothing Gummarus could say or do pacified his wife. To no one's surprise, they never had any children.

It must have come as a relief when King Pepin ordered Gummarus to join him on a prolonged military campaign through Germany and into northern Italy. Gummarus was gone for eight years. When he returned home, he found that Guinmarie had almost completely destroyed his estates. She had withheld the servants' wages, taxed the tenants to the point of near starvation, and let the house fall into ruins. Now that he was back, Gummarus made amends to everyone his wife had cheated and abused, and then he set to repairing his house. Naturally, he insisted on a separation.

The record doesn't say where Guinmarie went. Gummarus remained on his estate until, toward the end of his life, he built himself a hermitage and chapel in a quiet place and spent his last years there. He must have enjoyed the silence.

See holy card, page 403

ST. CYRIL & ST. METHODIUS

827–869 • 826–885 • FEAST DAY: FEBRUARY 14

Saints Cyril and Methodius have come to be seen as the link between the Churches of the East and the West. These two Greek brothers trained as priests in Constantinople and, in 861, were selected by the Byzantine emperor Michael III to lead an embassy to the Khazars, in present-day Ukraine. The mission had two goals: to cement an alliance between the Byzantines and the Khazars and to bring the Khazars (who had converted to Judaism) into the Church. It was a tremendous success. The Khazars signed a treaty with the emperor, and nearly every Khazar asked to be baptized. As for Cyril and Methodius, they realized that the Slavic lands were ready for conversion.

They chose Moravia (today part of the Czech Republic) for their next mission, but by now they realized that many obstacles impeded their success. The Bible, the liturgical books, and the Mass (or Divine Liturgy, as it was known in the East) were all spoken in either Latin or Greek, languages the Slavs didn't understand. Worse still, the Slavs had no written language of their own.

First the brothers created a new alphabet, known as Cyrillic (in Cyril's honor); then they translated the Bible and the Mass into Slavonic, the language understood by almost all Slav nations. Because of these innovations, a flood of new converts entered the Church from Moravia, Bohemia, Croatia, Serbia, and Slovenia. The Mass the brothers brought to the Slavic lands was the Byzantine liturgy of the East. But because they lived almost two hundred years before the Church split into Catholics and Orthodox, Saints Cyril and Methodius were loyal to the pope. With one foot in each world, so to speak, the brothers have become the saints invoked for the reunion of the Catholic and Orthodox Churches.

See holy card, page 404

ST. GUDULE

DIED 712 • FEAST DAY: JANUARY 8

Thousands of female saints never married, but almost all of them became nuns. St. Gudule is the rare exception—she chose chastity and a devout life without leaving the world for the cloister. As a result, she has become the patron of single women.

Sanctity ran in Gudule's family. Her mother, Amalberga, her sister Raineld, and her cousins Begga and Gertrude of Nivelles all became saints. Of them, Gertrude had the most profound influence on Gudule. She was the child's godmother, her teacher at the convent where Gudule went to school, and a model of holiness. After Gertrude's death in 659, Gudule returned to her parents' house at Hamme, in Belgium. The family belonged to the Flemish nobility and were well-off, so Gudule had both the leisure and the means to spend her days performing works of charity around the neighborhood.

Her daily routine began before dawn, when she arose and walked to her favorite church in the town of Moorsel, two miles away. Since it was usually still dark when she arrived at church, Gudule took a lantern to light her way. This mundane detail inspired a legend. It says that as she prayed, the devil would blow out the flame in the lantern, but by a miracle the candle always relit itself.

Gudule was buried in her parish church. About eighty years later, Charlemagne (who was distantly related to Gudule's family) had her relics moved to her favorite church in Moorsel and founded a convent there in her honor. During the Viking invasions of Belgium in the tenth century, the relics were moved to Brussels for safekeeping, to the large Church of St. Michael, thereafter renamed St. Gudule and St. Michael. Sadly, in 1597 Calvinist extremists attacked the church and destroyed St. Gudule's relics.

See holy card, page 404

ST. MARCELLUS OF PARIS

(DIED ABOUT 430) • FEAST DAY: NOVEMBER 1

According to legend, there once was a cemetery outside Paris that was home to a female vampire. In life, she had been a notorious adulteress; in death, she fed on the people of Paris and turned some into members of the undead. To protect his flock, Bishop Marcellus entered the woman's tomb, confronted the vampire, and killed her. Though dozens of saints had encounters with the devil and his evil legions, St. Marcellus is the only one said to have gone up against a vampire.

We don't know much about Marcellus (Marceau, in French, whose name now graces the St. Marceau district in Paris). It seems that he came from a family of Christians who were members of the working class. As a teenager, Marcellus was mature beyond his years—modest, quiet, and thoughtful, where other boys his age were boisterous and impulsive. While still in his teens, he began to study for the priesthood and showed such aptitude that the bishop of Paris, Prudentius, overlooked his youth and ordained Marcellus reader (one of the minor orders, an early step in the process that led ultimately to ordination as a priest). Even when he was made a priest, Marcellus was the youngest in his ordination class.

When Prudentius died, Marcellus was selected to succeed him. Yet, despite his high office, he remained unpretentious and hard-working. It is said that he was a wonderworker, with the vampire slaying being the most dramatic example of his feats.

After his death, Marcellus was buried in a cemetery outside the city. The village in which he grew up nearby was known as Saint-Marceau. Today the relics of St. Marcellus lie buried in the Cathedral of Notre-Dame in Paris.

See holy card, page 404

ST. NICHOLAS OF TOLENTINO

1245–1305 • FEAST DAY: SEPTEMBER 10

As a personal penance, St. Nicholas of Tolentino resolved never to eat meat. Once, when his host served him chicken, Nicholas made the sign of the cross over the dish and the chicken turned into roasted vegetables. In another version of the story, the meal was a dish of roasted partridges that Nicholas restored to life, watching happily as they flew out an open window.

An Augustinian priest, Nicholas spent his days and nights visiting prisoners, converting sinners, reconciling squabbling families, bringing relief to the poor, nursing the sick, and praying for the dead. But it is the miracles for which he is best remembered. His canonization process recognized as authentic three hundred miracles attributed to St. Nicholas. The investigation of inexplicable healings and other supernatural phenomena was rudimentary in the Middle Ages; nonetheless the stories are impressive.

St. Nicholas is said to have raised one hundred people from the dead; he saved the lives of nine passengers aboard a sinking ship; he gave sight to a blind woman; and he healed a sick child by touching him and saying, "The good God will make you well." When very ill, he had a vision of the Blessed Virgin Mary in which she urged him to eat a bit of bread dipped in water. Nicholas did as the vision instructed and recovered. On all future visits to the sick, he gave them a piece of bread dipped in water, praying to Mary as he did so. In this way, hundreds more were cured.

See holy card, page 421

ST. GODELIEVE

1049–1070 • FEAST DAY: JULY 6

In 1067, when St. Godelieve was eighteen years old, her parents married her to Bertulf of Ghistelles, a Flemish nobleman. Exactly how or why this arranged marriage came about remains a mystery, since from their wedding day Bertulf detested his bride, cruelly beating and abusing her. The one mercy in this wretched situation was that he didn't rape poor Godelieve.

After months of mistreatment, Godelieve returned home and told her parents about her misfortune. Her father was outraged and threatened Bertulf with a full range of civil and ecclesiastical penalties. Bertulf gave every appearance of being contrite, so Godelieve felt obliged to return to Ghistelles and try once more to build a life with her husband.

But Bertulf's conversion had never been sincere. In collusion with his mother, a woman just as wicked as Bertulf, he plotted Godelieve's murder. Two of his mother's servants took Godelieve by surprise, strangled her with a rope until she was unconscious, and then tossed her down a well, where she drowned.

The local people came to regard this innocent young woman as a saint and began making pilgrimages to the site of her murder. It was said that water from the well where Godelieve had drowned cured sore throats, and visitors to her grave reported other miracles as well.

In the meantime, Bertulf had remarried and, with his new wife, had a little girl who was born blind. Inspired by the stories of healing through the intercession of Godelieve, the second wife took her child to the grave of the woman her husband and mother-in-law had murdered. To everyone's astonishment, the little girl's sight was restored. This miracle, above all others, confirmed Godelieve as a saint.

See holy card, page 421

ST. FLORA OF CORDOBA

DIED 851 OR 856 • FEAST DAY: NOVEMBER 24

In 711 Moors from North Africa invaded Spain. Within twenty years, they had conquered almost the entire country, establishing a caliph in Cordoba to rule the realm. Although outbreaks of anti-Christian persecution sometimes occurred, the Moors were generally content to collect an annual tax from their non-Muslim subjects and leave them alone. Then, in 850, a new wave of anti-Christian violence erupted, possibly in response to the conversion of Muslims to Christianity.

Among the converts were St. Flora and her mother. Flora's father and brother, however, remained Muslims, and when the brother learned of Flora's renunciation of Islam, he handed her over to the caliph's men. The judge ordered Flora to be scourged and then turned her over to her brother, who was instructed to do everything in his power to bring Flora back to the Muslim faith. Instead of renouncing Christianity, Flora escaped and hid in a church.

There, she met a young woman named Mary, the sister of a deacon who had just been martyred by the Moors. Together the women resolved to return to court and declare that nothing would force them to renounce Christ.

The judge ordered the women to be imprisoned, swearing that he would sell them to a brothel. When St. Eulogius heard of Flora and Mary's case, he wrote them a letter, now known as "Exhortation to Martyrdom," in which he said: "They threaten you with a shameful slavery, but do not fear: no harm can touch your souls whatever infamy is inflicted on your bodies." Seeing that no threat would shake their faith, the caliph ordered them to be beheaded.

The women's bodies were buried in Cordoba, where they are still venerated as patron saints of the city. St. Flora is especially singled out because of her brother's role in her martyrdom.

See holy card, page 421

ST. MARIA GORETTI

1890–1902 • FEAST DAY: JULY 6

St. Maria Goretti's parents were tenant farmers on the estate of Count Mazzolini in southern Italy. The Gorettis lived with another family, the Serenellis, in a spacious loft above one of the barns. While the adults and older children worked in the fields, Maria stayed at home cooking, cleaning, and watching the toddlers of both families.

On July 5, 1902, while everyone was working, Maria sat in the shade of the barn's verandah, playing with her baby sister. Suddenly twenty-year-old Alessandro Serenelli appeared. He grabbed Maria's arm and dragged her up to the loft, where he tried to rape her. But Maria fought back, and her resistance enraged Alessandro. He pulled out a knife, stabbed Maria fourteen times, and then fled, leaving her for dead on the floor.

Hours later, when the Gorettis and Serenellis returned from the fields, Maria was still clinging to life. They managed to take her to a hospital, but the girl's injuries were too severe—there was nothing the surgeons could do to save her. She was conscious as she received the Last Rites; then she said that she forgave Alessandro and prayed that God would forgive him, too. On July 6, Maria Goretti died.

A court found Alessandro Serenelli guilty of murder and attempted rape, sentencing him to thirty years in prison. Eight years into his term, he issued a public statement expressing sorrow for his crime. Having served his full sentence, he was released in 1932. The first thing Alessandro did was to visit Maria's mother, Assunta Goretti, to beg her forgiveness. On Christmas Day, they went together to Mass and, kneeling side by side at the altar rail, received Holy Communion. "If Maria could forgive him," Assunta said, "I can, too."

So many miracles were reported at Maria's grave that the local bishop waived the customary fifty-year waiting period and opened the cause for her canonization. Alessandro Serentelli was one of the witnesses interviewed about Maria's life and merits. In 1947 Pope Pius XII declared Maria to be Blessed, and, three years later, proclaimed her a saint. A crowd of 250,000 packed St. Peter's Square for the ceremony, and among them was Assunta Goretti—the first time in history a mother had attended the canonization of her child.

As for Alessandro, in 1937 he joined a branch of the Franciscans called the Capuchins, enlisting as a lay brother. He did all the housekeeping and physical labor around the monastery but never became a priest. He died in 1970, with a picture of St. Maria Goretti on his bedside table.

See holy card, page 421

ST. JANUARIUS

DIED ABOUT 305 • FEAST DAY: SEPTEMBER 19

Every weekend in New York City, from spring through early fall, one neighborhood or another plays host to a street festival. But the city's biggest, glitziest, hands-down-favorite festival comes in September, when, for eleven days, more than one million visitors cram into the narrow streets of Little Italy to celebrate the Feast of San Gennaro. In English-language compilations of the saints, he is St. Januarius. But New Yorkers, even those without a drop of Italian blood, call him by his Italian name, San Gennaro.

In the first years of the fourth century, Januarius was a bishop, but sources differ about whether he served the Christians of Naples or nearby Benevento. About 305, during the emperor Diocletian's ferocious persecution of the Church, Bishop Januarius was arrested while attempting to visit imprisoned Christians. The governor condemned him, along with the priests and deacons arrested with him, to be thrown to the lions. When the beasts wouldn't touch the men, the governor ordered Januarius and his companions to be beheaded.

Almost immediately, devotion to St. Januarius began among the Christians of Naples. In the next centuries, the city came to regard him as one of their chief protectors—the saint whose prayers saved them from invasion, epidemics, and all manner of disasters. St. Januarius has been invoked against volcanic blasts at least since 1631, when a violent eruption of Mount Vesuvius threatened Naples. The people of the city called on their favorite saint to help them, and by his prayers the flow of lava stopped and Naples was saved.

See holy card, page 422

ST. ONUPHRIUS

DIED ABOUT 400 • FEAST DAY: JUNE 12

About 400, Paphnutius, an Egyptian abbot, traveled into the desert to visit the holy hermits who dwelt there. He had been wandering for seventeen days when he saw a wild-looking creature whose hair and beard reached almost to the ground. The man was naked except for a loincloth made of woven palm leaves. The frightened abbot began to run away when the creature called out to him, "Come to me, man of God, for I am a man like you, living in the desert for love of God."

The old man's name was Onuphrius. On the day Paphnutius met him, he had been living as a hermit in the desert for seventy years. Decades earlier his clothes had rotted away, so he wove his loincloth from the leaves of a date palm growing beside the cave that was his hermitage.

Seated inside the cave, Paphnutius asked Onuphrius if he should leave his monastery and become a hermit, too. Onuphrius said no, that God had chosen Paphnutius to be a father to his monks. Paphnutius hoped to spend a few days with Onuphrius, but upon awakening the next morning, he was distressed to find that the old hermit was dying. Onuphrius, on the other hand, took it as a final sign of God's goodness to him; his life had been prolonged until Abbot Paphnutius came to give him a proper Christian burial.

On his deathbed, St. Onuphrius promised that if anyone had a Mass said for him, or in his name was charitable to the poor and hungry, he would intercede for that person at the Last Judgment. Then the holy man closed his eyes and died in peace.

Abbot Paphnutius placed the hermit's body in the cleft of a rock, sealing up the opening with stones. Once the saint was buried, his cave collapsed, and the date palm that grew beside the entrance drooped and died.

See holy card, page 422

ST. BRENDAN

ABOUT 486–575 • FEAST DAY: MAY 16

Long before there were eco-warriors and endangered species lists, St. Brendan kept an eye on whales. He was abbot of a monastery that he'd founded at Clonfert in County Galway, near Ireland's Atlantic shoreline. While monks on the Continent savored the stability of spending their whole life in the same abbey, Irish monks craved travel. They yearned to venture either to isolated islands in the Atlantic, where they could live as hermits, or to the far corners of Europe, where they would combine preaching the gospel with seeing the sights.

Brendan's wanderlust lay dormant until one day a monk named Barinthus asked for shelter at his monastery. He told Brendan he'd just returned from a marvelous country far to the west, way across the Atlantic. He thought he must have surely found the Promised Land of the Saints because every rock there was a jewel, and every tree bore rich and satisfying fruit. The more Barinthus talked, the more Brendan felt the urge to sail off in search of this extraordinary land. He chose seven of his monks to come along, and a few days later Brendan and his companions set sail.

Their adventures are recorded in *The Voyage of Brendan*, a kind of Arabian Nights adventure told with an Irish brogue. It was a best seller in the Middle Ages, and it is still an entertaining read. One of the stories tells how, one morning, Brendan and his monks went ashore on a barren island to cook breakfast. They had just lit a fire when the island heaved up. It was not an island at all, but a whale.

See holy card, page 422

ST. PAULA

347–404 • FEAST DAY: JANUARY 26

St. Jerome was not an easy man to like, and he considered few people to be his friends. But, to the handful who were admitted into Jerome's inner circle, he was loving and loyal to the end. His dearest friend and most generous supporter, the person who financed the translation of the Vulgate Bible, was St. Paula. She was a Roman patrician descended from Scipio and the Gracchi, heroes of the old Roman republic. Her parents tried to elevate their lineage even higher by claiming Aeneas and Agamemnon as their ancestors, too.

Paula, who was wealthy in her own right, became immensely rich when she married a senator. They had one son and four daughters, two of whom—Eustochium and Blesilla—became saints. Paula was only thirty-two when her husband died, and the loss sent her into deep mourning. Marcella, her close friend who was also recently widowed (and would later be a saint, too), came to help. She showed Paula how, even as a widow, she could be happy again and, more important, useful and holy as well.

At this time, St. Jerome was one of the most famous priests in Rome, not only for beginning his great work of creating an accurate Latin translation of the Scriptures, but also for serving as the spiritual director for well-to-do Roman women. When Marcella introduced Jerome to her friend, Paula's life changed forever. At first she benefited from Jerome's advice on how to pray and make the best use of her great wealth. When Jerome learned that, like Marcella, Paula was fluent in Greek, he invited her to assist him in translating and analyzing the Greek-language books of the Bible.

Meanwhile, Paula's daughters, Eustochium and Blessilla, became Jerome's protégés. In Blesilla's case, the relationship ended tragically. She longed to live the life of an ascetic, and Jerome encouraged her. Unfortunately Blesilla's health was poor, and she fasted to excess. She contracted a fever, possibly malaria, and, not having the strength to resist it, she died.

After the death of Pope St. Damasus, Jerome's patron and protector, he, Paula, Eustochium, and several other Roman women from their inner circle moved to the Holy Land, settling in Bethlehem. Once again Paula did everything she could for Jerome, emotionally, financially, and even in terms of scholarship (she learned some Hebrew to help him translate the Torah). In Bethlehem, she built an enormous religious complex that included a monastery, three convents, a school, and a hospital for pilgrims. As her friend Marcella had promised, Paula did indeed feel happy, useful, respected, and beloved. She was on the path to sainthood. When she died in Bethlehem, a heartbroken Jerome, loving to the end, buried her in the holiest spot he could think of—beneath the altar of the Church of the Nativity.

See holy card, page 422

ST. VINCENT

DIED 304 • FEAST DAY: JANUARY 22

St. Vincent's connection to wine is hard to determine. Nothing in his life story suggests a link between him and the beverage. As with St. Agnes and her lamb and St. Bibiana and hangovers, St. Vincent probably became the patron of wine through a pun on his name. In French, the word for "wine" is *vin*, and in Spanish and Italian, it's *vino*. Another possible explanation is more gruesome—that red wine reminded Christians of St. Vincent's bloody martyrdom.

Vincent was a deacon in Saragosa, in northeastern Spain. When the emperor Diocletian began the last and most ferocious persecution of Christians, Vincent was arrested along with his bishop, Valerius. The men were starved in prison and then brought to trial, half dead. Neither would deny Christ; but where Valerius was sent into exile, Vincent was handed over to torturers. They stretched him on the rack, tore open his flesh with iron hooks, rubbed salt into his hid-eous wounds, and suspended him over a slow fire. Finding the deacon still faithful to Christ and still alive, the local magistrate had Vincent thrown into a bare prison cell and left to die. Even there he was tormented—the floor was covered with broken pottery shards that opened his old wounds and inflicted new ones.

Christians bribed their way into Vincent's cell to comfort the martyr and tend his injuries, but Vincent died of his wounds. Upon leaving the cell, the Christians of Saragossa carried with them the cloths and bandages stained with the martyr's blood; these they preserved as relics.

See holy card, page 423

ST. COLUMBA OF RIETI

1467–1501 • FEAST DAY: MAY 20

Her parents named her Angelella, but at the child's baptism, a dove flew into the church and perched on the edge of the font. Ever after the little girl was known as Columba, Latin for "dove."

Columba lived as though she were half in heaven and half on earth. In prayer she often fell into ecstasies, and it was said that she conversed with St. Catherine of Siena (1347–1380). Yet Columba also healed the sick with a touch of her hand, made peace between quarreling factions in the city of Perugia, miraculously brought an end to an outbreak of plague, and converted the most hardened sinners, including a convicted murderer. Her reputation was such that the citizens of the neighboring town of Narni tried to kidnap her, hoping to make her their miracle-worker.

Not everyone was taken with Columba. When Lucrezia Borgia met her, the two women took an instant dislike to each other. For centuries, persistent rumors claim that Lucrezia poisoned her enemies and committed incest with her brother. Documentary evidence for these accusations is scant, but perhaps Columba saw the real woman inside and didn't like what she saw. As for Lucrezia, a master of machiavellian politics, she may have resented encountering a person she couldn't manipulate. What is certain is that she spread rumors that Columba was not a holy woman but a sorceress who accomplished her "miracles" through witchcraft. No one believed the charges, but they did lead to Columba becoming the saint invoked against charms, spells, and all other forms of sorcery.

See holy card, page 423

ST. EDMUND THE KING

841–869 • FEAST DAY: NOVEMBER 20

St. Edmund was still in his teens when he was chosen to be king of East Anglia. Lying on England's east coast, the kingdom was an easy target for the Vikings, and in 865 tens of thousands of invaders stormed ashore. To save his people, King Edmund bought off the Vikings with a bribe of hundreds of horses. Satisfied with the tribute, the invaders left East Anglia in relative peace and then marched north to York.

Four years later, this immense pagan horde returned; led by a warlord named Ingvar, they burned everything in their path. Edmund assembled his army in November 869, but the Vikings routed the men of East Anglia and took the king as their prisoner. Ingvar offered to spare Edmund's life if he agreed to rule as a puppet king and renounced his Christian faith. Edmund rejected Ingvar's terms.

To teach a lesson to England's other kings, Ingvar ordered Edmund to be stripped and flogged. Then after tying Edmund to a tree, Viking bowmen lined up and shot him through with arrows—but carefully, to prolong his suffering. When the English king was dead, they cut him down, chopped off his head, and threw it into the woods.

Once the Vikings were gone, Christians came looking for the martyred king's body. They found the corpse, but not the head. Then they heard a voice crying, "Here! Here!" Following the sound, they discovered in a little clearing a gray wolf with Edmund's head between its paws. By a miracle the wolf had protected the saint's head from being mutilated by other wild animals, and it was the wolf who had called to the men searching for the relic.

As if he were a house pet, the wolf let the men take the head, and then it joined the procession that carried the dead king to the town of Sutton for burial. Once St. Edmund's relics were safe, the wolf trotted back into the woods.

See holy card, page 423

ST. MARGARET OF ANTIOCH

DIED 304 • FEAST DAY: JULY 20

St. Margaret's legend makes many modern readers uneasy. It is said that while she was in prison for her faith, Satan appeared in her cell in the form a huge dragon and swallowed her whole. In the beast's belly, Margaret brandished a little cross she had with her; at once the monster's stomach burst open, and Margaret emerged alive and unharmed. Although a disconcerting story to us today, it remains the origin of St. Margaret, the patron of women in labor. If pictures, statues, and church dedications are any indication, the tale comforted countless pregnant women living centuries ago. Throughout medieval Europe, St. Margaret was a much-loved saint. In England alone, more than 250 churches were dedicated to her.

The rest of the legend says that Margaret was the daughter of a pagan priest who disowned her after she converted to Christianity. With no place else to go, she left her home in Antioch and went into the countryside to live with her foster mother. While she was tending her foster mother's sheep, Margaret was spotted by the local governor. He proposed marriage, but she replied that she had dedicated her virginity to Christ. This candid admission led to Margaret's arrest, her run-in with the dragon, and ultimately her martyrdom.

That a Christian virgin named Margaret was martyred in Antioch during the persecution of Emperor Diocletian is almost certainly true, but those are the only known facts. One final point—St. Joan of Arc said that one of the three heavenly voices she heard belonged to St. Margaret of Antioch.

See holy card, page 423

ST. EDITH STEIN

1891–1942 • FEAST DAY: AUGUST 9

In 1984 Pope John Paul II initiated the celebration of World Youth Day to bring together thousands of Catholic young people from around the globe to confirm and strengthen their commitment to their faith. The second World Youth Day, held in 1987, coincided with John Paul's beatification of Sister Teresa Benedicta (Edith) Stein, a Jewish convert to Catholicism who entered a Carmelite cloister and was murdered by the Nazis at Auschwitz. She is an interesting and unexpected choice as patron saint of the WYD phenomenon; typically a young saint such as St. Agnes, or St. Aloysius Gonzaga, or St. Maria Goretti would have been held up as a model for Catholic youth. Nonetheless, St. Edith does represent a commitment to the life of prayer and good works, intellectual depth, and faithfulness to Christ unto death.

Edith Stein, the youngest of seven children of an Orthodox Jewish family, was born in what was then Breslau, Germany, but is now Wroclaw, Poland. By the age of thirteen, she had lost her faith. As a university student, she studied philosophy under Edmund Husserl, a proponent of the philosophical school known as phenomenology. At age twenty-five, Edith received her doctorate and began teaching at the University of Freiburg. While on vacation in 1921, she read the autobiography of St. Teresa of Avila—this event marked her first step toward Catholicism. She read more, took formal instruction from a priest, and was baptized in 1922. She continued to teach, although now at Catholic schools. Then, in 1934, Edith entered the Carmelite convent in Cologne, taking the name Sister Teresa Benedicta of the Cross.

By now the Nazis were in power in Germany. Although Edith had converted to Catholicism, the Nazis still regarded her as a Jew. As anti-Semitic legislation and persecution increased, in 1938 Edith's superiors decided to transfer her, for safety, to a convent in the Netherlands. It was not far enough. Two years later the Nazis overran the Netherlands, imposed anti-Semitic legislation upon the Dutch, and began deporting Jews to death camps.

On Sunday, July 20, 1942, every Catholic priest in the country read from the pulpit a letter from the Dutch Bishops Conference condemning Nazism as racism and denouncing the persecution of the Jews. Six days later, the Nazis retaliated by specifically rounding up Jewish converts to Catholicism. Edith Stein, along with her sister Rosa, who had also converted and become a nun, were seized and shipped off to Auschwitz, where they and all the Jewish Catholics of Holland were instantly marched to the gas chambers.

"Learn from Saint Thérèse [the Little Flower] to depend on God alone," St. Edith wrote, "and serve Him with a wholly pure and detached heart. Then, like her, you will be able to say 'I do not regret that I have given myself up to Love.'"

See holy card, page 424

ST. FRANCIS DE SALES

1567–1622 • FEAST DAY: JANUARY 24

Lots of saints were prolific writers, but St. Francis de Sales was persuasive. The little leaflets he published on the truths of the Catholic faith—written in clear, polished prose—brought thousands of Calvinists back to the Church. And for nearly four hundred years his *Introduction to the Devout Life* has been a beloved "how-to" book on giving up sinful habits and growing closer to God.

Francis hadn't planned to become a writer, but circumstances forced him to take up the pen. He was born in Savoy, a region encompassing parts of southeastern France and Switzerland. Although the de Sales family were staunch Catholics, most of their neighbors had become followers of the radical Protestant reformer, John Calvin. In 1533 Calvin and his followers overran the diocese of Geneva; drove out the bishop, the priests, the monks, and the nuns; and outlawed all practice of the Catholic religion.

Not long after his ordination to the priesthood, Francis, along with Louis de Sales, his cousin who was also a priest, began traveling through Savoy preaching to and debating with the Calvinists. Since it was impossible to visit every hamlet and farm in this mountainous region, Francis wrote a series of leaflets explaining and defending the essentials of Catholic doctrine, and he had them distributed throughout every corner of the diocese.

Success came slowly, but in five years the de Sales cousins had brought two-thirds of the Savoy population back to the Catholic Church. Impressed by such an achievement, the pope appointed Francis to be bishop of Geneva, the one city where the de Sales priests had made no headway. After Francis's consecration as bishop, the civic and religious authorities in Geneva refused to even let him set foot inside the city limits, let alone say Mass inside the cathedral. It was a crushing disappointment, but Francis's work kept him from dwelling on it. Since he had no seminary, he taught theology courses and personally examined each new candidate for the priesthood. He gave catechism classes to children. And he wrote on everything from how to teach religion to how to bring religious orders back to their original zeal.

Francis's most enduring legacy as a writer is his *Introduction to the Devout Life.* He wrote it, he said, "for those who live in towns, in families, and at court [and are] obliged to lead outwardly at least an ordinary life." The aim of this practical guide is to help Christians give up careless habits and old sins, bringing them step-by-step to a deeper love of God. It was the first religious self-help manual, and it became a best seller that has been translated into dozens of languages and has never gone out of print. The publisher made a fortune. But Francis, to the horror of every writer ever since, would accept none of the royalties.

See holy card, page 424

ST. CLEMENT OF ROME

DIED 101 • FEAST DAY: NOVEMBER 23

St. Clement's experience with boats was pretty unpleasant, so there's a touch of irony in his being patron of yachtsmen. During a wave of anti-Christian persecution, Clement was condemned to work in the mines in the Crimea. After toiling as a slave for a while, he was taken in a boat into the Black Sea, an anchor was tied around his neck, and he was thrown overboard.

St. Clement was the fourth pope, St. Peter's third successor. In his letter to the Philippians, St. Paul mentions a Clement who is one of his disciples, and it's possible that this man is the future pope. Also surviving is a letter written by Pope Clement to the Church in Corinth about the year 95. Reading between the lines, one gathers that the Corinthian Christians were torn by religious dissentions. They had not appealed to Rome for help, but Clement heard of their trouble and, as chief bishop of the Christians, wanted to teach them how to resolve their disputes.

"We are writing this, beloved, not only for your admonition but also as a reminder to ourselves," Clement says, "for we are placed in the same arena [as were Saints Peter and Paul], and the same contest lies before us. Hence we ought to put aside vain and useless concerns and should consider what is good, pleasing, and acceptable in the sight of him who made us. Let us fix our gaze on the blood of Christ, realizing how precious it is to his Father, since it was shed for our salvation and brought the grace of repentance to all the world."

In the ninth century, Saints Cyril and Methodius believed they had found St. Clement's relics in the Crimea, and they sent them back to Rome. Those relics are enshrined in the basilica of St. Clement, one of the oldest parish churches in Rome.

See holy card, page 424

Selected Bibliography

Anderson, Alan Orr, and Marjorie Ogilvie Anderson, editors and translators, *Adomnan's Life of Columba* (Thomas Nelson, 1961).

"The Arabic Gospel of the Infancy of the Savior," Ante-Nicene Fathers, volume 8 (www.ccel.org/fathers2/ANF-08/TOC.htm#TopOfPage).

Armstrong, Regis J., and Ignatius C. Brady, *Francis and Clare: The Complete Works* (Paulist Press, 1982).

Armstrong, Regis J., J. A. Wayne Hellman, and William J. Short, *Francis of Assisi: Early Documents* (New City Press, 1999).

Augustine, *Confessions*, trans. Henry Chadwick (Oxford University Press, 1992).

Barlow, Frank, *Thomas Becket* (University of California Press, 1986).

Bede, *The Ecclesiastical History of the English Nation* (E. P. Dutton, 1910).

Berenbaum, Michael, ed., *A Mosaic of Victims: Non-Jews Persecuted and Murdered by the Nazis* (New York University Press, 1990).

Bitel, Lisa M., *Isle of the Saints: Monastic Settlement and Christian Community in Early Ireland* (Cornell University Press, 1990).

The Book of Saints, 6th ed. (Morehouse Publishing, 1989).

Bowden, Henry Sebastian, *Mementoes of the Martyrs and Confessors of England and Wales*, ed. and rev. by Donald Attwater (Burns & Oates, 1962).

Brodrick, James, *Robert Bellarmine: Saint and Scholar* (Newman Press, 1961).

Brown, Peter, *Augustine of Hippo: A Biography* (University of California Press, 1969).

Budge, E. A. W., trans., "The Passion of St. George," *Bibliotheca Hagiographica Orientalis*, no. 310, 1888.

Buehrle, Marie Cecilia, *Kateri of the Mohawks* (Bruce Publishing Co., 1954).

Bury, J. B., *The Life of St. Patrick and His Place in History* (Book-of-the-Month Club, 1999).

Carr, John, "St. Gerard Majella," *A Treasury of Catholic Reading*, (Farrar, Straus & Cudahy, 1957).

The Catholic Encyclopedia, 1907 (www.newadvent.org).

Cavallini, Giuliana, translated by Caroline Holland, *Saint Martin de Porres: Apostle of Charity* (Tan Books, 1979).

Cepari, Virgilius, *The Life of St. Aloysius Gonzaga* (H. McGrath, 1884).

Chambers, R.W., *Thomas More* (University of Michigan Press, 1973).

Charbonneau-Lassay, Louis, *The Bestiary of Christ*, translated and abridged by D. M. Dooling (Parabola Books, 1991).

Clarke, W. K. Lowther, *The Lausiac History of Palladius* (Macmillan Company, 1918).

Colbert, Edward P., *The Martyrs of Córdoba (850–859): A Study of the Sources* (Catholic University of America Press, 1962).

Cross, Samuel H., editor, *Russian Primary Chronicle: Laurentian Text* (Medieval Academy of America, 1968).

Daniel-Rops, Henri, *Monsieur Vincent: The Story of St. Vincent de Paul* (Hawthorn Books, 1961).

de Cantimpré, Thomas, *The Life of Christina the Astonishing*, translated by Margot H. King assisted by David Wiljer (Peregrina Publishing Co., 2000).

de la Vega, Luis Lasso, *Huei Tlamahuitzoltica*, 1649.

Delehaye, Hippolyte, *The Legends of the Saints: An Introduction to Hagiography* (University of Notre Dame Press, 1961).

Demetrius of Rostov, *The Great Collection of Lives of the Saints* (Chrysostom Press, n. d.).

D'Evelyn, Charlotte, and Mill, Anna J., editors, *The South English Legendary*, 3 volumes (Oxford University Press, 1967).

de Voragine, Jacobus, *The Golden Legend*, 2 volumes (Princeton University Press, 1993).

Di Donato, Pietro, *The Penitent* (Hawthorn Books, 1962).

Dirvin, Joseph I., *Louise de Marillac*, (Farrar, Straus & Giroux, 1970).

Dirvin, Joseph I., *Mrs. Seton: Foundress of the American Sisters of Charity* (Farrar, Straus and Cudahy, 1962).

Donaldson, Christopher, *Martin of Tours: Parish Priest, Mystic and Exorcist* (Routledge & Kegan Paul, 1980).

Dorcy, Sister Mary Jean, *St. Dominic's Family: The Lives of Over 300 Famous Dominicans* (Tan Books, 1983).

Duffy, Eamon, *Saints & Sinners: A History of the Popes* (Yale University Press, 1997).

Eddius Stephanus, *The Life of Bishop Wilfrid*, translated by Bertram Colgrave (Harvard University Press, 1927).

Englebert, Omer, *The Lives of the Saints* (David McKay Co., 1951).

Eusebius Pamphilius of Caesarea, *The Life of the Blessed Emperor Constantine*, translated by Ernest Cushing Richardson, Nicene and Post-Nicene Fathers, volume 1 (Wm. B. Eerdmans, 1955).

Falasca, Stefania Falasca, "The Humble Splendor of the First Witnesses: The Catacombs of Saint Callixtus in Rome," *30 Days*, no. 4, 1996.

Farmer, David Hugh, editor, *Butler's Lives of the Saints: New Full Edition*, 12 volumes (The Liturgical Press, 1995–2000).

Fitzgerald, Allan D., editor, *Augustine Through the Ages: An Encyclopedia* (William B. Eerdmans Publishing Company, 1999).

Foley, Leonard, "Who Is St. Anthony?" (St. Anthony Messenger Press, 2001.)

Fraser, Antonia, *Faith and Treason: The Story of the Gunpowder Plot* (Nan A. Talese, 1996).

Freeze, Gregory L., *Russia: A History* (Oxford University Press, 1997).

Furlong, Monica, *Therese of Lisieux* (Random House, 1987).

Gallagher, Jim, *Padre Pio: The Pierced Priest* (HarperCollins, 1995).

Gheon, Henri, *Secrets of the Saints* (Sheed & Ward, 1944).

Goodier, Alban, *Saints for Sinners* (Image Books, 1959).

Graham, Edward P., translator, *Acts of the Hieromartyr Januarius, Bishop of Benevento*, 1909.

Grant, Michael, *Constantine the Great: The Man and His Times* (Charles Scribner's Sons, 1993).

Griffin, T. L., adaptor, *The Life of Philip Howard, Earl of Arundel, Saint and Martyr: Edited from the Original Mss by The Duke Of Norfolk* (www.geocities.com/griffin81au/HowardMartyr.html)

Grimal, Pierre, *The Concise Dictionary of Classical Mythology*, edited by Stephen Kershaw from the translation by A.R. Maxwell-Hyslop (Basil Blackwell, 1990).

Harrington, Daniel J., *The Gospel of Matthew* (The Liturgical Press, 1991).

Haskins, Susan, *Mary Magdalen: Myth and Metaphor* (HarperCollins, 1993).

Howatson, M. C., editor, *The Oxford Companion to Classical Literature*, second edition (Oxford University Press, 1989).

Huysmans, J.K., translated by Agnes Hastings, *Saint Lydwina of Schiedam* (Kegan Paul, Trench, Trubner & Co. Ltd., 1923).

James, M. R., translator, "The Gospel of Nicodemus, or Acts of Pilate," *The Apocryphal New Testament* (Clarendon Press, 1924).

Jerome, Letters (www.newadvent.org/fathers/3001.htm).

Jesch, Judith, *Women in the Viking Age* (The Boydell Press, 1991).

John Chrysostom, "Sermon 67 on Matthew," *Nicene and Post-Nicene Fathers*, series 1, vol. 10 (www.ccel.org/fathers2/NPNF1-10).

Jones, C. A., *The Life of St. Elizabeth of Hungary, Duchess of Thuringia* (Swift & Co., 1877).

Jones, Charles W., *Saint Nicholas of Myra, Bari, and Manhattan: Biography of Legend* (University of Chicago Press, 1978).

Jones, Frederick M., *Alphonsus de Liguori: Saint of Bourbon Naples* (Liguori Publications, 1992).

Jones, Gwyn, *A History of the Vikings* (Oxford University Press, 1984).

Kalvelage, Francis M., *Kolbe: Saint of the Immaculate* (Franciscans of the Immaculate, 2001).

Kelly, J. N. D., *Jerome: His Life, Writings and Controversies* (Harper & Row, 1975).

Kieckhefer, Richard, *Unquiet Souls: Fourteenth Century Saints and Their Religious Milieu* (University of Chicago Press, 1984).

Kowalska, Maria Faustina, *Diary: Divine Mercy in My Soul* (Marians of the Immaculate Conception, 2001).

Labarge, Margaret Wade, *Saint Louis: Louis IX: Most Christian King of France* (Little, Brown, 1968).

LaChance, Paul, translator, *Angela of Foligno: Complete Works* (Paulist Press, 1993).

Lappin, Peter, *Dominic Savio: Teenage Saint* (Bruce Publishing Company, 1954).

Leys, M. D. R., *Catholics in England 1559–1829: A Social History* (Sheed and Ward, 1961).

"The Life of Our Holy Mother Mary of Egypt," Internet Medieval Sourcebook, Paul Halsall, editor, (www.fordham.edu/halsall/sbook.html).

Lightfoot, J. B., and J. R. Harmer, translators, *The Apostolic Fathers*, second edition (Baker Book House, 1989).

MacDonald, Iain, editor, *Saint Brendan* (Floris Books, 1992).

———, *Saint Patrick* (Floris Books, 1992).

Martindale, C. C., *The Vocation of Aloysius Gonzaga* (B. Herder Book Co., 1927).

———, *Life of St. Camillus* (Sheed and Ward, 1946).

Maxwell, John Francis, *Slavery and the Catholic Church* (Barry Rose Publishers, 1975).

McLynn, Neil B., *Ambrose of Milan: Church and Court in a Christian Capital* (University of California Press, 1994).

McMahon, Norbert, *The Story of the Hospitallers of St. John of God* (The Newman Press, 1959).

McNabb, Vincent J., *St. Elizabeth of Portugal* (Sheed & Ward, 1938).

Mauriac, François, *Saint Margaret of Cortona* (Philosophical Library, 1948).

Meany, Mary Walsh, "Angela of Foligno: A Eucharistic Model of Lay Sanctity," *Lay Sanctity, Medieval and Modern: A Search for Models*, edited by An W. Astell (University of Notre Dame Press, 2000).

Medwick, Cathleen, *Teresa of Avila: The Progress of a Soul* (Alfred A. Knopf, 1999).

Meissner, W. W., *Ignatius of Loyola: The Psychology of a Saint* (Yale University Press, 1992).

Molinari, Paolo, translated by José María Fuentes, S.J., "Blessed Miguel Augustin Pro, Martyr for the Faith," *La Civiltà Cattolica*, 1988.

Monda, Andrea, "A Troublesome Saint," *Inside the Vatican*, April 1999.

Musurillo, Herbert, *Acts of the Christian Martyrs* (Oxford University Press, 1972).

New Advent, Inc., *The Fathers of the Church*, Electronic version, 1997.

Nixon, Virginia, *Mary's Mother: Saint Anne in Late Medieval Europe* (Pennsylvania State University Press, 2004).

Ogg, Frederic Austin, editor, *A Source Book of Mediaeval History: Documents Illustrative of European Life and Institutions from the German Invasions to the Renaissance*, (1907; reprinted by Cooper Square Publishers, 1972).

O'Malley, Vincent J., *Saints of Africa* (Our Sunday Visitor, 2001).

———, *Saints of North America* (Our Sunday Visitor, 2004)

Orsenigo, Cesare, *Life of St. Charles Borromeo* (B. Herder Book Co., 1943)

Panzer, Joel S., *The Popes and Slavery* (Alba House, 1996).

Pastrovicchi, Angelo, *Saint Joseph of Copertino* (B. Herder Book Co., 1918).

Pernoud, Regine, *Joan of Arc: By Herself and Her Witnesses*, translated by Edward Hyams (Scarborough House, 1994).

Phelan, Edna Beyer, *Don Bosco: A Spiritual Portrait* (Doubleday, 1963).

Poulos, George, *Orthodox Saints*, 4 volumes (Holy Cross Orthodox Press, 1990).

Riches, Samantha, *St. George: Hero, Martyr and Myth* (Sutton Publishing, 2000).

Roberts, Alexander Roberts, and James Donaldson, editors, *History of Joseph the Carpenter*, Ante-Nicene Fathers, Volume VIII, (Hendrickson Publishers, 1994).

Roberts, Alexander Roberts, and James Donaldson, editors, *The Protoevangelium of James*, Ante-Nicene Fathers, volume 8 (Hendrickson Publishers, 1994).

Roy, James Charles, *Islands of Storm* (Dufour Editions, 1991).

Rutler, George William, *The Curé of Ars Today: St. John Vianney* (Ignatius Press, 1988).

Schwertner, Thomas M., *St. Albert the Great* (Bruce Publishing Co., 1932).

Stinehart, Anne C., "'Renowned Queen Mother Mathilda': Ideals and Realities of Ottonian Queenship in the Vitae Mathildis reginae (Mathilda of Saxony, 895?-968)," *Essays in History*, vol. 40 (Corcoran Department of

History at the University of Virginia, 1998).

Sulpitius Severus, *The Life of St. Martin*, translation and notes by Alexander Roberts, A Select Library of Nicene and Post-Nicene Fathers of the Christian Church, Second Series, volume 11, 1894.

Talbot, Francis X., *Saint Among Savages: The Life of Isaac Jogues* (Harper & Brothers, 1935).

Taylor, Therese, *Bernadette of Lourdes: Her Life, Death and Visions* (Burns & Oates, 2003).

Trotta, Liz, *Jude: A Pilgrimage to the Saint of Last Resort* (HarperCollins, 1998).

Tylenda, Joseph N., *Jesuit Saints & Martyrs*, second edition (Loyola Press, 1998).

von Weinrich, Franz Johannes, *St. Elizabeth of Hungary*, translated by I. J. Collins (Burns Oates & Washbourne Ltd, 1933).

Urry, William, *Thomas Becket: His Last Days*, edited with an introduction by Peter A. Rowe (Sutton Publishing, 1999).

Valtierra, Angel, *Peter Claver: Saint of the Slaves* (Newman Press, 1960).

Weinstein, Donald and Rudolph M. Bell, *Saints & Society: The Two Worlds of Western Christendom, 1000–1700* (University of Chicago Press, 1982).

Wiedemann, Thomas, *Emperors & Gladiators* (Routledge, 1995).

Weisheipl, James A., *Friar Thomas D'Aquino: His Life, Thought, and Works* (The Catholic University of America Press, 1983).

Willey, David. "Magician priest wants patron saint of magic," BBC News World Edition, June 2, 2002.

Woods, David, translator, "The Passion of St. Christopher," *Bibliotheca Hagiographica Latina Antiquae et Mediae Aetatis*, number 1764, 1999.

———, "The Passion of St. Florian," *Bibliotheca Hagiographica Latina Antiquae et Mediae Aetatis*, number 3054, 1999.

Zimmermann, Odo J., and Avery, Benedict R., translators, *Life and Miracles of St. Benedict, by St. Gregory the Great* (The Liturgical Press, no date).

Index of Saints

About the Illustrations

The illustrations in this book are reproductions of antique and vintage holy cards, almost all of which come from the extraordinary collection of the Rev. Eugene Carrella of the Archdiocese of New York. Holy cards pair up naturally with patron saints because both are expressions of grassroots, folks-in-the-pews, popular devotion. Almost all the cards reproduced here date from the nineteenth and early twentieth centuries, the golden age of holy cards, when printers in Austria, Belgium, Germany, and France began to mass-produce holy cards of exceptionally high quality. Many of these printers used chromolithography, a complicated, time-consuming method of printing in which an image goes through the press many times, with a new color added with each pass. One of the finest printers of chromolithographic holy cards was the Society of St. Augustine in Bruges, Belgium, which turned out hundreds of different designs that are miniature works of art. Sadly, we almost never know the names of the original illustrators.

Nineteenth-century holy cards had a collectible dimension as well. The Dominicans, the Franciscans, and the Carmelites (among others) created whole series of holy cards depicting the saints of their religious orders. French chocolatiers slipped holy cards of martyrs, monks, or scenes from the life of Joan of Arc into each box of chocolates. (Buy more chocolate and collect them all!) At one point, a French manufacturer of beef stock packaged his product with scenes from the life of St. Francis of Assisi; printed on the back of each holy card was an advertisement for the company.

Acknowledgments

I would like to say a few words about the tight-knit group of people who produced this book. It's thought that writing is a solitary occupation, but in fact authors need a whole network of allies. First, an author needs a publisher who "gets" the idea he's trying to sell. I was very fortunate that my long-time friend Jason Rekulak, of Quirk Books, "got it" right away. I am very grateful to my editors, Melissa Wagner and Mary Ellen Wilson, who made my copy cleaner and sharper. Quirk's mega-talented art director Bryn Ashburn made the case that holy cards would make a good book about patron saints even better. May St. John Bosco, the patron of editors, St. Luke, the patron of artists, and St. John of God, the patron of booksellers, crown all their efforts with success.

Lastly, my profound thanks to Father Eugene Carrella for teaching me the history of holy cards and letting me borrow some of the finest pieces in his collection to illustrate this book. May St. John Mary Vianney, the patron of parish priests, shower him with blessings.

Thomas J. Craughwell is the author of Saints Behaving Badly: The Cutthroats, Crooks, Trollops, Con Men, and Devil-worshippers Who Became Saints (Doubleday, 2006). He has talked about saints and the canonization process on CNN, including a play-by-play of the pope's Christmas Eve Midnight Mass. He has also made several appearances on EWTN, the Catholic cable network, as well as the BBC, The Learning Channel, and Inside Edition.

The author of several articles about saints for The Wall Street Journal, Emmy, Inside the Vatican, Catholic Digest, St. Anthony Messenger, and Our Sunday Visitor, Craughwell writes a monthly column on patron saints for diocesan newspapers and catholicexchange.com. He has been a featured speaker on patron saints at conventions of the two leading associations of Catholic schoolteachers, the National Catholic Educators Association and the National Conference for Catechetical Leadership. He lives in Connecticut.